EMPIRE'S VIOLENT END

EMPIRE'S VIOLENT END

Comparing Dutch, British, and French Wars of Decolonization, 1945–1962

Edited by
Thijs Brocades Zaalberg
and Bart Luttikhuis

CORNELL UNIVERSITY PRESS   ITHACA AND LONDON

Thanks to generous funding from the research program Independence, Decolonization, Violence and War in Indonesia, 1945–1950, the ebook editions of this book are available as open access volumes through the Cornell Open initiative.

Copyright © 2022 by Cornell University

The text of this book is licensed under a Creative Commons Attribution-NonCommercial-NoDerivatives 4.0 International License: https://creativecommons.org/licenses/by-nc-nd/4.0/. To use this book, or parts of this book, in any way not covered by the license, please contact Cornell University Press, Sage House, 512 East State Street, Ithaca, New York 14850. Visit our website at cornellpress.cornell.edu.

First published 2022 by Cornell University Press

Library of Congress Cataloging-in-Publication Data
Names: Brocades Zaalberg, Thijs, editor. | Luttikhuis, Bart, editor.
Title: Empire's violent end : comparing Dutch, British, and French wars of decolonization, 1945–1962 / edited by Thijs Brocades Zaalberg and Bart Luttikhuis.
Description: Ithaca [New York] : Cornell University Press, 2022. | Includes bibliographical references and index.
Identifiers: LCCN 2021039990 (print) | LCCN 2021039991 (ebook) | ISBN 9781501764141 (hardcover) | ISBN 9781501764165 (ebook) | ISBN 9781501764158 (pdf)
Subjects: LCSH: Decolonization—Southeast Asia—History—20th century. | Decolonization—Africa—History—20th century. | Decolonization—Netherlands—History—20th century. | Decolonization—Great Britain—History—20th century. | Decolonization—France—History—20th century. | Political violence—Southeast Asia—History—20th century. | Political violence—Africa—History—20th century. | Anti-imperialist movements—Southeast Asia—History—20th century. | Anti-imperialist movements—Africa—History—20th century. | Counterinsurgency—Southeast Asia—History—20th century. | Counterinsurgency—Africa—History—20th century. | Netherlands—Colonies—History—20th century. | Great Britain—Colonies—History—20th century. | France—Colonies—History—20th century.
Classification: LCC JV241 .E49 2022 (print) | LCC JV241 (ebook) | DDC 325/.309405—dc23
LC record available at https://lccn.loc.gov/2021039990
LC ebook record available at https://lccn.loc.gov/2021039991

Contents

Preface　　　　　　　　　　　　　　　　　　　　　　　　　　vii

1　Introduction: Beyond the League Table of Barbarity: Comparing Extreme Violence during the Wars of Decolonization
Thijs Brocades Zaalberg and Bart Luttikhuis　　　　　　1

2　Not an Afterthought: Accountability for Colonial Violence in the Dutch and British Metropoles
Huw Bennett and Peter Romijn　　　　　　　　　　　25

3　Windows onto the Microdynamics of Insurgent and Counterinsurgent Violence: Evidence from Late Colonial Southeast Asia and Africa Compared
Roel Frakking and Martin Thomas　　　　　　　　　49

4　Cracking Down on Revolutionary Zeal and Violence: Local Dynamics and Early Colonial Responses to the Independence Struggle in Indochina and the Indonesian Archipelago, 1945–1947
Pierre Asselin and Henk Schulte Nordholt　　　　　71

5　The Places, Traces, and Politics of Rape in the Indonesian and the Algerian Wars of Independence
Stef Scagliola and Natalya Vince (in collaboration with Khedidja Adel and Galuh Ambar)　　　　　　　　　96

6　"The Normal Order of Things": Contextualizing "Technical Violence" in the Netherlands-Indonesia War
Azarja Harmanny and Brian McAllister Linn　　　120

7　"Bloodshed on a Rather Large Scale": Tactical Conduct and Noncombatant Casualties in Dutch, French, and British Colonial Counterinsurgency
Christiaan Harinck　　　　　　　　　　　　　　141

8 Comparing the Afterlives, Political Uses, and
Memories of Extreme Violence during the Wars of
Decolonization in France, the Netherlands, and Britain
Raphaëlle Branche   162

Contributors   181
Notes   183
Index   225

Preface

This book is the result of an intense and rewarding international collaborative effort. The project started in 2017 as part of a large-scale research program titled "Independence, Decolonization, Violence and War in Indonesia, 1945–1950," initiated and executed by three Dutch historical research institutes: the Netherlands Institute of Southeast Asian and Caribbean Studies (KITLV), the Netherlands Institute for Military History (NIMH), and the NIOD Institute for War, Holocaust, and Genocide Studies. As one of the program's eight constituent parts, our project pivoted around the spring of 2019, when we gathered with a group of twelve researchers at the Netherlands Institute for Advanced Studies (NIAS) in Amsterdam. During these three months of intensive discussions and collaborative research, the core of this book was developed. In teams of two historians, one from the Netherlands and one from overseas, the members of this research group explored various aspects of empire's violent end. Their comparative analyses, focused mainly on Dutch, French, and British cases, all revolved around the central questions of why, how, and to what extent security forces in service of the colonial powers in so many of these decolonization wars ended up using extreme violence. The first results of the collaborative effort were presented during a two-day NIAS conference that we organized in Amsterdam on 20 and 21 June 2019. Many other excellent scholars presented papers there during the second day. Some of the results of the first day of this event were published as a forum consisting of five short essays in Dutch in the *BMGN Low Countries Historical Review* in the 2020 summer issue. The present volume elaborates on these findings by adding a broad range of additional research, as well as three entirely new essays.

This book would not have been possible without the support of many people along the way. First of all, we would like to thank NIAS director Jan-Willem Duyvendak and the institute's wonderful staff. With facilities ranging from a top-service library, practical and financial support in organizing a vast array of academic events, and of course the famous NIAS lunches, they made those months at the institute a joy for us research fellows. Particular thanks are also due to Gert Oostindie, Ben Schoenmaker, and Frank van Vree, the directors of the abovementioned historical institutes, and of course to Mariëtte Wolf, who, as the program manager, supported so many aspects of our project behind the scenes.

We also owe gratitude to numerable colleagues who commented on, contributed to, or facilitated our work at various stages: our fellow researchers in the program, particularly Esther Captain for her early contribution to the project, the participants in the conference and other workshops, and our colleagues at Leiden University and the Netherlands Defense Academy in Breda, also for providing us with the time to work on this project. Finally, we would like to thank all the members of our research group, whose relentless energy, intellect, and humor have made this project a joy to lead.

Thijs Brocades Zaalberg and Bart Luttikhuis

EMPIRE'S VIOLENT END

INTRODUCTION
Beyond the League Table of Barbarity: Comparing Extreme Violence during the Wars of Decolonization

Thijs Brocades Zaalberg and Bart Luttikhuis

Extreme violence by colonial security forces during wars of decolonization has become one of the most hotly debated historical topics since the turn of the century. Much has been written about iconic cases of abuse such as "la torture" by the French during the Algerian War (1954–1962) and "Britain's gulag" in Kenya during the Mau Mau uprising (1952–1960). These painful legacies have attracted wide public attention as a result of the lawsuits filed by Kenyan victims against the British state and political gestures like President Emmanuel Macron's highly publicized acknowledgment in 2018 of systematic torture by French forces during the Algerian war.

Torture, executions, rape, and other forms of extreme violence during other wars of decolonization have also drawn varying levels of scholarly attention. The British counterinsurgency campaign in Malaya (1948–1960) has traditionally featured prominently as the paradigmatic case of a less violent approach to colonial counterinsurgency. But even this supposed poster child of the "hearts and minds" approach has become subject to a revisionist take that draws attention to its more violent early period and coercive aspects throughout.[1] The First Indochina War (1945–1954) is well known for its intense combat operations, culminating in the surprising French defeat at Dien Bien Phu. Yet atrocities by French security forces against the Vietnamese have remained largely outside the scholarly and public spotlights, which are still firmly locked on the Algerian war. Mainly owing to the late unraveling of the Portuguese African empire, research into extreme levels of violence during decolonization in Angola and Mozambique in the 1960s and early 1970s has been catching up only recently.

One particular war of decolonization that has created high levels of controversy on a national level in the past decade, but that has remained largely unknown internationally, is the Indonesian War of Independence (1945–1949), in which Dutch security forces committed many atrocities. When King Willem-Alexander apologized for "excessive violence on the part of the Dutch" in the late 1940s during his 2020 state visit to Indonesia, his gesture attracted a mere fraction of the international media attention received by Macron two years earlier.[2] The military aspects of the Dutch-Indonesian case—the very first in the long wave of post–Second World War decolonization wars—are also largely neglected by international scholars with an interest in the wars of decolonization. Even during the recent wave of attention for colonial counterinsurgency in the wake of the post-9/11 wars in Iraq and Afghanistan—conflicts with arguably similar characteristics—the Dutch-Indonesian case was all but absent from publications and conferences.[3]

The surge of attention in the Netherlands for its own violent colonial endgame, a topic clearly dissonant with the predominantly benevolent Dutch collective self-image, was prompted by a series of civil court cases on behalf of Indonesian victims against the Dutch state. The first of these court cases was filed in 2008 and decided in favor of the claimants in 2011, when it first attracted broad public attention. Ever since, Dutch society and politics have been in a process of reevaluating these dark pages of their colonial past.[4] Parallel to resurgent public attention, historians have taken up the mantle of studying these atrocities. In his seminal 2016 book *De brandende kampongs van Generaal Spoor* (The burning villages of General Spoor), Rémy Limpach led the way and concluded that "Dutch troops left a trail of burning *kampongs* and piles of corpses throughout the Indonesian Archipelago." Despite numerous earlier revelations and short spikes of public attention over the preceding decades, successive Dutch governments had downplayed any atrocities committed by Dutch troops as merely isolated "excesses" in an otherwise properly conducted military campaign. This new study showed that extreme violence had in fact been structural in nature.[5] After the mounting pressure of the continuing court cases and the publication of Limpach's book, the Dutch government in late 2016 decided to finally provide financial support for a 2012 initiative by three Dutch historical institutes for an independent comprehensive research program.[6]

This book is the outcome of one of this broader research program's eight subprojects. While the other seven Dutch research teams focused specifically on various aspects of the Indonesian case, our project set out to broaden the scope of analysis to a comparison with other wars of decolonization. In doing so, we not only seek to bring the Dutch-Indonesian case to the attention of a wider international audience, but also to place it at the heart of a much-needed comparative effort of juxtaposing extreme violence in Indonesia, Algeria, Indochina, Malaya, Kenya, and elsewhere. Throughout this book, therefore, the Dutch-Indonesian conflict runs as a thread that functions as a central case that also reveals new insights on these better-known cases.

The contributions to this book concentrate on escalations of violence by the colonizer's side of the respective conflicts. Even though local dynamics of violence, the often violent behavior of independence fighters and other armed groups, as well as victims' voices, feature centrally in some of the chapters (see the chapters by Frakking and Thomas, Asselin and Schulte Nordholt, Scagliola and Vince), the perspective of the different peoples on the receiving end of the colonial powers' violence—the victims—remains to be studied in more detail in future comparative research. Our focus on colonial transgressions also led us to exclude comparisons with both more peaceful transitions of power and the hasty British and Belgian withdrawals with extremely violent civil-war type aftermaths in India and Congo.

The starting point of our comparison, the Dutch-Indonesian case, perhaps requires some explanation for those less intimately familiar with its details. Two days after Japan's capitulation on 15 August 1945, the Indonesian Republican leaders Sukarno and Mohammed Hatta were the first in a wave of anticolonial nationalists to declare independence—to be followed two weeks later by Ho Chi Minh's proclamation of the independence of Vietnam. A violent anti-Dutch and internecine social revolutionary period coincided with the reappearance of Dutch authorities in the wake of the British occupying powers. The British initially militarily curtailed the Dutch and pressured them to negotiate with the Indonesian Republic. But after the Allied withdrawal, the gradual buildup of a 120,000-strong military force, and the breakdown of diplomacy, the Dutch government unleashed a first major military offensive in July 1947. They euphemistically labeled it a "police action" in order to signify to an international audience that this should be considered an internal affair. The aim of the offensive was to occupy the economically vital areas of Java and Sumatra. The operation was a success in conventional military terms, reclaiming large areas from the fledgling Indonesian Republic. However, the success was subsequently offset by a quite successful, yet costly, Indonesian guerrilla campaign.

US-dominated diplomatic intervention through the United Nations in this period initially favored the Dutch in their pursuit of a neocolonial federal construction within a Dutch-Indonesian Union—a model inspired on a French-Vietnamese agreement that was in the works simultaneously. But in the course of 1948, fears of communist insurgent success in Malaya and Vietnam at the time caused US policy makers (and in their wake other international actors) to switch sides, especially after they had become convinced that the nationalist Republic

FIGURE 1.1 During the partial Allied occupation of Java and Sumatra, British-Indian troops burn down houses in Bekasi on 13 December 1945. Large parts of the town were destroyed as a collective punishment for the brutal murder of five members of the Royal Air Force and twenty British-Indian riflemen whose Dakota aircraft crash-landed near the town. (Collection Netherlands Institute of Military History)

rather than the stubborn but weakening Dutch allies formed the best antidote against communism in Southeast Asia.[7] Ignoring the writing on the wall, the Netherlands nevertheless launched yet another major offensive in December 1948—the second "police action"—this time aimed at "decapitating" the Republic by conquering its capital and arresting its political and military leaders. This led to ever more intense guerrilla warfare, a similar faltering counterinsurgency campaign by the overstretched Dutch army, atrocities on all sides, and unprecedented international condemnation of the war-weary Dutch. All these factors together led to a speedy negotiated withdrawal in late 1949 and the formal transfer of sovereignty on 27 December 1949.

Indonesia thus became the first former colony in the post–Second World War era to gain independence through armed struggle, albeit in combination with successful diplomacy by its leaders. Several such struggles with varying levels of success would follow in Asia and Africa, with the last major decolonization wars ending in 1975 when the Portuguese finally withdrew from their African colonies. In this book, we have somewhat shortened our temporal focus. As our emphasis is on the Dutch-British-French comparison, Algerian independence in 1962 forms the endpoint of the major conflicts that we focus on (even though minor British colonial counterinsurgencies such as that in Aden would stretch into the 1970s).

In this introductory chapter, we will first explain the added value of a comparative approach in studying the topic of extreme violence during wars of decolonization. In making the case for a balanced comparison, we briefly reflect on how comparisons have previously been used by contemporaries, journalists and historians, in often opportunistic ways. We then give a more detailed definition of what it is that we compare in this volume: "extreme violence." Subsequently, we provide some essential comparative context on political and military aspects of the wars of decolonization studied here, in order to pave the way for our main conclusions: our reflections on the causes for and nature of the violent transgressions taking place within them. Finally, we elaborate on how we compare by introducing the other seven chapters, before recapitulating the key analytical findings that emerged from the collaborative effort of writing this edited volume.

Why We Compare: Beyond Guilt Ranking

Despite the wave of scholarly, public, and sometimes judicial attention in the United Kingdom, France, the Netherlands, and other countries, debates on extreme forms of violence have mostly remained nationally self-centered, one might even say parochial. This has hampered scholars' ability to fully understand the dynamics behind the escalation of violence. That is not to say that broader comparisons have never been made. In general, the field of colonial and imperial history has a rich tradition of comparative studies.[8] The processes of decolonization have also been contrasted, but mostly with a focus on the level of policy, diplomacy, and strategy for the French and British cases, for example by scholars such as Martin Thomas and Martin Shipway.[9] Surprisingly, however, academic comparisons focusing on the use of violence remain very scarce.

This scholarly void has not stopped various actors in the public sphere from using more superficial, ad hoc comparisons for their own, often opportunistic, purposes. Contrasting national "styles" of military operations during decolonization was already common practice in colonial times. The British "minimum force" approach in Malaya was typically contrasted with heavy-handed French practices in Indochina even before the British way was presented as the "population-centric" antidote to a US "enemy-centric" attrition strategy in

Vietnam after 1965.[10] The Dutch were another case in point. As early as 1946 the army commander General Simon Spoor contrasted—quite selectively and favorably for his own troops, of course—his colonial army's "direct methods" to the indiscriminate firepower unleashed by none other than the British military during the height of the battle of Surabaya (November 1945) and elsewhere during their partial post–Second World War occupation of Java and Sumatra. Attorney General Henk Felderhof, a central figure in the minimal prosecution of atrocities and in the legitimization of extreme violence in Indonesia, made a similar comparison in 1948 shortly after the British Royal Air Force started bombing communist rebels in neighboring Malaya at the outset of the communist rebellion. Felderhof's self-serving motive was to validate the wave of executions led by the infamous Captain Raymond Westerling on South Sulawesi in late 1946 and early 1947—much in the way that the captain himself, in his memoirs, later legitimized his campaign of terror (see the chapter by Harmanny and Linn).

Comparison has also frequently been used in later years in the public debate to underline lingering notions of Dutch exceptionalism, until this very day. When war veteran Joop Hueting in 1969 revealed on national TV widespread Dutch atrocities in Indonesia, one of many hundreds of angry fellow veterans ranted in a protest letter to the editors, "Dutch soldiers don't do such things. Germans, French and Americans do those things . . . but Dutchmen certainly DO NOT."[11] However, if recent historiography has proven anything, it is that—on orders by or with the consent of their officers—a significant number of young Dutch men as well as locally recruited colonial forces did resort to methods reminiscent of those of the former German and Japanese occupiers.

No matter the obvious differences in scale and intent, it is surprising that quite many soldiers themselves made this very comparison in their personal writings, such as that of a soldier writing home claiming in December 1948 that he could name many examples proving "we are no better than the Hun." Several of them even equated Dutch actions that they had witnessed to the infamous and iconic Nazi punitive razzia on the town of Putten in September 1944 (the Dutch equivalent of Oradour-sur-Glane or Lidice).[12] Dutch servicemen and administrators were not alone in seeing parallels between their own conduct and Nazi practices. Eric Griffith-Jones, the British attorney general in Kenya, described in a 1957 memo the abuse of detainees in internment camps as "distressingly reminiscent of conditions in Nazi Germany or Communist Russia."[13] French servicemen also made frequent comparisons with Nazi violence in France, referring particularly to the Oradour massacre of recent memory, asking, for instance, "how many Oradours in Algeria?" Or to quote another soldier describing in his diary the fate of an Algerian village under French attack, "Oradour without a church, French soldiers and not SS. Everyone is expelled, houses are burnt to the ground."[14]

Many of the more recent comparisons of excessive violence during French, British, Dutch, and other colonial counterinsurgencies also tend toward exercises in "guilt ranking," usually resulting in an assessment that downplays one's own culpability. Not only contemporaries and journalists but also respected scholars have occasionally made attempts at comparison. Nevertheless, even the best of this sort, by Van Doorn and Hendrix, remained no more than "a first sketch," as the authors readily admitted in 1985.[15] One of the key objectives in many of these attempts has been to establish that even though "we" may have been worse than previously assumed, the Dutch military was not quite as bad as the French in Algeria, the Portuguese in Mozambique, or the Americans in Vietnam. The often superficial comparisons have had a detrimental effect on public debate in the Netherlands, where this excuse has continued to hold sway.[16] In the United Kingdom, there has been a similar tendency. In our project, we are not interested in drafting what David Anderson has rightly disparaged as a "league table of barbarity." Instead, we explore the question why in fact *all* these wars escalated to the extent that colonizers so regularly engaged in serious human rights violations, despite the political and military-strategic differences.[17] Why, as Martin Thomas has put it, did "recourse to extreme violence seem not only logical, but defensible, even ethically imperative, to those authorizing it and performing it"?[18]

What We Compare: Definitions and Forms of Abuse

At this point it is important to clarify our central concept: extreme violence in decolonization wars. We are primarily interested in transgressions of violence, the moments when violence crosses certain boundaries, be they legal, normative, or political. In the respective historiographies of the conflicts studied in this volume, various terms have been used to identify this subject, each with its own problems. British debates about colonial counterinsurgencies for a long time revolved around theories of "minimum force" versus practices of "excessive force" or "exemplary force."[19] Many authors also use vaguer and under-defined terms like "brutality" or "atrocities" to identify their subject. Another favorite phraseology to signal the same topic without having to get bogged down in questions of definition is to talk about decolonization wars (and counterinsurgency in general) as "dirty wars."[20]

In the historiography on the Dutch-Indonesian conflict the discussion about terminology has likewise been highly contentious. An important marker was set in 1969 with the publication of a government report known as the *Excessennota* (memorandum on excesses). This hastily drafted document purports to give a survey (since proven to be highly incomplete) of "excesses" or incidents of "excessive violence" perpetrated by Dutch troops in the Indonesian war.[21] As its main author, Cees Fasseur, later admitted, the extralegal term "excesses" was chosen expressly by the Dutch government to avoid the use of "war crimes."[22] For decades these terms, with their euphemistic connotations, were largely uncritically adopted by Dutch historians. Only in the past decade has the usage started to shift. Some authors now prefer to speak of Dutch "war crimes" in Indonesia, irrespective of the difficult discussions about the applicability of the laws of war to the conflict.[23] The most commonly used term has recently become "extreme violence." However, these terms suffer from the same problem as all the previous ones: they are exceedingly difficult to define and demarcate.[24]

It is analytically problematic to treat transgressions of violence in isolation from violence in general. As we further illustrate below, extreme violence can also not be separated from the broader context of warfare—the type of war and its intensity—in which it takes place. Nevertheless, Stathis Kalyvas rightly warns us in his groundbreaking *The Logic of Violence in Civil War* that the study of violence needs to be analytically decoupled from war. After all, "a considerable amount of violence in civil wars lacks conventional military utility and does not take place on the battlefield." But Kalyvas also admits that violence cannot be properly explained without considering that a context of war crucially influences the forms and intensity of violence.[25] For instance, despite a recurrent belief over the past century in the effectiveness of the "hearts and minds" approach to counterinsurgency, it is hard to deny that few insurgencies have been successfully defeated without high levels of violence and coercive methods targeting the guerrillas' civilian support base.[26] However repulsive such measures may seem, these considerations have to be taken into account when explaining variations and parallels in the use of extreme violence against those striving for independence.

So where do we, for the purposes of this volume, draw the line between the transgressive violent acts at the heart of this study and "regular" violent acts of war that largely remain outside our scope? In essence, the authors in this book have converged around a commonsensical approach inspired by, but not solely focused on, the broad parameters of the human rights frameworks that were developed in the 1940s to 1960s. Important markers during the era of decolonization wars were the signing of the UN Human Rights Charter in December 1948, the emerging European Convention on Human Rights, signed in 1950, and the Fourth Geneva Convention of 1949.[27] However, precisely because of the fact that this legal framework was emerging only at the time of the decolonization wars, and because colonial powers most often tried to ignore it by claiming that these were internal conflicts, we do not intend to get fully embroiled here in the question of its applicability during the various conflicts under scrutiny. Others have done this to much greater effect.[28]

Instead, we take as an additional baseline to our commonsensical notion that, from the high command down to the level of the individual conscript or colonial soldier, individuals in most cases knew very well when they or their colleagues were crossing a boundary—for example when torturing, executing noncombatants, raping, pillaging, or razing entire villages. As elaborated above, many firsthand accounts in diaries by troops on the ground clearly establish this consciousness. As in official sources, these commentators often interpreted or legitimized such abuse as "a necessary evil," clearly implying their awareness of an ethical or legal line being crossed.

We do not mean to suggest that all violence during decolonization wars was "extreme," nor that decolonization wars necessarily saw more transgressions of violence than other wars. We are interested in the purpose, direction, and prevalence of some of the violence being used in the contexts of these wars. In our approach, a pivotal aspect making violence extreme—in other words, what made these wars "dirty"—is the deliberate targeting of those unable to defend themselves, be it noncombatant civilians or surrendered fighters as well as other unarmed suspects who have been taken prisoner.[29] Particularly in irregular warfare, delineating the former group—who is a civilian, and who is a guerrilla—is more complex than defining the latter category. Abuses that take place in captivity, such as torture, the execution of detainees, or rape and random sadistic acts (such as described in this volume by Scagliola and Vince), generally provide clearer examples of lines being crossed.

Extreme violence in the wars of decolonization took a range of forms. Targeting noncombatants encompasses not only inflicting well-known forms of bodily harm, but also the destruction of property and livelihood for nonmilitary purposes, such as (collective) revenge, intimidation, and punishment. Also included can be mass internment and the uprooting of whole communities in the context of population- and resources-control measures, such as in Kenya, Algeria, and Malaya (as mentioned in this volume in the contributions by Frakking and Thomas and Scagliola and Vince).[30] In each of these conflicts, hundreds of thousands of civilians suffered greatly as a result of these brutal and destabilizing but often strategically successful measures. Similar large-scale population-control was not used structurally by the Dutch in Indonesia. But a comparative perspective of strategic incentives makes one wonder whether the mass burning of houses and entire villages—which was a common practice in Indonesia—did not sometimes serve a similar resources-control function by denying insurgents a support base.[31]

What we quickly realized when comparing the historiographical literature on forms of violence is that the scholarly focus in relation to certain cases has often been driven by national obsessions, or what we call "iconic forms of extreme violence." Every former colonizing nation and every decolonization conflict seems to have acquired its own form of violence that is seen as the most striking expression of the conflict. For the French, this has been "la torture," the systemic use of torture in Algeria (as becomes clear in this volume in the epilogue by Raphaëlle Branche). For the British it is forced displacement and mass internment in what some have called "Britain's gulag" in Kenya, as well as the coercive "villagization" program in Malaya. For the Dutch case in Indonesia, so-called summary executions of noncombatants (especially those initiated by Raymond Westerling and his special forces on South Sulawesi) perform such a role of an icon of memory.[32]

Of course, certain forms of violence became iconic for the very obvious reason that they were very prevalent, very recognizable aspects of particular wars. Nevertheless, a more careful comparison shows—most clearly here in the contribution by Scagliola and Vince—that these icons of memory can also function as "black holes" absorbing most national scholarly attention, thus creating

FIGURE 1.2 French paratroopers question Omar Merouane, whom they suspect of having committed terrorist attacks in Algiers, on 14 March 1957. Systemic use of torture, or "la torture," has gained an iconic status in collective French memory of the Algerian war. (Jacques Grevin / AFP via Getty Images)

blind spots for other forms of violence. From our comparative work, we learned that in some cases the particular forms of violence became iconic not necessarily because of their prominence during the conflict. Other forms of violence were equally important but have not attracted the same level of attention in later debates. For instance, French torture has been heavily accentuated because it was systematic, but how much do we really know of the proliferation and scale of torture by Dutch security forces?[33] Similarly, can we really say that strategies of population and resources control had no functional equivalent in the Dutch campaign in Indonesia, as long as no one analyzes Dutch thinking and practices through this lens?

To be clear, these selective national memories have an obvious positive side: the fact that one particular violent phenomenon became iconic has consequently made these wars "memorable" in public consciousness. Simply put: if the Dutch public knows anything about atrocities in Indonesia it is probably *because* of Captain Westerling's mass executions, just as British and French audiences know about the decolonization violence because of the catchphrases "British gulag" and "la torture." By contrast, the French campaign in Indochina or British campaigns in Cyprus or Aden are much less known partly because of their lack of an iconic atrocity. But as we noticed, the iconic status of these forms of violence also has a more negative effect on memory and historiography. Iconic forms of violence tend to crowd out other forms of violence from our minds. As historians, we are as much a part of public debate as anyone else, and we can become afflicted by the same obsessions. Because collectively our research efforts have been focused heavily on certain forms of violence, we have not sufficiently researched other forms, leading to an unproductive confirmation bias that overly emphasizes national peculiarities ("national ways of war"). In this book, we highlight that these national obsessions are more a product of postwar narrative creation than a reflection of realities during the respective wars. In fact, we found that the forms of violence used in the wars studied here, as well as the causes for transgressions, were more closely comparable than a cursory reading of the various national historiographies would suggest.

Comparative Context: Decolonization, Warfare, and Atrocities

Before we can delve deeper into the causes and nature of extreme violence common to the wars we study in this volume, it is imperative that we introduce the most important cases within a broader analytical context. The many resemblances between the wars of decolonization notwithstanding, some general knowledge is warranted on the important variations in political, social, economic, strategic, and military contexts in Indonesia, Algeria, Indochina, Malaya, and Kenya. After all, these factors explain some of the significant differences in the scale and intensity of the wartime violence employed, which in turn *may* help explain the transgressions taking place in each case.

For instance, the political stakes for the French in Algeria were always higher than elsewhere, as the French considered "l'Algérie française" an integral part of the Republic, consisting of two *departements*. Algeria harbored a European settler community of over one million, making up almost 13 percent of the population. This contrasts starkly even with Kenya, whose white settler community of 0.2 percent was considered large in relation to other British colonies and—as in the case of Algeria—has often been presented as an explanation for the colonial power's tenacity and the draconian and violent methods it employed.[34] The estimated three hundred thousand Europeans in the Indonesian archipelago, more than half of them Eurasian, made up over 0.4 percent of its inhabitants. When it comes to economic relevance, it is crucial to consider that the Dutch "Jewel in the Crown" made an even larger contribution to the metropole's gross national product than British India did to that of the United Kingdom. Moreover, being the nation's only major colony, it was regarded as essential to the Netherlands' geopolitical relevance.[35] This all helps to explain Dutch political stubbornness and—in spite of a strategic potential dwarfed by France and Britain—the massive military deployment in times of post–Second World War austerity.

Clearly, the scale and intensity of military confrontations were also related to the respective colonial powers' willingness—or lack thereof—to address the legitimate grievances of those supporting the armed insurgencies, or ultimately to provide outright independence. The colonial powers' ability to internally contain insurgencies also played a significant role. The British were clearly most successful in politically and strategically isolating the insurgencies they faced in their relatively small colonies of Malaya and Kenya. This was partly because these insurgencies originated in a distinct ethic group, but also—at least in Malaya—due to the comparatively more timely and generous British offers of a pathway to negotiated autonomy and ultimate independence. The French and Dutch (let alone the Portuguese) were much more hesitant.

Another factor at play was the level of international military and diplomatic involvement, with the former having an escalating and the latter a de-escalating effect. The lack of outside interference in the dismantling of the British Empire and in military support for the communist resistance contrasted sharply with the highly internationalized Indochina War, which saw massive material Chinese military support to the Vietminh and increasing US political and military backing for the French.[36] Like Malay and Kenyan insurgents and in contrast to the

Vietminh (as well as the Front de Libération Nationale insurgents in Algeria), Indonesian nationalists remained isolated from outside military support, partly owing to geographical circumstances. But in stark contrast to the British or the French wars, the conflict in Indonesia was fully internationalized on the diplomatic level through British, US, and United Nations interference. While many Dutch contemporaries blamed the eventual loss of their colony on this meddling, US diplomatic intervention in 1949 is particularly likely to have saved the Dutch and Indonesians from an even longer and more intense guerrilla war that was in the end unwinnable for the Dutch.[37]

Figures on the scale and intensity of combat and other forms of violence are telling but extremely hard to come by. Those readily available, such as the numbers of military personnel involved on the part of the colonial powers, need to be weighed carefully. For instance, with a peak military strength of 150,000 personnel in Indonesia in 1949, Dutch troop levels may have seemed impressive, particularly in relation to the metropole's population of nine million, but the number of "boots on the ground" remained low relative to the seventy million Indonesians they were trying to control. Indonesia's population amounted to eight times that of Algeria, over two and a half times that of Vietnam, and twelve times that of Malaya and Kenya.[38] In comparison, French peak troop strength amounted to 450,000 forces in Algeria and 220,000 French Union Forces in Indochina, while the British-led military presence in Malaya and Kenya peaked at approximately 40,000 and 12,000 Commonwealth troops respectively. The fact that France over the course of the entire Algerian war mobilized close to two million men and the Dutch "only" 220,000 can be explained by the extremely long and often extended tours of duty of Dutch troops, lasting up to three or even four years. The resulting psychological wear and tear and the overall shortage of Dutch forces—and thus lagging willingness to punish troops for transgressions or to relieve officers—have been highlighted by some historians as among the key explanations for extreme violence. However, a comparison with, for instance, the French in Algeria leaves it doubtful whether more troops and shorter rotations would have resulted in less abuse.

Figures on military casualties on the colonial powers' side are fairly reliable. Algeria and particularly Indochina saw heavier fighting than Indonesia, which is partly demonstrated by the 25,000 deadly French casualties and over 90,000 French Union Forces dead, respectively. The Dutch, by contrast, lost close to 5,000 servicemen in Indonesia, half of the losses combat related, with the other half attributable to disease, exhaustion, or accidents, a ratio that was probably similar in most contemporary colonial conflicts. Bringing into the equation the deadly military losses of 1,450 Commonwealth forces during the conflicts in Malaya and 167 in Kenya immediately shows the lower overall intensity of those wars.[39]

When it comes to the numbers of deadly casualties among Indonesians, Algerians, Vietnamese, Kenyans, and Malays, levels of uncertainty rise exponentially. Moreover, as shown by Christiaan Harinck's chapter in this volume, the distinction between combatant and noncombatant casualties is highly problematic in all statistics. The most reliable estimates indicate that over 300,000 Vietnamese died during the nine-year Indochina War on all sides, including civilians. For Malaya, the official number of insurgents killed is 6,711. The estimated number of Kenyans killed at the hand of security personnel in British service ranges from the official figure of 11,503 to approximately 20,000, with some scholars even suggesting a multiple of that number. In Algeria, up to 300,000 Algerians died as a direct result of the war. Meanwhile, official Dutch figures say some 100,000 Indonesians died as a result of combat actions. A high ratio of noncombatant casualties might explain the massive asymmetry between Dutch and Indonesian victims. Moreover, certainly for the Dutch-Indonesian case and possibly for some of the others, these casualty figures represent the lower limit of the actual number of deaths.[40] In the end, establishing casualty figures is also highly dependent on whether we decide to focus on the anticolonial struggle or if we also include the civil war and fratricide often entangled in these wars.

Reliable statistics on atrocities and war crimes—figures that would be crucial to this study—are even harder to come by. A rare source is an internal French report of 1955 disclosing that over nine thousand Vietnamese war prisoners were executed, with a peak occurring in 1952–1953. The vast majority of the bodies were never recovered.[41] One of the few figures on victims of Dutch atrocities is provided by the iconic and thus relatively well-researched case of Dutch mass executions in South Sulawesi, which resulted in at least thirty-five hundred victims, mostly noncombatant suspects, in a three-month period (see the chapter by Asselin and Schulte Nordholt).[42] The vast majority of the incidents involving the murder of captives, or other forms of atrocities, are much harder to trace and reconstruct, as they took place during regular patrols and actions ("sweeps"). They went unreported and were at best marked as "prisoner shot while fleeing" in archival records.

The space and context in which violence and coercion took place thus largely determine the availability of sources and figures, as Scagliola and Vince, in their chapter, also highlight in relation to sexual violence. Somewhat more reliable figures are also available on the hundreds of thousands of Algerians, Kenyan, and Malay-Chinese civilians who were forcibly relocated and thus administered by the colonial powers. Again, no organized equivalent existed in Indonesia, but we do know that at the conflict's height tens of thousands of Indonesians were being held in makeshift Dutch prisoner of war camps.[43]

To conclude this contextual sketch, we want to emphasize the significant variations in intensity and scale of warfare between the conflicts studied most thoroughly in this book—with Indochina on one end of the scale and Kenya on the other. But it is altogether less clear how these differences affected the scale and nature of the excessive force being deployed. The intensity of combat was certainly not *necessarily* related to the use of extremely violent methods. It is striking how violence against noncombatants was used in all these conflicts (and on all sides, of course). So in spite of the relatively small and localized character of the insurgencies faced by British authorities, their methods were often viciously coercive. Particularly Kenya stands out for low combat intensity combined with high levels of violence. The Dutch case is also telling in this regard. The international involvement as well as the Netherlands' limited strategic potential restrained the Dutch militarily, resulting in peaks and lows in combat activity between 1945 and 1949. Yet despite the relatively short periods of months rather than years of truly intense guerrilla and counterguerrilla operations, the structural nature of the atrocities committed on all sides of the conflict is evident. Clearly, there are many other variables at work.

Causes and Nature of Extreme Violence

That brings us back to asking the "why" question: why did colonizers in all our cases resort to extreme forms of violence? This means that we have to further explore the causes and nature of the violence employed by the respective colonial security forces. As there is rarely a single cause or motive that sufficiently explains excessive levels of force used against noncombatants, our research led us to the conclusion that we have to think in terms of a causal hierarchy. Transgressions of violence are invariably the result of several, mutually reinforcing factors.[44] However, rather than merely listing these variables, we aim to weigh the relative importance of, on the one hand, specific causes for extreme violence such as failing leadership, lack of oversight and legal clarity, inexperience, psychological wear and tear on troops, individual psychology, and specific incidents triggering a "spiral of violence"; and, on the other hand, explanations emerging from more structural factors such as colonial legacies and cultures of violence, the nature of irregular warfare in general, and the legacy and brutalizing effect of the recent world war and long military deployments in the various colonies.[45]

Weighing and linking contributing factors by comparing different contexts opens up the opportunity to further the classic question whether the extreme violence of decolonization wars was an "unfortunate by-product" of combat or rather a deliberate strategy. In other words, was extreme violence during the wars of decolonization the product of the inability to restrain at least theoretically undesired extreme violence, and thus the result of inadequate leadership? Or was it the result of conscious decisions that the use of "exemplary force" was the most effective and sensible strategy? These questions have long dogged debates about violence in decolonization wars, including the Dutch debate. In the latter, Rémy Limpach most recently introduced the compromise solution that the bulk of extreme violence used by Dutch forces in Indonesia was "structural" but not "systematic."[46] What he meant by "structural" was that the strategy chosen by the Dutch leadership made extreme violence unavoidable and widespread, but that (except in a number of specific contexts) the use of extreme violence was not explicitly mandated. However, Bennett and Romijn's comparison here of processes of political accountability for violence suggests that even this solution may warrant further complication. Their study forces us to conclude that the system that facilitated the use (and continuation) of extreme violence was maintained with more conscious forethought than the formula of "structural but not systematic" perhaps suggests.

The chapters in this volume provide new insights that help start the work of better understanding, distinguishing, and categorizing structural and situational causes of extreme violence. What were the relations between the various causal factors identified by previous historians?[47] Were all causes that we have identified also necessary causes? Can we point out a certain pivotal driver throughout the cases of decolonization wars studied in this volume, or might we even generalize about a causal linchpin? These chapters force us to ask critical questions where assumptions—also our own—have tended to dominate.

Our conclusion from this exploration of causal hierarchies of violence is that one of the most crucial, and so far underappreciated, factors determining extremely violent behavior is *impunity*: the compound effect of a lack of governmental, media, and judicial oversight and lack of legal clarity. Notions of impunity are a thread through most of the chapters in this volume: from institutionalized avoidance of accountability on the political level (Bennett and Romijn), to institutionalized indifference on the level of military tactics (Harinck), to personalized impunity for perpetrators of rape and other abuses (Scagliola and Vince), to even a lack of retrospective reputational accountability in the various national memory cultures (Branche). Impunity emerged as the spider in the causal web binding many of the abovementioned factors together. For example, impunity exacerbates the brutalizing consequences of exposure to violent circumstances and overall psychological wear and tear on troops. Impunity also ties in with more structural factors such as the colonial system in which the white man was virtually untouchable. And impunity may also correlate with the nature of irregular warfare or counterinsurgency, which requires a high degree of dispersal of troops even down to platoon level—and thus lack of oversight. In sum, an institutionalized system of impunity at the tactical level, together with an often conscious lack of accountability at the strategic and political level, is something we can identify in all of the cases studied in this book, and seems to have been a linchpin connecting many other causal factors.

Our comparative exploration of structural causes of extreme violence also speaks to the broader academic debate on the nature of colonial violence, or, in our case, the nature of decolonization violence. In literature on colonial warfare, "colonial violence" often emerges as a distinct category. Dierk Walter, for instance, in his book *Colonial Violence*, speaks of the "conspicuous brutality" of colonial warfare and emphasizes that despite the relatively limited and irregular nature of combat in many colonial wars, colonial armies used "more brutal tactics" than their counterparts in "large-scale wars in the West." This argument builds on the premise that in a colonial environment, with Western powers fighting against a racially distinct enemy and a population deprived of equal rights, constraints were fewer and the ethical threshold for using force and coercion much lower than in "regular" theaters of war.[48] The fact that indigenous enemies often made the strategic choice to opt for guerrilla tactics reinforced this tendency, as contemporary Westerners often viewed this type of warfare as "uncivilized" or "savage." Some historians have also argued that colonial warfare and colonial policing were particularly brutal because the often fragile colonial regimes, colonial armies, and colonial societies were living in a constant state of fear: fear of their surroundings, fear of their colonial subjects, and fear for the potential of violent insurrection. As Kim Wagner (among others) has argued, this anxiety all too easily incentivized colonizers to use "exemplary force" through collective punishment or highly publicized executions as a key distinguishing feature of colonial violence.[49]

Should we then trace the regular occurrence of extreme violence during decolonization back to colonial cultural legacies, traditions, and mind-sets, as Dutch historians have also been inclined to do?[50] Were Western militaries in a colonial context more brutal than those fighting Europe'ws other twentieth-century wars? Because of the setup of our research, in which we have made thematically focused comparisons of various decolonization wars but not compared extensively with other wars, we cannot make definitive interventions in this debate. But as Clausewitz already observed, wartime use of force has an inherent tendency to escalate, though in different ways and to different degrees, depending on the constraints of the specific context.[51] In other words, the fact that violence escalates during warfare is not in itself noteworthy. But the explanations for why and how wartime violence transgresses are vital, which is precisely what this volume aims to provide.

Admittedly, our gut feeling tells us that the long-established practices of colonial racism, the denial of rights, white man's impunity, and the ever-present tendency to dehumanize the enemy played a role in making colonial forces particularly brutal. However, especially the contributions by Harmanny and Linn, and by Frakking and Thomas, do at least suggest that "colonial violence" is a highly problematic category. For one thing, as Frakking and Thomas argue, decolonization wars were generally experienced as something closer to civil war for many of the rural and urban communities among which they were fought, thus further erasing the difference with other twentieth-century conflicts. For another, the practice of culturally othering and dehumanizing the enemy has shaped patterns of violence in warfare on a much broader scale than just in colonial wars—a trend that goes back to early modern times, or even before.[52] It remains an open question whether the "othering" in colonial warfare is of a different nature than the "othering" occurring in all other wars, just as it remains a question whether colonial occupiers lived in a different state of anxiety for their surroundings than did any other military occupiers or authoritarian regimes.

Ultimately, to be able to answer these important, highly complex, and politically charged questions, we need to compare decolonization violence not only to "regular" combat operations in the context of interstate and intrastate warfare, but also to irregular warfare in a noncolonial setting. Harmanny and Linn in this volume set precisely such an agenda by comparing the war in Indonesia, for example, with the Greek Civil War and with the Korean War. One may further wonder about German abuse toward French civilians in a response to irregular *franc tireurs* in 1871 or about the so-called Rape of Belgium in 1914, let alone about massive abuse during the Second World War on the Eastern Front. As Sönke Neitzel and Harald Welzer argued in their study of German military experience, *Soldaten*, "the rigor with which German occupiers pursued alleged partisans was one reason that 60 percent of the casualties of World War II, an unprecedented proportion, were civilians."[53]

All this triggers the question whether the dominant driver for abuse was the nature of the colonial system—of which these wars were an extension—or rather the nature of irregular warfare with its inherently blurry lines between combatants and noncombatants (as both Frakking and Thomas and Harinck argue here). But even if irregular warfare is presumably by definition more "dirty" than conventional warfare, how should we evaluate the deliberate terrorization of populaces during the Second World War by strategic aerial bombardments on all sides? And what about the acceptance by the Western Allies of noncombatant casualties—including many thousands of French, Belgian, Dutch, and other allied civilians—in order to defeat Nazism? In what ways was the partially deliberate targeting of the enemy's civilian population for psychological effect in the age of "total warfare" different from collectively punishing sections of the Indonesian, Vietnamese, and Algerian rural populations through terror and destruction? Were these methods not also aimed at driving a wedge between them and the irregular fighters they were suspected to support?

Based on our extensive exploration of violence during decolonization conflicts we can still not answer these questions definitively. But at least it is our hypothesis that the notion of "colonial violence" as a sui generis category directly related to "colonial warfare" may obscure more than it enlightens. First of all, the violence taking place within a colonial war is not automatically or necessarily colonial violence. Automatically assuming that all violence in colonial war is also "colonial violence" leads to a tendency to assume that the origin or cause *must* also be "colonial."[54] Second, it is already hard enough in itself—probably impossible—to delineate colonial warfare analytically from other armed conflict related to foreign occupation. We certainly do not want to go down the road of stretching the concept of "colonial occupation" to the extent that it loses all explanatory power. Overall, then, we would hypothesize that colonial violence may need to be "de-exceptionalized."

How We Compare

Having placed our central topic of extreme violence in the somewhat broader frame of both decolonization conflicts and warfare in a noncolonial context, we can now elaborate on how we will compare our different cases. Because of the explorative character of our project, the book consists of focused and richly descriptive studies rather than bird's-eye comparisons with high levels of generics and statistics. We have opted to delve deeply into a small number of colonial conflicts, relating each of them back to the relatively unknown but highly instructive Dutch-Indonesian case. The selection of cases and themes of the individual chapters was determined by the availability of expertise and sources relevant to them, but also their contribution to the book's two central questions: why colonial powers used extreme violence and how we can characterize the violence we observe.

The first couple of chapters in this volume delve straight into the question we raised earlier: why resorting to excessive forms of force seemed inescapable, logical, and defensible to those perpetrating, ordering, or condoning it in all the decolonization wars studied here. Chapter 2, by Huw Bennett and Peter Romijn, focuses on the highest of political levels. They investigate processes of political accountability and impunity, comparing the ways in which policy makers dealt with—or did not deal with—information about atrocities in their colonies. The

FIGURE 1.3 Dutch troops pose with a captured mortar crew of the Indonesian Republic Army (TNI) in Central Java during the second major Dutch offensive, December 21, 1948. (Collection Netherlands Institute of Military History)

respective Dutch and British processes of denial, deflecting responsibility, and neutralizing scandals, while organized in different ways, had surprisingly similar outcomes in terms of institutionalizing impunity and thus condoning violence. Thus, while contemporary explanations for extreme violence preferred to place the blame on the aberrant behavior of individuals, a closer study of the evidence concerning what was known at the time and how that knowledge was processed points toward more systemic and structural causes.

By contrast to Bennett and Romijn's investigation of high politics, Roel Frakking and Martin Thomas in chapter 3 divert our attention in the exact opposite direction. They examine local microdynamics of violence in a broad-ranging comparison encompassing five cases. It was in the nature of decolonization wars that levels and forms of violence varied enormously between different areas even within the same conflict. Frakking and Thomas observe that targeting of noncombatants was especially rife in highly contested areas—what they call "interior borderlands." If we are to understand who used violence against whom and why, we cannot assume fixed or immutable affiliations. Supposedly fixed categories demarcating those who supported or opposed the warring parties, those who were colonizers and those who were colonized, anticolonial struggle and civil war, and those who were combatants or noncombatants, were in fact malleable and locally determined. This leads to an argument for de-exceptionalization.

The next two chapters take a closer look at the dynamics and contexts of violence in respective colonies by way of detailed symmetric comparisons. Chapter 4, by Pierre Asselin and Henk Schulte Nordholt, studies the period in 1945–1946 of early revolutionary violence and its suppression by comparing the Dutch-Indonesian confrontation with the emerging First Indochina War. In both former colonies, the sudden surrender of the Japanese on 15 August 1945 created a power vacuum that neither the British occupation forces and the returning Dutch and French, nor their Indonesian and Vietnamese adversaries, could initially fill. Asselin and Schulte Nordholt speak of a period of statelessness, which caused a chaotic contestation for power in which extreme violence emerged as a tool to assert control that (in the minds of all parties in the conflict) could not otherwise be attained. While these and other parallels between the two conflicts are striking, the processes showed obvious differences. These were caused partly by the Vietnamese communist insurgents already being much better organized than their Indonesian counterpart, partly by a radically different international context, and partly by differences in the strategic potential of the French and the Dutch, which resulted in variations in the degree to which extreme violence was directed top-down or initiated at the lower levels of command.

The second of these symmetric comparisons is Stef Scagliola and Natalya Vince's contribution on rape in the French-Algerian and Dutch-Indonesian Wars (chapter 5). Rape in wartime, they argue, is over-theorized but empirically under-studied. They compare and analyze the specific places and contexts in which soldiers raped, and delve into their motivations. Scagliola and Vince also explore the different ways in which rape in wartime has been politicized: discourses of rape are almost absent in the Indonesian case but dominate the narrative on the Algerian war. They ask the question to what extent the differing prominence of memories of rape can be explained by the different spaces—close to or far from the battlefield—in which abuse took place and the consequences this had for the victims' chances of redress.

The next two chapters further investigate the *nature* of violence during decolonization, both in their own way continuing the argument that these wars and their forms of violence should be de-exceptionalized. Chapter 6, by Azarja Harmanny and Brian McAllister Linn, deals with the notion of "technical violence." This term is current only among Dutch scholars of decolonization, and is used to refer to the employment of heavy weapons such as artillery and airpower. Among these Dutch scholars, "technical violence" is often considered almost inherently extreme. Moreover, they often suggest that the use of these weapons systems can be blamed for the majority of noncombatant victims.

By treating the Dutch case asymmetrically in the context of other wars—both colonial and other types of warfare—Harmanny and Linn critically assess both the ill-defined concept of "technical violence" and the sweeping assumptions about casualties, as well as the suggestion by contemporary counterinsurgents—inadvertently echoed by some scholars—that "direct" infantry methods were more selective and less deadly. Underlying all this is their analysis that, if anything, the use of heavy weapons in decolonization wars was in line with the broader nature of Western warfare in the mid–twentieth century.

Christiaan Harinck in chapter 7 is likewise interested in how the violence of decolonization wars fits in with wider contemporary Western military thinking. Harinck's broad comparative overview zooms in on the complex issue of noncombatant casualties. Based on a short survey of the available statistics, incomplete and unreliable though they may be, Harinck concludes that it is at least clear that in all decolonization wars casualties on the insurgent side far outnumbered casualties on the side of the colonizer. Also clear is that a significant share of those casualties were noncombatants. Harinck searches for explanations, first in the predominant military thinking of the time: impunity reigned because through most of the twentieth century Western militaries did not prioritize avoiding noncombatant casualties. Second, he points at the weapons on which colonial armies at the time relied for counterinsurgency: what he calls "weapons of collateral damage"—both the type of heavy weapons that Harmanny and Linn also address, and heavy infantry weapons such as machine guns and portable mortars. With this explanation and broader definition, Harinck deviates somewhat from the argument made by his colleagues in the previous chapter, in a sense representing precisely the predominant view in Dutch historiography that Harmanny and Linn critically examine.

This book is rounded out with chapter 8, by Raphaëlle Branche, who compares the political uses, afterlives, and memories of extreme violence during the wars of decolonization waged by France, the Netherlands, and Britain. All these three former imperial nations have struggled for decades with the uncomfortable place that these histories occupied in their respective collective memories. Each has gone through a long process, mostly separate from each other, but nevertheless with surprising similar steps. Branche traces the steps, from early narratives of success, through denial and defensive narratives, to recent hesitant and controversial attempts at reparation. She concludes that the recent past suggests we might be coming toward the end of a cycle of silencing and entering a new phase in which states have started recognizing at least a portion of their responsibility in the violence of the wars of decolonization. One could say that this volume is a symptom of that new phase.

The wars at the heart of this comparative study clearly show substantial variation in scale, intensity, purpose, and the methods employed. When we started this research, we received plenty of warnings not to compare apples with oranges. This saying has always struck us as confusing. Apples and oranges have much more in common than what sets them apart—they are both fruits, they are healthy, and full of vitamins and fiber. Similarly, while comparing the transgressions of violence in the context of decolonization, our research team quickly noticed that beneath the different surfaces, there was much more that united than divided our cases. This led to our first more general conclusion emerging from the series of thematically and methodologically rather diverse case studies: the need to de-exceptionalize. In a sense, every colonizer was attempting to square the same circle, each with its own tools: how to win a war among a population that most often did not see them as legitimate rulers. All the attractive words about restoring peace and order, winning heart and minds, and selective use of force could not hide that ultimately insurgencies could not be defeated by fighting armed opponents and persuasion alone. It always required forcing large swaths of the population into submission with the use of punitive and exemplary force and coercive methods against noncombatants.

The fact that the many commonalities surprised us somewhat could be interpreted as an indictment against the various national historiographies. Studies of extreme violence in the wars of decolonization from national perspectives have resulted in groundbreaking histories that have formed indispensable building blocks for our work here. Yet the isolation in which these various conflicts have often been studied has nevertheless led to a tendency in the literature to overemphasize national peculiarities and particular causes or forms of abuse. This observation leads us to our second conclusion. Our comparison shows that the notoriety of supposedly peculiar national forms of violence—the "iconic atrocities" such as "la torture" in Algeria, "Britain's gulag" in Kenya, or the summary executions of Westerling's troops in Indonesia—is partly the product of later historiographical obsessions, and less an actual reflection of their prominence in the respective sources. This iconic status of certain forms of violence has had the negative effect on memory and historiography that other forms of violence have been crowded out from our collective minds. Because much of historians' collective research efforts has gone into exploring certain forms of violence, they have insufficiently researched other forms, leading to a sort of confirmation bias.

Our third conclusion from our comparative explorations is concerned with the causes of extreme violence in decolonization wars: why does violence in all these wars escalate to this extent, and why did resorting to excessive forms of force seem inescapable, logical, and defensible to those perpetrating, ordering, or condoning it in all these wars? As elaborated above, previous historians have come up with a range of causal factors. Our contribution to those studies is, for one, that it is high time to put to bed the discussion whether occurrences of extreme violence in these wars were merely incidental "excesses" or rather of a structural nature. The fact that violent practices in all these wars escalated in similar ways, if in sometimes differing intensities, shows definitively that there are structural factors behind the escalation: from factors to do with the asymmetrical nature of the conflicts, to legacies of the Second World War and wider Western thinking about proper ways of war, to longer-established cultures of violence. Second, and most importantly, our contribution to discussions about the nature and causes of extreme violence is that among that spectrum of contributing causal factors, one stands out as a causal linchpin: the lack of accountability and thus the institutionalized impunity for extreme violence that was a common denominator throughout the conflicts studied in this forum. It is the glue that binds most of the other important causal factors together.

These conclusions are not only relevant to our own small circle of historians doing research on wars of decolonization. All those interested need to realize that what we are coming to terms with is not merely a Dutch, French, or British, but a common Western or at least European predicament. As shown in Raphaëlle Branche's final chapter to this book, an effort to compare should also inform the ongoing public use of history in our respective societies, the collective-memory battles and public reckoning related to these troubled pages of Western history. That is not to judge whether one form of coming to terms with the past is "better" than the other. But at least it might be possible to learn from each other, instead of pointing out the splinter in the other's eye while ignoring the beam in our own.

2

NOT AN AFTERTHOUGHT
Accountability for Colonial Violence in the Dutch and British Metropoles

Huw Bennett and Peter Romijn

In January 1949, the Dutch Senate discussed the recent military offensive against the Indonesian Republic, which had been halted by Resolution 63 of the United Nations Security Council. Communist member Jan Haken quoted letters sent by Dutch conscripts. One case concerned an act of revenge for the death of two Dutch soldiers, when the company burned down the nearest *kampung* and randomly shot at least ten local men. The soldier wrote, "If you tell the men this is just like the Huns had done, they answer that 'these blackies' are to blame themselves."[1] Nearly four years later, in the British House of Commons, the colonial secretary, Oliver Lyttelton, was pressed to explain military methods in Kenya. Labour Party member of Parliament Maurice Edelman asked whether the "sinister proportions" of killed to wounded Kenyans indicated the security forces were pursuing a "shoot to kill" policy, including executing the wounded. Lyttelton refused "to allow British soldiers . . . to have to fight entirely with their hands tied behind their backs."[2] In both the Dutch and British cases, attempts to hold ministers accountable for human rights violations signally failed. This chapter asks why such attempts failed, because accountability failure meant extreme violence could continue unchecked. We build on scholarship that analyzes the politics of international law to investigate how colonial powers attempted to bypass universal human rights standards. As Fabian Klose points out, European powers violated in the colonies the very same principles they championed at home.[3] We argue that the politics of domestic governmental accountability must be understood to properly account for the success of this sustained hypocrisy.

In the spring of 1949 an unstable truce was reached after pressure in the United Nations, enabling negotiations to start between the governments of the Republic of Indonesia and the Netherlands. The final settlement resulted in a "transfer of sovereignty" on 29 December 1949. The conflict cost at least one hundred thousand Indonesian lives and approximately five thousand lives of the Dutch military. From the early stages onward, tens of thousands of Dutch and Eurasian civilians were either killed or forced to migrate. Just across the Straits of Malacca another colonial conflict was in its early stages: the Malayan Emergency, declared by the British authorities on 16 June 1948. The Malayan Communist Party, supported mainly by ethnic Chinese, launched an armed bid for independence from a Britain severely weakened, in material and moral terms, by the wartime Japanese occupation. In October 1952 another "emergency" was declared. In Kenya the Mau Mau movement sought to achieve national liberation by building on widespread discontent over land distribution, primarily in the Kikuyu, Embu, and Meru communities. Both British "emergencies" lasted until 1960, though the serious fighting was over earlier.[4]

Colonial wars were fought outside the field of vision of metropolitan peoples. Did imperialism in general "infuse . . . every organ of British life"? Or was public opinion apathetic to empire? Only a minority of Britons participated in the empire's wars after 1945.[5] In the Dutch case, society assumed the nation's economy and international status depended on the empire.[6] In all, 220,000 men were deployed as members of the Dutch armed forces in the effort to restore colonial rule, among them some 70,000 in the colonial army.[7] Yet the war happened far away, and preconceived ideas may have mattered more than news about bad military conduct. If there was a prevailing detachment, this expanded the opportunities for manipulating information and framing interpretations in desirable directions. Decolonization occurred after the Second World War, when attributing the qualities of good and evil had become an instrument of mobilization. Such discourses lingered after the war, even though the European powers refused to apply the concept of "war" in colonial conflicts. As Europe demobilized after 1945, in the colonies formal and virtual states of war remained. Domestically the United Kingdom and the Netherlands returned to liberal democracy and political accountability; at the same time they restored authoritarian colonial structures. In the discussion quoted above, another member of the Dutch Senate, A. B. Roosjen of the conservative Protestant Party ARP, urged politicians "not to destroy what the military had accomplished: restoring law and order in our overseas territories."[8] Advocates of these policies felt they could compare their methods favorably to the uniquely harsh violence employed by Nazi Germany. Even the purposes underpinning these projects were contrasted: the Nazis as selfish aggressors; the British and Dutch as enlightened powers, wisely guiding underdeveloped peoples.[9]

In the opening section of this chapter, we explain why the British and Dutch cases are worth comparing, how the comparison is conducted, and reflect on several important similarities. The second section of the chapter argues that the general picture of limited accountability in these cases must be related to the transmission of information about the violence taking place in the colonies. We dissect the multiple official channels by which information passed from the local level in the colony up to regional centers and thence on to the metropole. At each point we analyze the ways in which violence was framed, to assess whether the information channels constituted a filtration system, whereby knowledge about transgressive violence became downplayed or even eliminated. If the process as a whole tended to sanitize violence, then we need to account for the times when this did not happen—during scandals about atrocities. In its third section, the chapter compares the thresholds for scandal: what constituted "scandalous" violence, who brought about the complaint, and how were these scandals inflamed in public discourse? Finally, in section four, the chapter examines scandal management. The techniques of evasion, denial and delay, and diversion were enacted to prevent senior leaders from taking responsibility for atrocities. The chapter comparatively analyzes the extent to which these methods were used in the case studies to evade accountability. To conclude, the chapter evaluates the extent to which successful information management contributed to the ongoing perpetration of transgressive violence.

Comparing the Dutch and British Cases

The Dutch and British cases share a central outcome, which shapes the comparison to follow: no government minister ever accepted responsibility for transgressive state violence, despite being formally accountable.[10] Responsibility might have meant resignation from office or even conviction in a criminal court. We do not attempt to produce a replicable theory about accountability in wartime. Rather, the purpose is to understand the causal mechanisms involved in the Dutch and British cases.[11] The literatures on both countries emphasize the national particularity involved in their responses to colonial disorder. The comparative method is well suited to problematizing this assumption.[12] To ensure coherence between the cases, the analysis is structured around the phases of information management, scandal emergence, and scandal management. The comparison is focused by attending directly to these questions, avoiding a detailed narrative about the conflicts in general.[13] By disaggregating the cases into the phases whereby accountability was avoided, the chapter identifies the importance of timing in the causal mechanisms and allows for within-case comparisons about the relative causal weight to be accorded to each phase.[14] Combining within-case analysis and cross-case comparisons in this manner can assist in drawing out the implications for future research.

Accountability exists only if elected representatives and the public can access accurate, timely information about government actions. In this section we analyze information management processes to demonstrate how knowledge about violence could be hidden, minimized, or lost. But first we describe an essential context for both cases: the prevalence of state propaganda. Measuring propaganda's effectiveness is difficult. But the state's efforts to influence thinking about the conflicts, in the war zone, at home, and internationally, is telling. In the Dutch case, the wartime trauma of occupation turned into a plea for restoring national strength after 1945. The government promoted *volksweerbaarheid* ("popular fighting spirit") in its press policies to connect morale at home to the troops overseas.[15] The domestic Rijksvoorlichtingsdienst (RVD–The Hague: National Information Service) coordinated relations with the press. The war also witnessed an intense interconnection in the colony between the propaganda organized by the civil Regeringsvoorlichtingsdienst (RVD-Batavia: Government Information Service) and the military information services. Officials and journalists circulated between the two spheres all the time. News was framed in "positive" ways: by claiming to restore order for "the peace-loving paddy-growers," in pointing at the cruelty of the enemy, or by avoiding sensitive topics, like not showing pictures of casualties.[16] Embedded journalists and documentary film makers were instrumental, and control over them was closely maintained.

Britain ended the Second World War with a highly sophisticated propaganda apparatus. Though the Ministry of Information was abolished, the emerging Cold War prompted the government to make propaganda a central element in foreign and colonial policy.[17] The Information Research Department was created within the Foreign Office in January 1948 to counter the communist threat. From 1949 the IRD operated against "anti-British" elements (including those in the empire), alongside the information services run by the colonial authorities in each territory.[18]

Civil servants in The Hague as well as in Batavia (Jakarta) received reports from administrators and military commanders in the field.[19] They were able to steer reporting by speaking to editors and embedding journalists.[20] Embedding happened under the aegis of the military information services, who provided as well as vetted information. Moreover, many media outlets were connected to their affiliated political parties. For example, the leader of the

Roman Catholic Political Party (KVP) in Parliament was the political editor of two leading Roman Catholic newspapers. The same applied to his counterpart in the previously mentioned ARP, while the editors of the Labor Party (PvdA) newspaper and the Socialist Broadcasting Society (VARA) were leading members in the Labor Party.[21] The independent Dutch News Agency ANP (Algemeen Nederlands Persbureau) was closely connected to the government. An example pinpoints how positions in the chain of information might be blurred: W. A. van Goudoever, a former editor-in-chief of the Semarang newspaper *De Locomotief*, was recruited by the RVD-Batavia and conducted fact-finding missions about military operations. He was part of a network that extended from the army commander's headquarters and the lieutenant governor-general's cabinet in Batavia to the Ministry of the Colonies at The Hague.[22] Thus the line between "official" and "unofficial" information was difficult to distinguish. In the colonial context, small communities of decision makers, administrators, and ranking officers communicated all the time, sharing assumptions about "military necessity" and "responsible reporting."

In the British case the government sought to restrict criticism by delegitimizing colonial opponents as mere criminals. These messages were essential to turn the populations in Malaya and Kenya against the insurgents and to convince domestic and international audiences that the violence was nothing worth bothering about. In a defining move on 12 November 1948 the Colonial Office decreed that those "engaged in acts of violence in Malaya should be referred to as 'bandits.' On no account should the term 'insurgents,' which might suggest a genuine popular uprising, be used." The terminology mattered for economic reasons, too. Insurance companies only covered the lucrative rubber estates for losses in an emergency—not those incurred in war. By December 1949 the Foreign Office was pressing for official terminology to refer to "communist terrorists," to align British and American Cold War strategy.[23] In Kenya the dominant propaganda themes changed several times. At first, propaganda emphasized insurgent brutality, such as the Lari massacre in March 1953, when the Mau Mau killed 120 African loyalists. This presented the conflict as an intra-tribal dispute, rather than as anticolonial. After a new Department of Information was created in January 1954, a more "positive" tone came about. Kikuyu were told about the opportunities open to them as alternatives to joining the Mau Mau. A final shift occurred in 1955: officials removed any references to the Mau Mau in public discourse, instead focusing on the achievements made in colonial development programs, such as land reform. Vilification had given way to diversion, and then in turn to distraction. In the process a tremendous expansion took place. The personnel working on propaganda in the colony rose from 46 in 1952 to 331 by the end of 1954.[24]

As in the Dutch experience, the British attempted to control understandings about colonial violence by influencing journalists. Officials went to great lengths to cultivate journalists covering colonial conflicts, keeping them supplied with information so that they were less likely to seek out sensational news of their own. In Nairobi the press received situation reports three times a day. Paradoxically, the media's commitment to objectivity sometimes resulted in stories about atrocities being omitted. The *Times*'s archive, for example, contains several draft stories about abuses in Kenya, never to make it into print. In December 1952 and December 1953, officials confessed to correspondent Oliver Woods that police and military forces were torturing suspects. But Woods never wrote a story about these revelations, fearing the evidence was not reliable enough to meet the newspaper's standards.[25] The local *East African Standard* newspaper toed the government line throughout the emergency, and even produced the Swahili newspaper, *Baraza*, on the government's behalf.[26] In terms of the domestic audience, the British government benefited from the media taking little interest in Malaya. Most fighting took place in the jungle, making it difficult to report and not very interesting. The Colonial Office successfully countered critical stories in the *Daily Worker* and *Malayan Monitor* newspapers by cultivating the trade union movement, where concerns about British policy were being voiced. Trade unions received special information to correct the "misunderstandings." Colonial Office lobbying exploited the emerging anticommunism on the British left to discredit the Malayan Communist Party. Kenya proved to be more visually rewarding for the media. But the frequent depictions in the press and in newsreels of mass roundup operations gave the security forces favorable treatment.[27]

Information Management from Colony to Metropole

Political awareness about events in the colonies was not a neutral property resulting from the acquisition and interpretation of information and coming to tenable conclusions. Information flows from the battlefield to the nodes of responsibility were manipulated to serve the interests of those who compiled the reports and guided attention.[28] Information is managed to produce desired results. In a liberal democratic polity, accountability is regulated along formal political lines, at the higher end of which parliament, government, and cabinet ministers share the ultimate responsibility. Although the Netherlands and the United Kingdom have different political systems, in principle accountability should function with the same logic. Neil Mitchell's analysis proposes that leaders apply broad repertoires to evade accountability for acts of extreme violence committed by their armed forces. The "management of blame" is subject to "political gravity": the highest responsible authorities generally manage to transfer the blame to the lowest possible level, such as troops in the field or local administrators.[29] Doing so is only possible if leaders possess information that can be subjected to the "correct" presentation.

Accountability avoidance derived partly from structural factors common to both Dutch and British cases. In the first place, military information systems are geared toward achieving victory. Rapidly gathering, processing, and acting on a vast quantity of information can give an army a decisive edge in war. These information streams were derived from the general staff systems introduced in the 1890s, when political accountability for military atrocities was hardly a priority.[30] A second factor concerns the military propensity for optimism. During military operations, positive news tends to be transmitted up the chain of command, whereas bad news is likely to be downplayed or quashed.[31] Armies in combat need to maintain a positive outlook to endure the horrors they face. It is also due to the fact that armies are hierarchical organizations that reward success: painting an uplifting picture can improve an officer's career prospects. Third, the European powers depended on locally recruited security forces during their decolonization wars, to provide capacity at a cheaper cost than metropolitan manpower.[32] Knowledge about these forces' misdeeds could be denied, as they often operated in a confused or incomplete chain of command. Finally, all military organizations depend on secrecy. The British state was exceptionally secretive after the Second World War. Cabinet ministers were easily excluded from decision making on nuclear weapons, for example. Parliament's ability to investigate defense topics was severely circumscribed.[33]

The Dutch information system was more diffuse. Formally, communication between Batavia and The Hague was the responsibility of the governor-general (from 1948 onward, the high commissioner of the crown) and the minister of colonies (from 1946 onward, of overseas territories). The governor-general was the supreme authority in the colony, responsible for the administration, the judiciary, and the armed forces (expeditionary force and colonial army, but Royal Navy excluded). In the Parliament, the minister of colonies was responsible for all matters colonial. In practice, other information channels existed. The Ministry of Foreign Affairs created an agency to liaise with Batavia—DIRVO (Directie Verre Oosten: Directorate for the Far East)—to support diplomacy worldwide.[34] Other ministries had their own contacts in the administration, as well as in the public relations organizations—Defense and Navy in the first place, also Finance and Economic Affairs. Such contacts raised mutual suspicions when matters got tense. P. J. Koets, the chief of cabinet of the high commissioner, complained in January 1949 about "anonymous telegram exchanges" between field commanders and their counterparts in the Dutch defense organization. He explicitly criticized "the romanticism" in the reporting by the army commander, General Simon H. Spoor. Overoptimistic reporting on the impact of his recent military offensive could have a dangerous impact on politicians at home who had no experience of the situation on the ground, Koets argued.[35]

Troops in the field reported daily to their headquarters on operational and intelligence issues. Tactical reporting routinely included mention of enemy fighters "laid down" or "shot while escaping."[36] The army commander's office compiled information in comprehensive surveys, often on a daily basis, for the governor-general while leaving out most details.[37] Batavia would add the accounts received from the field administration before sending them to the ministry at The Hague.[38] Next, the Colonial Office compiled weekly reports that went to the cabinet and a select committee of Parliament.[39] Thus, a multistaged practice of information management influenced the opportunities for accountability. In the reports from Batavia, actions by the enemy were highlighted, whereas those of the Dutch troops were mentioned much less, if at all. The responsible civil servants and politicians continuously received accounts of violations of truce, infiltrations, ambushes, attacks, and cruelties by the enemy. A sense was stimulated that harsh action had to be taken. Reports from Batavia paid attention to the internal political situation within the Republic of Indonesia, building an expectation that moderate leaders would get the upper hand if the Dutch held firm. The fear was expressed that the position of the supposed moderates would be undermined by radicals, being the "real enemies." If relying on such "official streams of information," judgment would unavoidably be tainted by thinking in terms of "military necessity" as a political instrument for mastering the situation.[40] The same tendency defined the reporting by the government information services.[41]

These formal exchanges were complemented by communications along private, professional, political, and military avenues. Civil servants added private annexes to reports for their trusted counterparts overseas, senior officers exchanged opinions, politicians traveled frequently on the expanding KLM airline, and soldiers wrote letters home. Censorship of letters home was hardly effective. Nevertheless, troop commanders tried to suppress "undesirable political activities," particularly monitoring communist and former National Socialist soldiers. All services acted on the understanding that "facts, of which publication is considered impossible or undesired" should be suppressed.[42] Yet the Netherlands lacked a version of the British Official Secrets Act. On several occasions in 1946 and 1947 the Dutch cabinet discussed the possible introduction of such a law, explicitly referencing the British example.[43] During the Indonesian War of Independence, it did not materialize, however. In any case, no strong culture of secrecy existed. The colonial administrators and military moved around in small circles. People had shared education, careers, and experiences, worked together closely, visited parties, and drank together. In Batavia and elsewhere, Indonesians, also including Republican officials, shared news and gossip. Secrets did not remain secret for very long. What mattered was the capacity for steering and framing information. And this was challenged, even in government circles. In late 1949, as negotiations with Indonesia drew to a close, former minister of colonies J. A. A. Logemann wrote to his successor Johan van Maarseveen about the weekly reports to The Hague: "as in earlier times, this weekly report does not provide facts at all, only highly speculative and tendentious comments." In his reply, the minister of the Roman Catholic Party in the coalition admitted the reporting from Batavia "did not excel in terms of objectivity."[44]

Official reporting chains in the British case must be seen in the context of a different constitutional situation. In the United Kingdom, Parliament's authority over colonial matters was never clear, owing to the wide powers devolved to colonial governors, and the existence of legislative councils in many territories. Parliament legislated on imperial issues, such as defense and finance, but most legislation pertaining to a particular colony was enacted through Orders in Council, effectively ministerial decree.[45] Information reached the cabinet as a whole, and the responsible secretaries of state for the colonies and war, via three channels. Firstly, the joint intelligence apparatus coordinated secret and open-source information. The Joint Intelligence Committee (JIC) presided over a well-oiled machine with several levels. The committee comprised representatives from the three armed services, the Secret Intelligence Service (foreign intelligence), the Security Service (domestic intelligence), the Foreign Office, and, from 1948, the Colonial Office. Other departments attended meetings as necessary. Each department gathered intelligence; the committee then produced assessments on specific threats, several hundred each year.[46] However, the JIC only became seriously involved in colonial intelligence after 1955.[47] Before then, much was devolved to each colony's local intelligence committee. During the Malaya and Kenya emergencies a hierarchy of committees took information from the district to the provincial and then the colony level. These committees normally met at least fortnightly and produced reports for their superior organization. Intelligence was gathered by the colonial administration, the police Special Branch, and the army. The Special Branch was normally the lead agency, receiving periodic advice from the Security Service, which had liaison officers in colonial territories.[48]

The second avenue for reporting was from the governor to the Colonial Office in London. British colonial administration rested upon the belief that decision making should be devolved as far as possible.[49] The governor and his senior officials corresponded with the Colonial Office, which liaised with other departments where necessary.[50] For Malaya, the office of the commissioner-general for

South-East Asia (in Singapore) was also involved in information management. Within the colonies a system of emergency committees operated. In Kenya the Provincial Emergency Committees, and their subordinate committees at district level, directed operations in their area. Chaired by the leading colonial official for the area, they brought the administration, military, and police together. They reported ultimately to the War Council presided over by the governor, which decided policy. Finally, the military chain of command stretched back to the War Office. Battalions in the field gave reports to their superior brigade at the end of every planned operation, in addition to real-time updates by radio signal. These were then sent to the headquarters commanding the campaign: Malaya District, or East Africa Command. Malaya District was responsible to the commander in chief, Far Eastern Land Forces. His assessments were sent weekly both to the

FIGURE 2.1 During the Kenyan Emergency, a British Army patrol searches a man suspected of being a member of the Mau Mau insurgent movement. (© Imperial War Museum [MAU 552])

regional Defense Co-ordination Committee (Far East), and direct to the War Office. For Kenya the superior headquarters was the Middle East Land Forces, subject to the same regional arrangements as in the Far East. From October 1952 the governor's military staff officer in Nairobi directed operations. In June 1953 General George Erskine was sent to become the new commander in chief, East Africa Command. He had authority over all security forces and reported to the War Office.[51]

Low-level reports covered tactical incidents in detail. These described events that may have constituted illegal or excessive violence. In Kenya, "On the 19th August [1953] an alleged informer, leading a Police party up the Telaswani River in the Timau area, tried to escape. Failing to halt when challenged he was shot dead."[52] At times, this phrase could be a euphemism for an illegal execution. Or it could represent a legitimate response to a dangerous situation. There is seldom any discussion in the sources—once the matter had been briefly itemized, it normally disappeared from the agenda. In any case there were simply too many of these tactical records produced for senior politicians and commanders to read them. At the next level up, province summaries still mentioned violence. Again a Kenya example is instructive: "An operation was mounted on the 7th May, 1954, on Kilombe Hill by the Devons, which resulted in the killing of one unidentified Kikuyu, who ran when challenged, and having no identification documents."[53] The lack of documents serves to close down any interest in the case. Without even knowing the deceased, how could any inquiries proceed? The top-level reports, such as the minutes of the Colony Emergency Committee, generally omitted specific incidents. These were the records most likely to be seen by politicians and generals in Britain. They did contain a clear sense of the repressive policies being pursued. A Kenya Colony Emergency Committee meeting in May 1953, for example, agreed to permit the security forces to open fire during ambushes without giving the normal legally required warning beforehand.[54] Clearly granting such license was dangerous in creating a permissive environment for excessive killing—which is precisely what took place. Yet the absence of any language conveying human suffering connected to abstract policy decisions made the paper easy to skim over and quickly be forgotten. Sanitizing how events were described as the paper trail reached the top of government effectively rendered willful ignorance an irresistible choice.

The Eruption of Scandals

Scandals had the potential to disrupt the normal state of ignorance, or apathy, about extreme violence. In this section we demonstrate how scandals remained exceptions to the rule. Most often, potential scandals were defused before they threatened to throw policy off course. During the first months of the Indonesian struggle for independence, much emphasis was put on the fate of the Dutch internees who were forced to remain secluded to escape the waves of violence occurring in several areas, the Bersiap/Berdaulat. Consequently, the Dutch mindset assumed the violent character of the Indonesian Revolution and the need to restore colonial authority. This is not to suggest the public sphere was under an iron regime suppressing information contrary to the official view. In the postwar Netherlands, there was much space for critical voices opposing the war.[55] After the proclamation of Indonesian independence the debate evolved in two directions: either a new relationship with an autonomous or independent Indonesia, or restoring colonial rule. These issues were passionately discussed in the media, in Parliament, as well as in meetings at grassroots level. The conservative spectrum (Roman Catholics, Calvinists, Conservative Liberals) rejected negotiations with Sukarno's Republic, advocated military force against "bandits" and "communists," and refused to acknowledge the right of Indonesians to self-determination. Socialists, Progressive Liberals, and Liberal Protestants believed in a common future for the Netherlands and Indonesia in a voluntary union of sovereign states under the Dutch crown. The Communist platform promoted complete Indonesian independence and resisted deploying the military for recolonization.

One of the most active critics was Frans Goedhart, a socialist MP, founder and former editor of the resistance paper *Het Parool*. Goedhart traveled regularly to Indonesia and reported on Dutch atrocities. He worked with fellow Labor MP Nico Palar, an Indonesian who soon became disillusioned with Dutch politics and joined the Indonesian delegation at the United Nations. Another leading ex-resistance paper editor was Henk van Randwijk, who had many connections in the Indonesian freedom movement. He received letters from conscripts pointing to acts of indiscriminate violence. All this suggests the public sphere in the Netherlands concerning the war was as divided as the top political leadership. The left was pushed into a minority position, because of the political cleavage between socialists and Communists; the latter proved to be the most ardent adversaries of the war, but during the Cold War they were brandished as unpatriotic. Thus, the actions of Communist MPs and the reporting in the Communist newspaper *De Waarheid* did not get as much resonance as the subject matter deserved.[56] In the spring of 1946 the socialist MP Palar was the first to intervene in Parliament concerning Dutch atrocities. This related to a case occurring in April, as the British military administration in West Java reacted furiously after a Dutch action "purging" the village of Pesing.[57] Goedhart had been informed about the case by a Dutch journalist, who introduced him to an army captain of the Reserve, who was appalled by the behavior of the troops. He asked Palar to intervene in The

Hague. The minister of colonies instructed Batavia to investigate the case, but a committee whose members belonged to the colonial army and administration accepted the explanations of the implicated military. Later in the same year the administration let the case drop, basically exonerating the troops.[58] Nevertheless the Pesing case was an early example of a practice developed by the military and civil authorities in the colony during the conflict when dealing with the communication of atrocities. Time and again, critical voices would be discredited and muffled by repertoires of blaming the whistle-blowers, blaming the enemy and his propaganda, blaming the circumstances, pointing at the fog of war, denying facts, denying responsibility, and indicating the importance of the mission.

Over the years 1945–1949, information on an array of atrocities by Dutch troops reached the metropole. MPs called to account the government in specific cases. In 1946 these matters included, besides the Pesing incident, a reprisal at Meester Cornelis. In 1947 letters from conscripts were cited in the left-wing press and Parliament about the mistreatment and killing of prisoners.[59] In December Dutch troops killed unarmed men in Rawagede, West Java (120 according to Dutch sources, 431 by Indonesian accounts). The news was brought into the open by United Nations representatives.[60] The most outrageous episode of the war was the "Westerling affair" developing in late 1946. Directed to "pacify" South Sulawesi, Captain R. P. P. Westerling and his special forces conducted a campaign of summary executions. His unit went from village to village, collecting the population on the central square, and interrogating presumed "terrorists," assisted in this task by informers. In the process, special forces and regular colonial troops that joined the campaign shot at least thirty-five hundred persons. In February 1947, as the campaign was drawing to an end, the authorities in Batavia decided things were getting out of hand and withdrew the special forces (see also Asselin and Schulte Nordholt). When in July 1947 the press broke the news, the minister promised an investigation committee, but the report was only finalized in December 1948. The delay was blamed on a "lack of staff" for the committee. Moreover, the report was restricted to members of Parliament. In late 1950, the prime minister announced that no prosecution against Westerling was to be undertaken.[61]

In 1948 and 1949 more letters from soldiers found their way into the press and Parliament. A letter detailing atrocities during the occupation of Yogyakarta in January 1949, published by the left-wing *De Groene Amsterdammer*, provoked questions in Parliament. Prime Minister Willem Drees was forced to promise another inquiry. As the inquiry proceeded, the minister of overseas territories complained that information about atrocities tended to be vague. Fact-finding was thus extremely difficult. The scandal was defused by means of delaying tactics, beyond the transfer of sovereignty to Indonesia in December 1949.[62]

In the final year of the war, military operations escalated before a final round of negotiations started. Journalists and MPs on the left kept appealing to ministers about atrocities. These included the killing of prisoners in East Borneo and Malang and the shooting of Red Cross workers at Peniwen.[63] The official reply remained the same: the army command had issued orders against excessive violence, and the authorities in Batavia remained committed to bringing to justice those who broke the rules of engagement.[64] Once again, the socialist MP Frans Goedhart pressed for an inquiry. He was told by the colonial secretary that such an initiative might endanger the peace negotiations.[65] The government and its agencies stuck to publicly supporting the assumption that the war had to be won first, that the purpose was right, and that atrocities were in essence caused by derailed individuals, not by the actions of the command structures and their civilian allies.

In the British case, only the Suez invasion in 1956 caused a major political crisis back home—and this was a dispute about the conflict's legitimacy, rather than the violent methods employed during its course.[66] Popular culture reflected uninterest in state violence toward the colonized. Memoirs written by soldiers and officials with frontline experience, and published while the conflicts simmered on, treated their deployment as a big adventure, often replete with hunting metaphors. References to transgressive violence by the state were notable by their absence.[67] By the mid-1950s, newspapers, radio, and newsreels gave considerable coverage to the conflict in Kenya. But these reports paid little attention to the security forces' behavior, instead sympathizing with the plight of European settlers subjected to the Mau Mau's bestial violence. Any references to state violence usually framed it as defensive, necessary, and restrained.[68] Three feature films about Kenya appeared while the conflict was under way. *Simba* (1955) and *Safari* (1956) conformed to official propaganda in portraying the Mau Mau as a brutal, anti-Christian movement; Europeans were clearly depicted as victims, not perpetrators. Hollywood's *Something of Value* (1957) offered a more subtle account, leading the viewer to draw critical conclusions about colonialism, especially of the white settler variety.[69] Overall, popular culture did little to lead public opinion toward a sustained critique of colonial violence. Cultural representations of insurgents as remarkably brutal shrank the political space for standing up for the rights of Malayan and Kenyan civilians subjected to colonial violence.[70]

A range of anticolonial organizations operated on the left of British politics. Immediately after the Second World War the left prioritized domestic reconstruction and the expanding welfare state over anything in the colonies. Perhaps the best-known group, the Movement for Colonial Freedom (formed in 1954, *after* the most extreme violence in Malaya and Kenya was over), never attracted more than a thousand individual members. Though criticism of Prime Minister

Clement Attlee's administration arose in relation to policy in India and Palestine, these controversies surrounded partition and withdrawal, rather than military action.[71] The public's interest in Britain's international affairs was largely sated by policy makers' success in sustaining the country's image as a great power, even in an age of relative decline.[72] Decolonization violence made no difference to the British voter's life, in stark contrast to the Dutch situation.[73] Consequently, attempts by activists to expose atrocities were consistently knocked back. Between December 1951 and December 1952 Labour MPs repeatedly criticized the recently elected Conservative government for the collective punishment measures applied in Malaya and Kenya. Their condemnation failed to hit home, as these measures had been authorized by the prior Labour administration. A motion against collective punishment attracted 131 signatures; yet another motion, applauding the tactic as "just and firm," achieved 138.[74] Public indifference melded with parliamentary arithmetic to neutralize the potential for change.

Labour MPs Leslie Hale and Fenner Brockway visited Kenya in November 1952 to investigate. On returning to the House of Commons they called for extensive arrests and detention without trial to be halted. In July 1953 a Kenya Committee was publicly launched in London, attended by Communist Party members, trade unionists, Labour Party members, and Kenyan representatives. The group, which continued to be dominated by the Communist Party, produced leaflets and held further public meetings to condemn British repression. These criticisms tended to be neutralized by official propaganda emphasizing Mau Mau savagery—thus British supporters for Kenyan nationalism could be written off as apologists for barbarity.[75] The likes of Hale and Brockway remained on the Labour Party's fringes. The party's mainstream, and their allies in the Trades Union Congress, prioritized Atlanticism and anticommunism in foreign policy, not colonial liberation.[76] In the two-party British system, an inability to make opposition to state violence a party priority effectively disarmed the issue entirely. Conservative MPs would never vote against their own party on a topic as emotive as supporting the troops in combat.[77]

Critics outside Parliament were similarly sidelined. In May 1956 Eileen Fletcher, who had worked from December 1954 as a rehabilitation officer in the Kenyan detention camps, raised concerns in Britain. She expressed her reservations about detention practices in pamphlets, specialist journals, and the mainstream press. In June Fletcher spoke at twenty-four meetings and press conferences in a bid to win public attention. The campaign attracted interest partly because she spoke out for female and child victims, striking a chord with popular attitudes about vulnerability. On 6 June the House of Commons debated the case. Particular attention was paid to the legality of detaining children; the colonial secretary argued that as all girls held in detention were over fourteen, their handling was perfectly legal. The government convinced Parliament that all was in order, partly by attacking Fletcher, and partly by describing the Mau Mau violence the detained girls were implicated in. Overall the episode failed to achieve a change in detention practices.[78] Even the International Committee of the Red Cross became implicated in covering up state violence. Having avoided colonial conflicts on the basis that they were outside the ICRC's remit, delegations eventually visited Kenya in 1957 and 1959. The 1957 inspection of detention facilities not only missed the systematic abuses then happening, but resulted in the delegates applauding the colonial authorities in the local press. Over the following two years government ministers exploited the ICRC's favorable comments to rebut critics in Parliament who complained about detention conditions.[79]

A notorious scandal did eventually hasten decolonization in Kenya. Eleven prisoners were beaten to death by guards at the Hola detention camp in March 1959, as a result of a coercive policy to force inmates to work. The authorities' attempt to cover up the deaths as being caused by drinking contaminated water was destroyed by a damning coroner's report. Despite a ferocious parliamentary outrage over the incident, the government managed to defend their detention policy in general terms as successful in rehabilitating the deranged Mau Mau. Even critical newspapers such as the *Manchester Guardian* accepted this logic. While the camp commandant and the commissioner for prisons in Kenya left office as a result, no senior official or politician in Nairobi or London was held to account. Prime Minister Harold Macmillan actually refused to let his colonial secretary, Alan Lennox-Boyd, resign in case Africans conclude that "they had now got the white man on the run." The Conservative government won the general election that year with an increased majority.[80]

Scandal Management

Whereas the preceding instances can be seen within the framework of avoiding scandal, both in the Dutch and British cases the emergence of open scandals could not always be avoided. Information management was scaled up to scandal management. There are reasons for leaders to indulge in willful ignorance or cover-ups. Foremost among these is the leaders' reliance on their agents in the field. For example, when an intelligence organization is accused of torture, leaders may ignore the accusation because they depend on intelligence to continue making policy. If the agents are punished, an adverse impact may be had on their colleagues' morale, leading to a drop in intelligence, or even a mutiny. Another motivation derives from domestic politics. Elected politicians stand to gain little from criticizing their own military and security forces.[81] A first step in managing scandals is outright denial, accompanied by attempts to discredit those who have raised the allegations. Once denial becomes implausible, leaders attempt to delay a reckoning until other events take over the news agenda. The next stage is for leaders to divert attention from the events by relativizing them. As abuses or atrocities happen in a conflict, leaders attempt to trivialize their own security forces' misdemeanors while exaggerating the barbarous nature of the enemy. These claims are situated within longer-term propaganda by the government to shape public opinion. As a final stage in the process, leaders delegate responsibility to the most junior actor possible, and limit the blame to as small a number as possible in order to avoid demoralizing the security forces. A scapegoat must be found to validate the assertion that although there may be rotten apples, the barrel is fine. Often the scapegoat will be permitted a "soft landing" of very limited punishment.[82]

In the Dutch case, the management of scandals in 1949 became closely tied to the unfolding military-political endgame. The Dutch had been condemned by the United Nations Security Council for their second large-scale military offensive aimed at eliminating the Indonesian Republic. This endeavor backfired, as the Indonesian Republic displayed military and political resilience, and the international community forced the Dutch to withdraw and negotiate. During the following months, however, a settlement was not reached while the military struggle escalated, and mass violence became commonplace. Dutch politicians and administrators were concerned that reports of atrocities would undermine their negotiating position. Correspondence between the minister of overseas territories and the high commissioner in Batavia illuminates the nervousness about the potential impact of scandals and the repertoire of denial, delay, and diversion deployed to keep these matters out of the public sphere. Colonial administrators wanted to continue with their policy of "pacification," to strengthen their position during the negotiations. High Commissioner A. H. J. Lovink wrote about the dilemmas of restoring "peace and order" to his minister in The Hague, Johan van Maarseveen. Alluding to the Westerling scandal, he mentioned his recent visit to South Sulawesi, where, as compared to Java and Sumatra, "perfect degrees of law and order" existed. "If one considers," he continued, "how this situation has been reached, one can only come to the conclusion that terror has been countered by terror, obviously successfully. I would prefer not to enter an inquiry into the methods applied."[83] In this context, information could be seen as harmful, and something requiring management.

At the same time the authorities tried to manage information offensively. A recurring element in the practice of diversion was discrediting whistle-blowers.

In 1947, leading missionary G. J. de Niet had written to the minister of colonies Jan Anne Jonkman, a fellow socialist. He damned the refusal to recognize Indonesian independence and branded the counterinsurgency operations as "Japanese measures of terror." When Dutch troops took Yogyakarta in December 1948 they captured the letter.[84] Military intelligence was eager to expose the Labor Party as unpatriotic. The director of Central Military Intelligence, Colonel Dr. J. M. Somer, sent the letter to the army commander, General Spoor, who warned the high commissioner about the "irresponsible tone" of De Niet's correspondence.[85] High Commissioner Louis Beel forwarded the document to the minister, who answered that he read the content with "much surprise."[86]

The distribution of the letter was used to discredit De Niet, and by implication Jonkman, and not to consider the issue of atrocities. What happened in 1949 was a combination of delay and diversion. Ironically, when sending the letter two years earlier, De Niet had encouraged Jonkman to share the letter widely. From his point of view, the matter should not remain secret. Jonkman then talked to the chairman of the Labor Party and with the government representative in

FIGURE 2.2 Netherlands forces commander General Simon Spoor (*center*) receives parliamentary leaders from The Hague at his headquarters in Jakarta in December 1948. Spoor was frequently informed of abuse by his forces, but he and Dutch policy makers mostly frustrated prosecution of those responsible and were themselves never held accountable. (Photo: R. G. Jonkman, National Archives / Fotocollectie Dienst voor Legercontacten Indonesië)

Batavia, the independent minister of reconstruction L. Neher. Neher discussed the accusations with Spoor, finding them "rather vague" and difficult to address. Neher added that he would monitor the result of this intervention, as he had concluded that "reports and letters were written, but none of the authors would be in touch with the institutions whose actions were put to blame."[87] As a matter of fact, nothing further happened, until the "revelations" of early 1949. Thus, the repertoire of delay, diversion, nonresponse, blaming the whistle-blower, and political framing of criticism was applied to defuse a scandal.

These techniques would continue during the final year. In April 1949, Frans Goedhart addressed the Labor Party conference, criticizing the atrocities committed by Dutch troops during and briefly after the recent military offensive. Goedhart was countered in Parliament by the former minister of colonies and founder of a dissident Roman Catholic party Charles Welter. Welter, a colonial diehard, stated that Goedhart had no right to criticize the troops fighting a wily enemy. The leader of Labor in Parliament, M. van der Goes van Naters, approached Minister Van Maarseveen, defending Goedhart and asking for a public inquiry. Van Maarseveen said he preferred an inquiry to stay under the radar, in order not to endanger the Dutch position at the negotiating table. He promised to send legal specialists to discover if crimes had taken place on a scale that warranted prosecutions. Van der Goes assumed these specialists would be put at the disposal of the high commissioner in Batavia, so objected when it became clear they were to operate under the prosecutor-general in the colonial capital. This implied their assignment was limited to an investigation of criminal offenses under the supervision of the highest prosecutor in the colonial system—who had refrained from prosecutions so far. Despite his objections, Van der Goes did not press the matter in the interest of coalition politics.[88] In the end, it was decided by the minister, in conjunction with the army commander and the prosecutor-general, to send three public prosecutors from the Netherlands, C. van Rij and W. H. Stam, to join the office of the prosecutor-general. They only departed on 22 September, after delays over their tropical outfits and pensions.[89] Consequently, they arrived just more than two months before the end of colonial rule. Nevertheless, Van Rij and Stam wrote a thorough and revealing report founded on the files of the prosecutor. It was, however, submitted as late as August 1954, and then relegated to the drawers by Prime Minister Drees, only to resurface partially in 1969. Thus, the fact-finding about actual transgressive violence would be successfully relegated to the afterlife of the conflict, for decades to come.[90]

Whereas in the Dutch experience the government seemed to be hit with multiple potential scandals at the same time, the British avoided simultaneous crises until 1959. The Hola detention camp furor made an impact precisely because it happened soon after a scandal about police repression in Nyasaland and alongside criticism about policy in Cyprus.[91] Earlier on, this cumulative effect was missing. During the Kenya emergency a major scandal over abuses by the security forces threatened to derail the government's campaign against the Mau Mau. As a matter of fact, allegations of brutality by the colonial state had been raised since the counterinsurgency's early days. Many of these implicated local forces. The Kenya Police Reserve, a force largely recruited from white settlers, was notorious for beating up suspects during questioning, sometimes with lethal consequences. These cases gained little traction in mobilizing political opposition in Britain, because they were dismissed as one-offs and, more effectively still, as wrongheaded actions by the settlers, who understandably were incensed at Mau Mau savagery.[92] General Sir George Erskine's appointment as military commander in June 1953 was partly intended to control the brewing controversy. He discovered that torture during interrogations and indiscriminate shootings were the rule rather than the exception. So he issued a directive to all officers in the security forces: "I will not tolerate breaches of discipline leading to unfair treatment of anybody. . . . I most strongly disapprove of 'beating up' the inhabitants of this country."[93]

Shortly after arriving, Erskine discovered that soldiers from the 5th Battalion, King's African Rifles (KAR), had executed twenty-one prisoners. This case was potentially much more damaging for the army and the British government than any earlier controversy, and therefore called for active scandal management. First, nobody had "accidentally" shot a single person in the heat of action. On the contrary, twenty-one deaths indicated premeditation. Second, twenty-one deaths implied direction by an officer. Third, the political and ethnic identity of the officer in question mattered. Crimes by settlers in the Police Reserve, or loyalist Kikuyu in the Home Guard, were condoned as impassioned acts by those with an emotional stake in the conflict. But the King's African Rifles were commanded by white, British Army officers. Such men were expected to maintain a higher standard. Finally, as an army regiment, the KAR came under the military chain of command, reporting directly back to London, and fell under military discipline. The political stakes were thus extremely high. As Erskine's investigations proceeded over the next six months, he discovered abuses by the army to be more widespread than he at first believed. Erskine came to realize the terror unleashed at the emergency's outset could not easily be reined back in. He chose to punish offenders where possible, to cover up where not, and to continue with a military strategy that had violence against civilians at its very heart.

At first a court of inquiry was held by 70th Brigade, responsible for the 5th KAR. The court failed to fully establish what had happened on 17–18 June 1953, which contributed to Brigadier D. M. Cornah being replaced a few months later. A Major Griffiths and ten of his soldiers were placed under open arrest, while further investigations took place. Military policemen discovered Griffiths's unit had also shot dead two more civilians on 11 June. General Erskine hoped these matters could be resolved by court-martialing Griffiths, in what he described as a "revolting and unforgivable case." At the trial in late November, the court heard how Major Griffiths executed two civilians at a checkpoint. He was acquitted because of a technicality that arose from the prosecution's incompetence—they pressed one murder charge, and then proved he murdered the other man. Erskine was incensed by this verdict. Investigators began to prepare for a second trial covering the later events. Opposition leader Clement Attlee led questions in the House of Commons, demanding to know whether the case reflected broader practices in the army. The controversy centered on allegations about a competitive military culture that encouraged killing, regardless of whether the victims were legitimate targets or not.[94] For the army, any blame needed to be appended to the most junior person possible, and make him a scapegoat. The Griffiths court-martials served to hold to account a rogue, relatively junior, officer, without looking into the wider practices in the army. However, the parliamentary pressures for more systemic questions to be addressed could not be completely ignored. If they must be answered, then General Erskine would follow a fundamental principle in military leadership—by taking the initiative.

On 5 December 1953 Erskine asked London for permission to establish a court of inquiry into military misconduct. The cabinet agreed, announcing the move to Parliament five days later. Lieutenant-General Sir Kenneth McLean flew out to chair the inquiry. His remit covered three areas: monetary rewards to soldiers for kills; whether units kept scoreboards to compare kill rates; and deliberate stoking of a competitive killing approach by commanders. Over twelve days he heard evidence from 147 witnesses. McLean found one instance of officers offering cash rewards to soldiers for kills. Scoreboards were deemed to exist for keeping track of statistics rather than to encourage killing. Finally, McLean discovered a normal rivalry between units, with no "unhealthy" attitude toward killing the enemy. The inquiry concluded the army's reputation for "restraint backed by good discipline" remained intact. These findings were warmly welcomed in Parliament. Even critical MPs, such as Richard Crossman, now believed the army was operating to acceptable ethical standards. This outcome resulted, however, from careful stage management. Prime Minister Winston Churchill personally blocked the inquiry from examining all aspects of the army's conduct, and insisted the evidence be heard behind closed doors. Erskine agreed that a "full enquiry" might well "do more harm than good." McLean was prevented from looking into events before 1 June 1953, when the use of violence against civilians had been most unconstrained. Some witnesses were asked leading questions, and the inquiry ignored evidence presented to them of military rapes. Despite the presentation in Parliament, the McLean inquiry as scandal management represented more a cover-up than a cleanup. Griffiths was finally convicted at his second court-martial, in March 1954, for grievous bodily harm and disgraceful conduct. No officer or soldier faced prosecution for the murder of the twenty-one people on 17–18 June: such a case would have exposed three officers, several noncommissioned officers, and a whole platoon as being involved in torturing and murdering members of a formation supposed to be their allies, the Home Guard.[95] The image of the army as a whole was safeguarded behind a curtain of secrecy, which Britain's democratic institutions failed fully to notice, let alone tear down.

Sociologist Kees Schuyt has stated that the quality of a nation as a moral community is strongly defined by the way in which political accountability is conceived and expressed.[96] In liberal democracies, like the British and Dutch political systems, the core of that principle (accountability) is that leaders at the highest level should take responsibility for the mistakes of those at the lower levels. Moreover, they should provide all information relevant to the way in which they exercise their responsibility. This chapter points out that in the wars of decolonization, this principle did not work at all. Accounting for atrocities and mass violence was founded on information streams manipulated and framed by military and political leaders. These practices contaminated the quality of the polity as a political community. Being prepared to wage war and to make "dirty hands" systematically is one thing; to do so in a conspiracy of silence is even worse. The question in this chapter concerns the how and why of evading and refusing accountability, including urging action. The Dutch-British comparison shows that the processes of providing, framing, and withholding of information may have been different, as far as the working of the political and colonial contexts were dissimilar. Nevertheless, the outcome of the processes remains highly comparable. In both cases, the metropoles engaged in wars with colonial liberation movements that were not allowed to be called "war," and the crimes committed by their own troops were not allowed to be called "crimes." As a rule, information about what happened in the field was manipulated, filtered, framed, and in some cases made to disappear.

Maintaining colonial relationships and controlling the territories and populations were prioritized. To that purpose the armed forces and order troops could claim a large amount of freedom of action, as well as a strong benefit of the doubt. The management of information, if politically urgent, scaled up to management of scandal, and consisted of operating the military, administrative, and political channels of information. At the same time, the news media were used to influence the public sphere. Thus, the people in responsible positions were able to avert or evade accountability. Concerned citizens, journalists, and in particular members of Parliament were in a position to ask critical questions and put pressure on the governments. Nevertheless, in both Parliaments there were stable majorities set to defusing such criticism. Politically speaking, almost all critical voices were heard from the left. In the Netherlands, as well as in the United Kingdom, the left was divided between communists and socialists, and the emerging Cold War was a decisive factor in these two groups operating separately. The socialists were divided as well, between a mainstream inclined to support the government's position, and a highly critical minority on the left.

There are, of course, differences between the two cases, indicating how the specific national properties of institutions and sentiments have worked out—and these differences may enlighten some matters as well. Institutional secrecy is one of those: in the UK it was a defining element in the culture of governance, whereas in the Netherlands matters need not be officially secret to be stashed away anyway. The British media were more docile than the Dutch, but in the latter case the manipulation of the press was a more subtle game, owing to greater political and ideological pluralism. Despite all this, the Dutch press found more space for "bad news" than the British, even though the impact might be conformist and not necessarily shocking to the system. Moreover, during both world wars, the British had experienced and generally accepted government propaganda and steering of the media. In the Netherlands, owing to the German occupation, such propaganda was suspect and required subtler ways of influencing by those in power.

Domestic and international susceptibility to such propaganda underwent a change in the latter half of the 1950s, in step with an expansion of the global human rights regime. In Algeria the national liberation movement successfully internationalized its struggle to gain traction on the world stage.[97] Insurgents in Cyprus (1955–1959), Aden (1963–1967), and then Northern Ireland (1969–1998) applied diplomatic, propaganda, and legal strategies to delegitimize the British with local, national, and international audiences. Brian Drohan has shown how through techniques of "cooperative manipulation" the British attempted in these conflicts to evade accountability while appearing to accede to normative pressures for restraint. From the second half of 1956, activist lawyers in Cyprus started to exert increasingly effective pressure on the security forces to comply with the law.[98] The British fought back with tough emergency legislation, an extensive propaganda campaign, and a protracted diplomatic dispute with Greece that threatened to destabilize progress toward European political and military integration.[99] Three factors enabled Cypriot activists to mobilize the human rights regime in a fashion not seen in Indonesia, Malaya, or Kenya: support from the Greek government, transnational inspiration from other liberation movements, and the ability to have recourse to the European Convention on Human Rights, applicable in colonial territories only from October 1953, when the Dutch had left Indonesia and the worst fighting in Malaya and Kenya was over. The convention only had an effect on decision making about counterinsurgency after the Greek government lodged the first-ever interstate complaint with the European Commission of Human Rights in May 1956, over the draconian nature of the emergency legislation then in force on the island.[100] The Cyprus case underscores the requirement to approach the decolonization conflicts with great sensitivity to the legal and political distinctions between time and place. Even within the apparently fairly homogeneous British experience, the early postwar legal-political context differed markedly from that evident from the mid-1950s.

In the Dutch case, the dynamics of the decolonization conflicts were more tangible than in Great Britain. The main issue was always of a political nature: would the nation be prepared to accept Indonesian independence or not? If so, one had to let go of the colonial maxim that the ties between the Netherlands and Indonesia should be considered as a manifest destiny. This was a highly emotional issue for many Dutch of the time, who had been socialized in that idea ("Indië Verloren: rampspoed geboren!"—If the Indies are lost, catastrophe will be at hand!). The British were much more sober about such prospects: they kept believing in the global importance of their empire, and they had more colonies anyway, so the existential threat to their nation was not perceived that strongly. In both cases, however, the struggle to maintain the colonial relationships was addressed in terms of purpose and means to be applied. Those who believed that this was a noble purpose accepted the fact that a price had to be paid. That the price one was willing to pay could contaminate the political community for generations to come was not a matter that concerned those who were evading responsibility for the atrocities. Later generations in both nations would, however, make efforts to reconstruct accountability.

3

WINDOWS ONTO THE MICRODYNAMICS OF INSURGENT AND COUNTERINSURGENT VIOLENCE

Evidence from Late Colonial Southeast Asia and Africa Compared

Roel Frakking and Martin Thomas

This chapter pursues a microdynamics approach to political violence.[1] Essential to its argument are two elements, which might at first glance seem contradictory: variation and comparability. The challenge is to explain why civilian populations faced greater levels of repression and violence in some places and not others (the variation element) while at the same time tracing similar patterns in multiple colonial conflicts (the comparability element). To do so, we explore local experiences of insurgent action and consequent repression by imperial security forces. Evidence is drawn from selected territories in late colonial Southeast Asia and Africa. The final years of empire breakdown in Dutch-occupied Indonesia, French Indochina, and British Malaya are considered alongside the French-ruled African territories of Madagascar and Algeria, where clashes between insurgents and security forces produced opposite outcomes: a rapid collapse of rebellion in Madagascar and its eventual triumph in Algeria. We concentrate on rural communities subjected to organized violence as insurgencies triggered counterinsurgencies by colonial security forces and their local auxiliaries. Our concern is not so much with differences in political outcome between territories. Rather, our approach demonstrates that strategies of colonial violence against civilian populations reveal comparable microdynamic patterns across empires.

Three core themes are addressed. The first looks beyond the analytical preoccupation with asymmetries in decolonization conflicts by focusing on the local grievances that give rise to outbreaks of ostensibly anticolonial violence. Asymmetric conflict, and the question inherent to it—how the weak defeat the strong—are familiar to scholars of violent decolonization, and of counterinsurgencies more generally.² We approach this question differently, focusing on the social pressures that lead communities to involvement in decolonization conflicts. We view strategy in a biopolitical sense, as derived from the countervailing efforts of insurgents and counterinsurgents to impose lasting control over the means of life—access to food, to shelter, and to basic welfare services—which marked the decolonization conflicts fought out in rural societies. Grievances over such fundamental issues, and the ways they changed over time, were the critical microdynamics at work here. We attach particular significance to the singular demographic advantage enjoyed by those opposed to European colonial control: their ability to conceal themselves within indigenous society. No matter how sophisticated the informant networks and intelligence-gathering apparatus created by colonial security forces, their starting point was that of the outsider.³ It was at this epistemological level of knowledge creation about local communities that insurgents could offset the imbalance in military capacity between their fighters and the security forces they engaged. Armed with fuller local knowledge about their opponents' actions and intentions, insurgents might evade capture, escape to sanctuary bases across frontiers, disrupt communications lines, or embark on ambushes or acts of sabotage.⁴

Our second theme considers the nature and composition of the irregular units, often locally recruited paramilitary formations, which we categorize as "violence workers."⁵ These groups, often rudimentarily armed, enacted a high proportion of village-level violence, typically at the behest of others but also to improve their security or otherwise advance their interests. Their histories remind us that categories typically regarded as fixed, whether those of insurgent versus loyalist or combatant versus noncombatant, were sometimes more fluid in practice. What interests us are those local pressures that lead people to traverse the line between participation and nonparticipation in acts of political violence. Rarely was there a linear progression toward involvement in an anticolonial struggle or, conversely, toward definitive loyalty to the incumbent regime.⁶ Our proposition is that binary constructions of insurgent or loyalist are overly rigid.

Closely connected to this issue of "who fights?" our third and final theme is the targeting of local populations, colonial subjects whose precarious—and often unrecognized—status as "civilians" left the individuals and communities involved acutely exposed to insurgent and security force violence. Such targeting might be evidenced by demonstrative insurgent punishment of local authority figures and others accused of collusion with colonial state agencies or settler enterprises. But others without clear attachment to any political side also faced heightened risks as rebellions escalated and legal clampdowns ensued. Colonial populations without legally defensible rights as citizens found themselves criminalized for performing workaday activities such as moving outside their village to a place of work, traveling after dark, or socializing in groups.[7] Greater legal restrictions on freedom of movement—the *Staat van Oorlog en Beleg* in Indonesia, emergency restrictions in Malaya, *états d'urgence* in Algeria—which some have characterized as "lawfare," undermined any notional idea that noncombatants were easily distinguishable from the combatants caught up in a decolonization conflict.[8] Our interest here is in the inverse relationship between the multiplication of laws and regulations and the heightened exposure to violence that rural populations faced. For such people, law rarely protected. It persecuted.

Our objective, overall, is to tease out local experiences that either do or do not enable us to identify violent decolonization as a discrete form of conflict. In doing so, our perspective is strongly influenced by analytical shifts in the study of civil wars, in which the work of Stathis Kalyvas stands out.[9] Kalyvas has transformed our understanding of social conditions in civil war by focusing on the motivations of those caught up in it. His recognition that conflict narratives are as multivalent as are the individual and community experiences that inform them rests on several key insights. One is that the explanations of—and justifications for—conflict participation at the macro-level of the nation, the regime, or the insurgent group may jar with those at the microlevel of the village or the extended kin network. At the local level, the microdynamics of participation in violence appear to be shaped by the perception of insecurity, itself conditioned by the continuity or otherwise in administrative services and judicial authority and the attendant presence or absence of security forces and their insurgent opponents.

The mounting difficulties of tax collection in rural Algeria during 1955, the first full year of the country's war of independence, illustrate the point. French tax assessors and the Algerian village elders required to provide information about households, livestock, and landholdings were targeted by the Front de Libération Nationale (FLN) and, at the same time, vilified by angry residents confronted with both governmental fiscal demands and the exactions of FLN fund-raisers.[10] Already issued with sidearms, tax assessors complained that they faced assassination as soon as army units moved on from the districts or settlements in question. Obedient householders who paid colonial taxes were similarly threatened.[11] By October of that year tax collectors struck off certain communes in eastern Constantine, an FLN stronghold, as a no-go zone.[12] The point of this example is to indicate that macro-level explanations of conflict may not coincide with the microlevel dynamics that generate violence.[13] This is not to suggest that we ignore the national perspective to focus wholly on the local. Quite the reverse: it is to argue that our understanding of the spread of late colonial conflicts and the different ways in which they were experienced between regions and communities must accommodate these microdynamic variations alongside the major shifts in policy and action among combatant groups.

From these preoccupations, first with the contest between insurgents and security forces to impose biopolitical control over rural communities, second with those engaged in acts of violence, and finally with the erosion of noncombatant status, we derive the concept of interior borderlands. These were the places where the efforts of security forces and insurgents to compel compliance and achieve meaningful social control were most contested. Contestation over access to resident populations and their resources and the consequent absence or impermanence of tangible administration made such areas politically liminal. Hence, our descriptor of "interior borderlands," because such places marked the edges, the outer margins of colonial authority. Thinking about these areas as interior borderlands helps us explain local variations in levels of violence against resident populations living in places where colonial state authority and insurgent control were constantly disputed.

Consider for a moment the Aurès-Nememchas (hereafter Aurès), rugged hill country in eastern Algeria. Rivalries between insurgent commanders in this region were acute, but the region remained a hub of FLN resistance from the start of the Algerian war in the winter of 1954–1955.[14] Germaine Tillion, the influential ethnographer brought in by colonial governor Jacques Soustelle to help diagnose the source of Algerian resentments in this region, concluded that the Aurès was so under-administered that rural populations had no sense of a governing French presence. At the village level, the political authority of *caïds* (headmen) and *djemâas* (councils) was more tangible, but neither was integrated within a larger colonial administration.[15] Often left unprotected, these village representatives were the first to face punishment by FLN fighters if they refused to work with the insurgents.[16] To remedy things, in June 1955 the French government released 155 million francs to the Algiers authorities to fund the purchase of two-way radios for all subprefectures and some two hundred village councils in areas where FLN activities were reported. For the first time, the central colonial administration could communicate in real time with its local auxiliaries.[17]

Physically isolated from Algeria's external frontier with Tunisia to the east, contested villages in regions like the Aurès were borderlands even so. For these were liminal spaces in which state power frayed at its edges.[18] Whether deep inside Madagascar's eastern highlands or at the perimeter of the Malayan new village, the competing efforts of state and anti-state forces to change patterns of landholding, to regulate family life, to transform cultural behavior, or, more basically, to render colonial subjects legible to officials or recruiters, were fought with particular intensity. In such interior borderlands, whether isolated villages or relocation centers, colonial subjects were especially vulnerable to the everyday violence practiced by paramilitary guards, policemen and soldiers, or, outside the confines of the settlement, by insurgents and their supporters. Rarely did these violence workers face judicial consequences for harming colonial subjects physically, sexually, or psychologically. From punitive acts of terror to rape and other abuses against civilians, the connection between the microdynamics of violence and the nature of these interior borderlands is, we will suggest, a strong one.[19]

Asymmetries, Local Grievances, and Violence

Postwar uprisings in French Madagascar and British Malaya provide our case studies in this first section, with a focus on connections between community grievances, outbreaks of violence, and asymmetric repression.

We might view the outbreak of rebellion in French Madagascar in the spring of 1947 as two histories, macro and micro, running in parallel. One is the better-known account of a nationalist uprising coordinated by a political movement, the Mouvement Démocratique de la Rénovation Malgache (MDRM). In this master narrative, political marginalization of the ethnic groups that formed the backbone of MDRM support, inflated expectations of reform, and a police clampdown on the MDRM leadership all contributed to the outbreak of a clearly anticolonial insurgency.[20]

The other, locally focused history is subtler. It paints a variegated landscape of overlapping village-level concerns. In this reading, struggling families take precedence over the MDRM's ideological claims. Sharp postwar increases in the price of foodstuff staples, including rice, coffee, and flour, caused widespread hardship—in some regions, even hunger. Provincial administration was meanwhile restructured during late 1945 and 1946, with budgetary responsibility devolved to provincial governors. Central to this program was the establishment of sixteen regional tax offices. Their revenue inspectors turned to the local gendarmerie, the *Garde indigène*, to enforce higher poll tax payments.[21] Resultant village-level grievances about unaffordable food and an insupportable tax burden were sharpened by the fact that the colonial government had no functioning native affairs service. In other colonies it fell to the native affairs office—the bridge between district administrators, or *commandants de cercle*, and the colonial governor's office—to evaluate local opinion and to relay policy proposals from administrators in the field. The *commandants de cercle* could also be petitioned in person by village, clan, workplace, or other community representatives. In postwar Madagascar no such connection existed. This peculiarly colonial problem was compounded by the suppression of chiefly authorities in areas where cash crop production on settler-owned farms predominated.[22]

These problems came together in the areas of Eastern Madagascar worst affected by the 1947 rebellion. The new tax offices were targeted. Most were forced to close. Beyond the towns, armed rebels and day laborers joined in acts of political violence: burning settler-owned coffee plantations and ambushing vehicles traveling between farmsteads. Classic acts of peasant resistance—crop destruction and attacks on farm trucks loaded with produce—underscored two things: the local grievances at the heart of the rebellion and the attackers' lack of weapons with which to "take on" colonial security forces. Peasant violence served clear politico-economic purposes but was also performative: a culturally resonant act that signified a community's limits of tolerance.

The tragedy was that the principal audience—the French administration—was missing. The absence of a functioning native affairs service left the colonial government starved of information and thus prone to dangerous exaggeration about the scale of the uprising and its underlying causes. Only later did it emerge that in the rebellion's opening months between April and August 1947 all commercial traffic in three heavily settled districts on Madagascar's East Coast had ceased because of the breadth of social unrest. Unable or unwilling to identify peasant support for the rebellion as a form of protest against chronic poverty, the colonial authorities instead chose a blunt military response. Madagascar's eastern coastal belt was saturated with army reinforcements, some of them Foreign Legion and other assault troops en route to fight in Vietnam, diverted instead to the island.[23] They were expected to act fast in order to resume their original itinerary. If the rebellion's economic and cultural dynamics were never wholly understood, they were acknowledged, albeit indirectly, in terms of political ecology: of control over natural resources and their disposition.[24] The "restoration of order" was to be measured in the resumption of movements of people and goods from farms to markets, something that for several months required military escort.[25]

If the violence of the Madagascar rebellion was clearly asymmetric, the Madagascar case is also instructive as an example of an ostensibly "postwar" insurgency, but one that was catalyzed by wartime political crisis and economic destabilization.[26] Violence was triggered as much by wartime disruption as by anticolonial sentiment, meaning that it makes sense to analyze it within the broader framework of a "greater" Second World War whose ripple effects pervaded the global South for years after 1945. There is nothing particularly original in this insight.[27] Decisive wartime changes, whether events or processes, are commonly applied to explain the widespread emergence of anticolonial insurgencies in the late 1940s. But, perhaps most important from our perspective as analysts of violent political processes, discussion of decolonization's violence as a social practice is substantially absent. Yet understanding collective violence as what political scientist Adria Lawrence terms a discrete *form* of conflict rather than just its *escalation* is surely crucial if we want to explore the proliferation of insurgencies and the nature of the counterinsurgencies adopted in response to them in the aftermath of bigger wars between states.[28] Standing back to view Madagascar's 1947 insurrection as an escalation or, perhaps more accurately, as an explosion of social conflicts worsened by the local impact of world war is easy enough. But it requires the microlevel analysis to work out why the forms of Malagasy violence described above predominated.

In Malaya similar "greater war" dynamics were in evidence. The combination of prolonged Japanese occupation, an abortive British Federation scheme, and Malayan Communist Party (MCP) success in building support among the colony's immigrant Chinese workforce laid the ground for the outbreak of insurgency.[29] On 16 June 1948 the MCP launched an uprising against the British and their local clients within the Malay and Chinese communities. Communist guerrillas of the Malayan National Liberation Army (MNLA) murdered three planters in Perak and two Chinese laborers elsewhere. The British declared a state of emergency in response, outlawing opposition movements and conducting mass arrests.[30]

Few ethnic Chinese supported MCP goals, and the conservative Malayan Chinese Association (MCA) became a focal point for growing communal resentment against the guilt by association confronted by the 2.3 million Chinese in Malaya.[31] Justifiable Chinese complaints of indiscriminate repression went unheeded. Colonial administrators and the Malay elites favored by the colony's political apparatus dismissed Chinese grievances, proclaiming a Malayan Federation that cemented Malay primacy while marginalizing the colony's other minorities.[32] Security forces first embarked on a brutal "counterterror" campaign before turning to a compulsory resettlement scheme, the "Briggs Plan," which forcibly relocated some five hundred thousand ethnic Chinese by December 1952.[33]

Initially at least, the resettlement scheme, or villagization as it was known, deepened Chinese alienation. Entire communities were displaced without warning, their homes destroyed. Cultivatable land and basic amenities often proved inadequate at new resettlement sites, condemning the expellees to "slumification." By flooding Malaya's rural interior with workers forcefully removed from elsewhere, the British created a chronic labor surplus in villagization areas. Barbed-wire perimeters, curfews, and persistent police violence became routine for the "New Villagers," whose every movement was subject to punitive surveillance.[34] In some cases, those resettled found themselves labeled as detainees, their ID cards marked with red ink. This rendered them unemployable, because managers refused to hire "communist suspects."[35] Malaya's forcible resettlement was "counterinsurgency inside the wire" at its rawest.[36]

Life in the New Villages began to improve during 1951. With resettlement nearing completion, additional funds were allocated to improving the sites.[37]

British counterinsurgency tactics also evolved as isolated MNLA cadres faced worsening attrition. The MCP's reaction, codified in its "October 1951 Directives," was to retrench. A quarter of its frontline units were reassigned from fighting to agricultural work intended to sustain the guerrillas over the longer term.[38] The Malayan Chinese Association exploited these more favorable conditions to validate its self-appointed role as protector of Malaya's ethnic Chinese population. With British endorsement, MCA funds brought improved sanitation, civic amenities, and educational facilities to the New Villages.[39] Little by little, MCP insistence that New Villages were "concentration camps" lost credibility.[40] Communist reportage from localities such as Kedah lamented a loss of contact with village populations too closely monitored to lend any support to the insurgency.[41] These changes did not signify that the British had addressed local grievances *or* that the MCP was entirely defeated. In 1954 New Villagers still faced grinding rural poverty and continuing harassment from all sides.[42] Two years later, rubber tappers across six villages in Pahang protested stringent food control measures, apparently pushed into action by relatives supportive of the MNLA.[43] Home Guards who during the day toiled in British-owned fields still fell to MNLA bullets in supposedly safe resettlement villages.[44] In early 1956, Semenyih New Village became a cause célèbre after British security forces and local auxiliaries strip-searched women, making them run for their clothes.[45] A resulting public inquiry into these abuses was overshadowed by media concentration on the suspects arrested during the British raids.[46] Contrary to the top-down perspective of steadily improving security, these examples of the microdynamics of political violence indicate that, to the very end of Malaya's Emergency, the colony's interior borderlands exemplified by the New Villages remained an insurgency front line and a communal fault line.

Violence Workers and Paramilitaries

To pursue violent political solutions, insurgent groups first had to organize by placing themselves beyond the reach of the colonial state.[47] This the Malagasy fighters were never able to do. In other cases—Algeria, French Vietnam, and parts of Republican-held Indonesia—insurgent organization rested on networks of transnational connection, on cross-border evasion, on international streams of munitions, and on sanctuary bases in neighboring territories. How far, though, did these same dynamics condition the activities of local militias, "self-defense forces," and other violence actors whose contacts were more limited, whose freedom of movement was more constrained, or whose organization was more informal? These questions inform our second theme, focused on selected paramilitaries caught up in decolonization conflicts.

Through our microdynamics-of-violence lens, we can see that, locally, these violence workers behaved in ways inimical to colonial interests. In this connection, we look at two quite different militia groups in Indonesia: plantation guards (PG) and the ethnic Chinese paramilitary group, the Pao An Tui (PAT). Local enforcers' actions and the motives behind them illuminate that murky area where European domination stops and colonized cooperation starts. Dutch reliance on locally recruited forces increased dramatically as a function of the additional Indonesian territory brought under nominal colonial control following the first "police action" of July 1947. Still, Indonesian Republican forces compelled Dutch units to concentrate in key areas, so General Simon Spoor's command chose to arm auxiliary formations in Java and Sumatra to patrol plantations, gather intelligence, and, in the case of the PAT, protect Chinese communities. The twenty thousand or so plantation laborers formed into armed cadres are prime examples of violence workers. Armed by the colonial state to police interior borderlands, they retained some independence of action by either remaining neutral or compromising with insurgents. Plantation guards, who generally were reluctant to engage in violence, are at one end of the violence

FIGURE 3.1 During a large demonstration in Medan, Sumatra, in September 1947, Chinese protesters carry a banner demanding the means to protect themselves from the violence by Indonesian forces against their minority community. Their use of English shows they aim at an international audience. (Collection Netherlands Institute of Military History)

worker spectrum, while the Pao An Tui—better organized, but also more locally coercive—stand at the other end. What unites them is their ambivalence about serving as adjuncts of the colonial state.

Our suggestion is that, while plantation guards and the PAT tried to remain neutral during Indonesia's independence struggle, circumstances forced them to make choices based on self-preservation. By 1948 plantation guards increasingly bowed to Republican demands. The PAT also broke free of colonial control, but in a different way: taking local law enforcement and economic power into their own hands. Placing the different trajectories of the plantation guards and the PAT into comparative perspective, our argument is that one category of colonial violence workers may morph into another category of paramilitaries operating beyond state control.

Thus we suggest that the five thousand or so Chinese paramilitaries of the Pao An Tui might be described not just as violence workers, but as violence entrepreneurs. These were paramilitaries whose prime motivation was to protect their movement and the section of the population, whether ethnic, religious, or kin-based, they served. Violence entrepreneurs typically used their coercive power to carve out a sphere of influence, whether working for colonial authority or not. The PAT were violence entrepreneurs in the sense that they operated *apart* from both the Dutch colonial regime and the authority structures that coalesced into the Republic of Indonesia. Their raison d'être was distinct: the protection of a Chinese population widely accused of being compromised by a long history of association with Dutch colonial authority.[48] Another characteristic of violence entrepreneurs is that from the perspective of those who armed them—in this case, the Dutch—militia autonomy translated into an unwelcome capacity for independent action.[49] Financed by Chinese interest groups, the PAT controlled black markets in the towns they patrolled, sometimes bullying local police forces to turn a blind eye to illegal PAT activities.[50] Dutch sources allege that PAT intelligence gathering went hand in hand with kidnapping, molestation, and, in some cases, murder.[51] Some PAT members also exploited their status as armed enforcers for the Dutch to settle local scores (with local Royal Netherlands Indies Army units, for example), thereby creating another dynamic of violence.

The Indonesian resistance targeted plantation guards and the Pao An Tui as collaborators. But whereas plantation guards generally sought accommodation with family or acquaintances in the resistance,[52] the PAT was so specifically Chinese that compromise with the resistance was unavailable as an alternate survival strategy. Throughout the five years of the Dutch-Indonesian conflict, Chinese were murdered in large numbers.[53] Even so, the Chinese organizations that initially provided funds and recruits to the PAT scrambled to declare the force neutral shortly after the organization's founding in Medan, Sumatra.[54] In practice, PAT autonomy resulted in units making enemies *and* working alongside both Republican and Dutch armies.[55]

Indiscipline among plantation guards became endemic as the war reached its climax. By 1948 planters were complaining that their guards were disloyal, ineffectual, or uncontrollably violent. In one infamous case, a single guard leader persuaded an entire guard unit to stand aside when local resistance fighters, led by the guard leader's brother, attacked the plantation, killing the estate manager.[56] The pattern of forceful PG members determining the actions of complete guard units was repeated elsewhere.[57] In general terms, plantation guards refused to risk their lives by barring attackers from destroying factories and plantations. As Republican victory became imminent in 1949, policemen and local plantation guards either deserted or handed over weapons to the resistance in a bid to avoid (post-independence) retaliation.[58] As one planter frankly conceded, "[the guards] were Indonesians tasked to protect us from other Indonesians. What I'd call precarious safety."[59]

Dutch authorities, aware their position was becoming untenable, disbanded the plantation guard and the Pao An Tui. Planters also wanted to rid themselves of unruly guard units because Tentara Nasional Indonesia units roaming the countryside were drawn to the weapons caches stored on the plantations. For its part, the incoming government of the federated Republic of United States of Indonesia (RUSI), soon to be transformed into the unitary Republic of Indonesia, was equally reluctant to leave plantation laborers with reserves of weapons. Immediately after independence, the president of the RUSI duly declared the plantation guards dissolved.[60] Disbanding the Pao An Tui was a tougher proposition. Where circumstances allowed, from the spring of 1948 onward the Dutch authorities negotiated local arrangements with Chinese communities and their PAT units. Elsewhere, PAT organizations endured, although they were increasingly marginalized as independence drew closer.[61]

Parallels might be drawn between the actions of the plantation guards as well as the increasing autonomy of the Pao An Tui militia on the one hand and, on the other hand, the rural counterinsurgent militias put in place by the French colonial administration from the start of the Algerian War in 1954–1955. In anticipation of the implementation of martial law in the northern regions where FLN activity was severest, on 24 January 1955 the Algiers government announced the creation of rural police militias, the Groupes Mobiles de Police Rurale (GMPR). French-officered but recruited among the communities they were to oversee, GMPR units reported to the local prefect, whose responsibility it was to assign them to particular towns and settlements.[62] The underlying purpose here was two-fold: to free up army and gendarmerie units to chase down FLN fighters, and to provide the protection forces needed to convince village communities that the Algerian rebellion would be contained. Additional static forces for policing rural settlements were also a prerequisite to Operation *Sauterelle*, a roundup of nationalist sympathizers accused of involvement in killings of local officials, settlers, and their livestock.[63] The original government decree creating the GMPR defined their core task in terms of restoring a "climate of confidence" in the countryside. Although some GMPR units were motorized and therefore capable of mobile operations, their judicial powers were tightly limited.[64] In theory, Algerians serving in the GMPR could only conduct house searches, make arrests, or take people into custody when gendarmes or members of the *police judiciaire* were present.[65] In practice, their agency was greater. GMPR members furnished vital intelligence about which houses to search and which suspects to detain, creating ample opportunity to shape police operations and to safeguard their interests.[66]

As with the plantation guards, doubts persisted within the colonial administration over the loyalties of individual units of the GMPR. General Gaston Parlange, a former native affairs officer who directed army operations against the FLN in the Aurès during 1955, judged the new militia critical to French counterinsurgency. Together with Governor Jacques Soustelle, he lobbied hard for GMPR units to receive modern equipment, including heavy machine guns, mortars, and jeeps. Both men insisted that GMPR personnel be paid on time, highlighting official anxieties about their loyalty.[67] Revealingly, Parlange admitted that the rural population of eastern Constantine, the larger region in which the Aurès was situated, was "completely silent" about the estimated four hundred FLN fighters in their midst.[68] The general identified various microlevel factors to explain the local population's refusal to cooperate with the French authorities: chronic rural poverty, lack of basic administrative services, and sentimental attachment to anti-authority figures. Six months later, one of Parlange's colleagues, Colonel Constans, a senior commander in eastern Constantine, turned this logic of microdynamic pressures on its head, insisting that the FLN, and not the colonial system, was the root of the problem. He advised the Algiers authorities of the opportunities presented by the unremitting cycle of insurgent demands on villagers in his sector of operations: "Different sources confirm that the populations of the *douars* are tired of the exactions of *fellaghas* [slang form, for "peasant rebels"] and are seeking our protection. [FLN-]forced exactions, demands for supplies, summary executions, punishments, etc. ruin peasant livelihoods and create a climate of fear. Every Muslim can be denounced as a government informer by an enemy and executed without any form of trial."[69] For all that, Parlange's primary solution was punitive: levying collective fines and coercing villagers into working with the GMPR.[70]

It was a hopeless task. Between 1955 and 1957 the quickening rhythm of attacks by the Armée de Libération Nationale (ALN) on villages and farmsteads supposedly under GMPR protection raised new questions about GMPR effectiveness.[71] ALN incursions were often timed to coincide with the absence of French officers or in the knowledge of where GMPR personnel would be at a particular time. ALN insurgents sometimes escaped after having seized the entire cache of GMPR small arms: the principal prize involved. The combat performance of particular GMPR units in several such encounters was judged so poor that more reliable formations, with a higher proportion of French personnel, were brought in to replace them.[72] GMPR units complained in turn that army sector commands either failed to provide force protection when insurgent attacks were threatened or, worse, fired on GMPR personnel mistaken for insurgents. Rural communities were left unconvinced that their security situation was improving.[73]

The war's local vicissitudes and mounting tensions in the GMPR-army relationship became grimly apparent on the night of 20–21 April 1956. ALN fighters launched coordinated attacks on five villages in the eastern Algerian *communes mixtes* of Guergour and Lafayette, situated northwest of Sétif. All five villages had allegedly either come over to the French or sought army protection. A diversionary attack was launched against the GMPR post situated between them, leaving the surrounding population unprotected throughout the night. In the village of Ticsi, twenty inhabitants had their throats cut, and the homes of those accused of collaboration with the French authorities were burned. Two other villages in the same *douar* were destroyed by arson, their occupants having fled as news reached them of attacks nearby. Twenty-eight corpses were found in two villages in the neighboring *douar* of Ikadjadjen. Unconfirmed reports of civilian deaths in other settlements were lent credibility by the discovery of a further twenty-five bodies in the Beni Chebana *douar*, making this the largest ALN reprisal raid in the Constantine *département* since the massacres ordered in the Philippeville region by local FLN commander Youcef Zighoud on 20 August 1955. Significantly, even after these attacks were reported and reinforcements requested, the French sector command lacked sufficient forces to station any troops in the affected villages.[74]

The loss of trust between army commanders, the prefectural authorities, and GMPR units under their authority deepened as factionalism and competition intensified among the insurgents fighting the French.[75] The infamous defection of self-styled general Mohammed Bellounis, commander of the Armée Nationale du Peuple Algérien, the largest insurgent force loyal to Messali Hadj's Mouvement National Algérien, antagonized numerous GMPR cadres.[76] Bellounis reportedly came over to the French in disgust at the FLN's killing of scores of his fellow Kabyles in a July 1957 massacre near the settlement of Melouza, always a contested interior borderland of the Algerian conflict. Local GMPR units were sidelined as a result, a poor reward, some said, for their longer-term loyalty to the colonial authorities next to Bellounis's more recent change of heart. Anger within the GMPR boiled over after another high-level 1957 defection, that of Larbi Cherif, a prominent ALN commander in southern Algeria. Cherif, who spent over a decade in the French army before joining the FLN, was derided as an opportunist, a regional strongman whose harsh exactions from the local Muslim population continued regardless of his change of sides.[77]

Whether Cherif was simply better at extracting local advantages than GMPR units, whose opportunities for gain were constrained by their working partnerships with French security forces, is open to question. Whatever the case, during 1958 the nature and composition of this rural police militia changed fundamentally. An FLN propaganda campaign was by then under way, seeking to persuade young Algerians to join either the GMPR or its civil administrative partners in the Sections Administratives Spécialisés (SAS). This paradox was easily explained. Once assigned to the GMPR or the SAS, these new recruits were expected to relay intelligence, to purloin supplies, and, most importantly, to steal weapons for use by the ALN.[78] Little wonder that the GMPR was excluded from French strategic planning as preparations began for General Maurice Challe's major offensive against the ALN insurgency conducted in 1959.

The GMPR's brief history, as these examples suggest, was shaped by the interaction between major shifts in the conduct of the Algerian war and the microdynamics of village politics and community interest. Drawn into the war as the conflict escalated in 1955–1956, the GMPR was, by late 1958, marginalized from French counterinsurgency plans.[79] The effectiveness of this rural militia was called into question as it became harder for serving GMPR personnel to navigate a path between protection of their local communities, outward loyalty to colonial authority, and, in some cases, a willingness to accommodate FLN/ALN demands. Ultimately, these local factors proved determinant. Although never wholly co-opted by the FLN, the GMPR was not the colonial security instrument that its French architects had hoped.

Problems of Civilian Status and Targeting

Issues that have surfaced repeatedly in this chapter—the ability or inability of colonial security forces to protect isolated settlements, the composition of the units assigned the task, and the shrinking space for neutralism as insurgencies intensified—crystallized in the ways in which civilian populations were targeted by competing combatants.[80] This, perhaps the most important of the microdynamics in decolonization conflicts, also presented the most visceral dilemma for those living in the interior borderlands we have studied thus far.

To illustrate the point, we again focus at the microlevel on local communities, this time in Indonesia, French Vietnam, and Algeria. Their responses to the violent decolonization unfolding around them mirrored the vulnerabilities of living along interior borderlands. Our first example is the Sundanese, an ethnic group consisting of between eight to ten million Indonesians concentrated in West Java. On 4 May 1947 in Bandung's central square, the Partai Rakyat Pasundan (PRP), led by Suriakartalegawa, proclaimed the autonomous State of Pasundan, or Negara Pasundan. The culmination of sustained Sundanese pressure, the establishment of the Pasundan State in West Java was cemented by the Malino Conference of July 1946, during which Lieutenant Governor-General Hubertus van Mook urged distinct polities to seek autonomy under the Federated Indonesian States.[81]

The PRP's victory was hotly contested. Dutch authorities accused Suriakartalegawa of corruption, and infighting made day-to-day governance difficult.[82] Worse still, the Pasundan's creation outraged the Republic of Indonesia. Under the March 1947 Linggajati Agreement, the Dutch ceded de facto sovereignty over Java and Sumatra to the Republic. The latter saw an autonomous state in West Java as yet another Dutch betrayal.[83] Prospects for the Pasundan were further diminished by divisions among the Sundanese. Some reported to Dutch strongholds to signify their support. Others, not wanting the ascription of Sundanese identity abruptly foisted upon them, accused Suriakartalegawa of fomenting discord among Indonesians.[84]

In the short term, proclamation of the Pasundan State helped both the Dutch and those sympathetic to the Republic solve a problem that had plagued them since 1945: distinguishing friend from foe. Each wanted to deny civilian populations the option of neutralism by compelling adherence to its respective side. For the Dutch, the Pasundan State functioned as a lever to draw in those Sundanese who sought protection from Republican demands. Conversely, for Sukarno's Republic the sudden visibility of supporters of the Negara Pasundan afforded its troops civilian targets who were now condemned as collaborators.[85] This tension between Sundanese and Indonesian (Javanese) identities produced specific forms of violence. Its distinguishing feature was the ascription of collective guilt to the Sundanese community, and most especially to those living along the expanding interior borderland of the frontiers between West and Central Java.

Both inside West Java and beyond it, anti-Pasundan organizations sprang up. Sundanese village leaders were cajoled into signing standardized forms that signed over entire villages to the Republic at the stroke of a pen. The Indonesian National Army (Tentara Nasional Indonesia, TNI) units forced villagers into public acts of repudiation, mocking portraits of Suriakartalegawa. Soon, Pasundan's information service had collated long lists of retaliatory acts, including arson and murder, against Sundanese who refused to comply with Republican demands. All took place as the direct result of this new polity, the Pasundan, and the interior borderland it created at the edge of Republican territory in Java.[86]

In sum, proclamation of the Negara Pasundan made waging war against the Dutch in West Java synonymous with ethnic violence against the Sundanese. In Republican eyes, the Pasundan had to be destroyed. The Dutch, meanwhile, used the creation of this autonomous state to force increasing numbers of Sundanese to take their side. At the macro-level, too, the Pasundan's leaders oscillated between Republican and Dutch forces, mirroring the divisions experienced among village communities.[87] But it was at the microlevel that the TNI won the battle for West Java over the course of 1949.

Recalling our discussion of the Pao An Tui, one might ask whether there was much difference between Republican targeting of the Sundanese and the ethnic Chinese. In both cases the combination of lasting intercommunal frictions and locally specific microdynamics was crucial. Whereas ethnic Chinese had for a long period been cast as unreliable outsiders unsympathetic to the Indonesian national ideal, for the Sundanese such accusations were a direct outcome of the ways violent decolonization played out. They were placed outside the Indonesian Republican nation because of their presumed ideological choice to oppose it.

FIGURE 3.2 In Padang, West Sumatra, an Indonesian villager is forced to tell those who have fled that it is safe to return to their homes and to not fear the Dutch presence. 1947. (Collection Netherlands Institute of Military History)

Phrased differently, by 1947 the required level of performance of loyalty to either the Republic or the Dutch increased, as did the penalties for making the wrong choice. Neutrality became unsustainable, making "civilian status" meaningless.

Similar dynamics of shrinking civilian spaces can be observed in French Vietnam and French Algeria, one at the end of a decolonization conflict, the other at a decisive moment of escalation. On 15 May 1954 dignitaries in the North Vietnamese urban center of Phúc Yên, in the Red River delta fifty kilometers upstream from Hanoi, submitted a petition to the commander of the local French colonial garrison. Phúc Yên's petitioners made a simple plea. They wanted an hour's extension, from 9:30 to 10:30 p.m., before the nightly military curfew was imposed. Three days later, the French sector commander, Lieutenant Colonel Pierre Huot, responded with a polite *non*. It was precisely because of the army's nighttime patrols that life in Phúc Yên remained so calm. Vietminh insurgents were active nearby, and experience proved that attacks were usually launched under the cover of darkness. Far better for Phúc Yên's townsfolk to put up with continuing curfew restrictions than risk more numerous Vietminh incursions.[88] Apparently mundane, this workaday exchange between civilian petitioners and their counterinsurgent "protectors" is actually peculiar.

Why? Because ten days earlier, 435 kilometers due west of Phúc Yên's emptied streets, the People's Army of Vietnam (PAVN) had won a signal victory at the Dien Bien Phu fortress complex. News of Dien Bien Phu's fall had an electrifying effect locally and globally. In a peace conference then in session at Geneva, the pace of international negotiations for a definitive French withdrawal from Vietnam quickened.[89] Meanwhile, at the heart of Huot's patrol sector, in the towns and settlements outlying Hanoi, desertions from local "home guard"–type units surged from a trickle to a flood.[90] These colonial reverses were not unforeseen. Conscious that the prospect of victory in the war in Indochina was slipping from their grasp, in October 1953 French commanders in Saigon established a grandly named "War Committee"—in reality, less a strategic policy forum than an improvised solution typical of a bureaucracy no longer fit for the purpose.[91] This macro-level initiative was, at least in part, a response to microlevel problems. The war's enormous financial costs—more than 70 percent of which were met by the US Treasury—had stifled French schemes for inward investment or the reconstruction of local administrative services of the type commonly tied to counterinsurgency efforts. The former "Associated States" of Cambodia and Laos were by then edging toward self-government.[92] Larger tracts of northern Vietnam were slipping into Vietminh hands, with refugees streaming southward in anticipation of a Communist victory.[93] Operationalizing French military plans in these circumstances was impossible politically or practically. At all levels, the Indochina War's dynamics were clearly working against France.

Yet, at the microlevel, throughout these turbulent months the inhabitants of Phúc Yên stuck by their curfew. Or did they? Huot's sanguine remarks in May 1954, patiently advising the disappointed petitioners to be indoors by 9:30 p.m., masked the fact that the town's fringes were already infested with Vietminh fighters. Strict curfew restrictions in the town center were essential to free up troops for more intensive patrolling of Phúc Yên's unruly outer districts. In short, the town was not some aberrant oasis of calm, but a microcosm of the war. Its internecine conflicts—between affluent center and impoverished edges, between the committed and the noncommittal, between Communist and non-Communist—were starkly apparent to the French commanders on the ground.[94] As in Indonesia, taking sides could no longer be avoided.

Two years after the Indochina War's endgame, in spring 1956 French armed forces were immersed in an even bigger conflict, this time in Algeria. Again, the paradoxical combination of harsh realism and dislocated unreality is striking in the welter of day-to-day military correspondence.[95] Analysts at the army's military intelligence bureau in Paris sifted through incoming weekly reports on the incidence of ALN killings, the progress of army security sweeps, and consequent changes in local Algerian opinion. Administrative difficulties within each and every sector command were meticulously described. Summarizing the reportage received in the final week of March 1956, the bureau chief, a Colonel Dalstein, was cautiously upbeat.[96] His timing was significant. This was the first full reporting period after Guy Mollet's Socialist-led government enacted its infamous Special Powers legislation in Algeria.[97] Martial law was extended in juridical and geographical reach. And French national service personnel were for the first time assigned to begin a massive expansion of the army's presence throughout the territory.[98]

These measures, a huge about-turn for a newly elected French government that had promised a negotiated end to the Algerian war, were preemptive.[99] High-grade intelligence indicated that the ALN's recent intensification of attacks prefigured a general offensive in which the insurgents would try to seize control of a major Algerian town from which to proclaim a "free Algerian government." The threat of an attempted urban occupation, the French intelligence now indicated, was overblown. There was, as yet, no genuinely nationwide rebellion, no "general terrorist uprising" in Dalstein's more loaded words. Nevertheless, the intensity of ALN violence was steadily increasing in the regions of the Algerian interior worst affected by rebel exactions. Public servants faced mounting threats. The buildings they worked in—police stations, government offices, schools, and the like—were being systematically destroyed. Weekly markets, another favored target, were forced to close, bringing rural commerce to a virtual standstill. The fabric of French administrative and economic control was being systematically torn away.[100]

Two months later, in May 1956, with emergency restrictions and accompanying French reinforcement in full swing, Dalstein mulled over the latest incoming military intelligence with greater confidence. The arrival of French conscript reinforcements had enabled the army's frontline units to mount search-and-destroy operations against even the most intractable rebel bands. ALN losses looked unsustainable. Most importantly, Algerian inhabitants caught in the crossfire understood that the balance of the war was shifting France's way. Dalstein dwelt on encouraging indications from two regions in particular. In and around the eastern market town of Guelma, epicenter of an earlier Algerian uprising in May 1945, local people were asking French garrison units to protect their homes and farmland. Meanwhile, south of Algiers in the Soummam Valley, another region of persistent rebel activity, villagers were forming self-defense units to resist ALN incursions. Week after week, these units demonstrated their willingness to fight off ALN insurgents.[101] Or so it seemed.

Eight weeks after Dalstein filed his report, ALN commanders and FLN party leaders would gather in that same Soummam Valley. Far from facing eviction by army pursuers or worrying about loyalist vigilantes, the rebellion's senior leadership debated the next stage of the Algerian war. The Soummam conference attendees eventually decided to sustain the rural insurgency while at the same time opening a new phase of urban guerrilla warfare and investing greater effort in the conflict's internationalization.[102]

What do this final section's three cases from Indonesia, Vietnam, and Algeria tell us about the civilianization of decolonization conflicts? Certain aspects might seem familiar. Of these, perhaps three stand out. First, both Indochina and Algeria were asymmetric conflicts in which the occupier's military preponderance and other technological advantages proved insufficient to prevent defeat. In Indonesia, though, the situation was more complex, the asymmetries less obvious, and certainly not consistently working in favor of one side or the other. Second, across each of the three cases, varied methods of war fighting and population control apparently did little—or not enough—to prevent colonial administrative control from ebbing away. Neither fixed defense of key strategic redoubts (as practiced in North Vietnam) nor the military saturation of territory and aggressive mobile warfare (as practiced in Algeria) changed the course of conflicts in which the hostility of civilian populations intensified over time. French security forces tried unsuccessfully to combine what David Kilcullen, in the context of Indonesian counterinsurgency actions in 1950s East Timor, has termed "counter-force" and "counter-value" strategies.[103] The former used blunt military violence—napalm bombing and free-fire tactics—in an effort to overwhelm insurgents. The latter combined political promises with social welfare initiatives, plus an intensive concentration on the domestic economy of the household, in an effort to weaken popular support for independence movements.[104] Applying both strategies, whether sequentially or in combination, proved fruitless in Algeria. For all that, specialist commanders, whether in the elite French army units integral to "counter-force" or the psychological warfare bureaus supportive of "counter-value," rejected any change of course.[105]

A third facet of these French conflicts, and one intimately connected to the preceding point, was the reliance on bureaucratized counterinsurgency, on data collection and statistical analysis of "kill rates" and other supposed indicators of security force advance.[106] This flattered to deceive. Its rationale, that human geographies could be understood and, with that, controlled, was visible in British-occupied Malaysia and Dutch-occupied Indonesia. British officials busied themselves applying statistical analyses on "Surrendered Enemy Personnel" to understand what made them tick. To the south, Dutch general Spoor kept tallies of incidents while divvying up the countryside into "*rayons*" he felt the security forces should be able to control.[107] By the time Spoor had conceived of this idea, the Republican grip on the countryside already precluded its implementation.[108]

In Algeria, by mid-1956 ALN commanders were facing dreadful attrition and struggled to keep large bands of fighters in the field. The insurgency's complexion altered in response. Greater strategic onus would be placed on bringing the war from the countryside to Algeria's northern cities. And, post-Soummam, the FLN-ALN would refine their methods of social control, from collecting funds and recruiting informants to enforcing boycotts and punishing "traitors" to the national cause. Security force reportage offered little insight into any of this, missing the decisive shifts in local politics. Indeed, the army's focus on wearing down the ALN masked the longer-term microdynamics of wars in which civilian populations were compelled to make life-or-death choices in conditions of heightened insecurity.

This chapter has connected local experiences of insecurity with more familiar narratives of conflict between security forces and their opponents—or macro-histories of decolonization. The argument is that the violence adopted by insurgents and counterinsurgents is contingent on the options available to them. The forms this violence took might appear excessive, insofar as exemplary, highly performative killings and lesser forms of bodily violence predominated. But the violence itself was conditioned by endogenous factors that, we suggest, are better comprehended in terms of available options. In this sense, the supposed extreme nature of violence we have considered can be understood as a series of logical, if troubling, choices. These options might be spatial, conditioned by geography, remoteness, and the logistics of communications and supply. They might be technological, a matter of available weaponry and other instruments of violence.

Most often, we suggest, they were political: a reflection of the level of restrictions imposed on freedom of movement, of association and therefore of organization. To test these propositions, we have analyzed cases relating to three topics: local grievances and degrees of asymmetry; violence workers and paramilitaries; and, lastly, problems of civilian status and targeting.

Our findings confirm that some common assumptions should be rethought. One is that colonial conflicts were highly asymmetric, the greater resources of colonial security forces compelling insurgents to focus on strategies of population control. We suggest that this is too reductive a view. For one thing, there was enormous variation in forms and levels of violence between areas that were more or less politically secure. In other words, even where incumbent forces (or their opponents) had "solved" the asymmetry puzzle and imposed seemingly uncontested control, rural communities were not safe from incursion and its violent consequences. For another, supposedly fixed categories demarcating those who supported or opposed the warring parties were in fact malleable and, for the most part, locally determined. Our first chapter section illustrated this point. It seems clear, for instance, that in 1947 the French government never grasped the political economy of the Madagascar revolt and the microdynamics of rural impoverishment that drove communities to violence. Determined to justify a repressive military response, ministers and colonial administrators, as well as army commanders in situ, instead misrepresented the revolt as an entirely macro-process, a nationalist uprising coordinated by a single political movement, the MDRM. In the geographically compact space of peninsular Malaya, by contrast, British security forces and their Malay auxiliaries gradually imposed tighter political control through the coercive containment of a rural ethnic minority population within the closely monitored confines of the "New Villages."

In the more diffuse interior borderlands of the Algerian highlands and the Indonesian archipelago the work of counterinsurgency proved much harder. Even after several years of decolonization war in both countries, loyalties among the civilian majority were primarily conditioned by their lived experience of local violence and not by the "national" history of competing ideological visions for a colonial or post-independence future. It was in this context that our second chapter section examined distinctions between violence workers and violence entrepreneurs, disaggregating between those enacting violence and those directing it. Local enforcers' actions shed light on those interior borderlands, places where state control was fitful and was only one of several endogenous factors shaping the actions of those caught up in decolonization violence. In this context, our examples of paramilitary units called on to do violence work—plantation guards in Indonesia and police militia in rural Algeria—might be construed as "victims" of the colonial system insofar as they were coerced into supporting it.[109]

Depicted as "loyalist" collaborators, these violence workers were anything but. Their ambiguous position and the alliance-making strategies it demanded reveal something deeper about the interior borderlands that such groups policed.[110] If sustaining the colonial system was dependent on the very communities it sought to restructure and control, then the proposition that decolonization conflicts were, at least in part, civil wars seems especially persuasive.[111] Viewed from above, the use of local proxies is a persistent, even defining feature of counterinsurgency strategy. Viewed from below, it looks much different: in part, the displacement of violence work onto local community members; in part, a means for those same community members to enhance their access to material resources, to social capital, and to biopolitical power.[112]

Violence work, then, presented agonizing life-and-death choices. Significantly, despite the efforts made in Indonesia and Algeria to professionalize the plantation guards and the GMPR respectively, neither militia proved either willing or capable of protecting its interior borderlands against insurgent forces. Members of the Pao An Tui, by contrast, were active community protectors with greater autonomy to exploit their role as an autonomous militia. Their willingness to do so lent the entrepreneurial dimension to their violence work, but also precluded compromise with encroaching Republican forces.

The issue of civilian exposure to violence discussed in our final chapter section made clear that insecurity persisted, despite the security force preoccupation with securitization, with martial law, curfews, punitive restrictions, and other facets of so-called "lawfare." Community members still faced the threat or actuality of violence, whether for defying restrictions or, alternatively, for obeying them.[113] Many adapted as best they could, performing multiple identities in an effort to achieve greater security. Public behavior and even intimate private lives mirrored these shifts. Sometimes that required outward compliance with authority, at others, a readiness to support anticolonial movements, or, depending on circumstances, both. These variations, particularly in the interior borderlands on which we have concentrated, underline the importance of a microdynamics approach if one is to grasp who used violence, who suffered it, and why. Contested decolonization, as a consequence, was experienced as something closer to civil war for many of the rural and urban communities among which it was fought.

4

CRACKING DOWN ON REVOLUTIONARY ZEAL AND VIOLENCE

Local Dynamics and Early Colonial Responses to the Independence Struggle in Indochina and the Indonesian Archipelago, 1945–1947

Pierre Asselin and Henk Schulte Nordholt

Both Indonesia and Vietnam suffered tremendously during the Second World War. That suffering compounded decades—centuries in some places in Indonesia—of exploitation, humiliation, and torment under colonial rule. Soon after Japan formally surrendered to the Allies on 15 August 1945, new cycles of violence engulfed both Indonesia and Indochina. Internecine at first, the violence increased as the French and Dutch undertook efforts to recolonize what they still considered theirs. Consistent with past practice, both colonial powers manipulated and exploited existing cleavages among the indigenous population and created new ones to meet their ends. The tendency of their armed forces to resort frequently to acts of extreme violence, and their rationale for these acts, are focal points of this comparative study.

Interestingly, few works have compared the experiences of Indonesia and Vietnam in the immediate postwar period.[1] Analyzing those experiences in tandem, Stein Tønnesson has argued that the power vacuum that followed Japan's surrender allowed revolutionary regimes to seize power in both Java and Hanoi. As neither Paris nor The Hague was prepared to part ways with its Southeast Asian colony, conflict ensued.[2] This study builds on Tønnesson's work. It assesses comparatively the causes, nature, and direction of the violence perpetrated by all sides following the new revolutionary authorities' declaration of independence in Indonesia and Vietnam. The comparative analysis allows us to better grasp the violent dynamics in both countries in the period 1945–1947. This chapter first attempts to explain local outbursts of violence against certain segments of the indigenous population by local forces in each country right after their respective declarations. Who was primarily responsible for that violence in each case and to what extent was it embedded in and informed by former colonial structures and the recent Japanese occupation? Subsequently, we turn to the diverging effects of the intervention by the British military forces, who occupied parts of both countries as agreed by the Allies during the Potsdam Conference (17 July–2 August 1945). Did their presence after September 1945 attenuate or exacerbate the violence? Ultimately and most importantly, we assess how the violence in both Indonesia and Vietnam reached new, "extreme" heights following the return *en force* of the French and Dutch.

This chapter demonstrates that virtual statelessness in Indonesia and a much better organized, but still weak communist state in Vietnam produced bloody contestations for power in which extreme violence against noncombatants became a tactical means, used by all sides, for achieving strategic objectives. It also shows that while some of the parallels between the two cases are striking, the process in each state was unique, owing to different styles of revolutionary governance, diverging international contexts, and different colonial potentials.

The Japanese Occupation and Its Aftermath

Japanese rule impacted Indonesia and Vietnam in profound and meaningful ways. It proved not only oppressive and violent in the extreme, but also produced famine that claimed the lives of millions in each nation. At the same time, the occupation variously enabled, emboldened, and strengthened indigenous nationalists. In addition to halting Western colonial control—in March 1942 in Indonesia and March 1945 in Vietnam—Japan created conditions conducive to assertions of limited self-governance and partial autonomy. The latter gave Indonesians and Vietnamese an unshakable aspiration to independence and sovereignty. The occupation also caused the balance of power in Indochina and Indonesia to change dramatically after the Second World War. The Japanese occupation of Indonesia resulted in years of detention under abominable circumstances for forty-two thousand military personnel of the Royal Netherlands East Indies Army (KNIL), as well as one hundred thousand Dutch civilians, including an increasing section of the Eurasian community in the course of the war.

Asians tended to welcome the Japanese as liberators. Soon, however, it became obvious the Japanese were not inclined to facilitate the national movement or independence. On Java, Japanese military leaders initially bet on the Indonesian urban middle classes to win popular support following the overthrow of Dutch rule. This policy failed because urban leaders were unable to reach the rural masses.[3] In 1944–1945, when the military situation of the Japanese was seriously weakened, a mass mobilization of youth, labor, and resources was implemented in Java through the indigenous Javanese administrative elite. In total, almost two million young men were mobilized and received military training. Notions of discipline, sacrifice, and an anti-Western fighting spirit became important elements of their mental and physical outlook and increased their willingness to fight. As indigenous administrative elites thus played a crucial mediating role, nationalist leaders joined Japanese propaganda efforts to mobilize the labor force. The Japanese increased forced rice deliveries, sometimes up to 70 percent of the harvest. The forced rice deliveries were badly managed but enriched local administrators and Chinese middlemen.[4] In total, ten million men were put to work as *romusha* ("volunteers") under appalling labor conditions. Malnutrition, exhaustion, and illness were widespread; thousands died. Aggravated by bad harvests and the breakdown of the transportation system, famines caused the death of approximately 2.5 million people in Java.[5] Social dislocation, economic hardship, and deep resentment toward corrupt administrative elites and Chinese middlemen became an explosive mixture in the hands of mobilized militias.

For years the Japanese in Indochina worked alongside the pro-Vichy French colonial authorities and ignored Vietnamese aspirations to independence. Desperate to muster more support locally as they faced mounting challenges in the Pacific War, the Japanese overthrew the French colonial government on 9 March 1945. In a *coup de force* that day, they disarmed French military and police forces, incarcerated upper-echelon civilian and military leaders, and confined to their barracks rank-and-file colonial troops of European descent. In approximately two days, the Japanese fulfilled the greatest aspiration of indigenous sovereigntists, realized three years earlier in Indonesia: suppression of the European colonial system. That same month, as they created the Investigative Committee for Indonesian Independence in the archipelago, the Japanese authorized the Vietnamese to form their own ostensibly autonomous government under Emperor Bao Dai to govern the presumably sovereign Empire of Vietnam. As it turned out, the new government was nothing more than a puppet regime loyal to the Japanese, who dictated its foreign policy and remained in charge of internal security. When a severe famine hit Tonkin and parts of Annam, Bao Dai's government was unable to react or even persuade the Japanese to help. The famine claimed nearly two million Vietnamese lives and generated an upswell of anger toward the Japanese and their local collaborators.[6]

Following Japan's surrender on 15 August, a power vacuum ensued in both Indonesia and Vietnam. All major actors on Java were taken by surprise; nationalist leaders were not prepared to take control. Instead, the initiative was taken by young radical and impatient revolutionary militants (*pemuda*) who distrusted senior nationalist leaders like Sukarno and Mohammad Hatta because of their close cooperation with the Japanese. The *pemuda* actually pressured Sukarno and Hatta to proclaim the independence of the Republic of Indonesia on 17 August 1945. The Republican leadership appointed throughout the archipelago local National Committees (KNI) consisting of moderate nationalists and experienced local administrators, and created formal Security Forces (BKR). As it turned out, most of the committees had little authority, while the emerging Security Forces were unable to prevent outbursts of violence.

Meanwhile in Vietnam, the Indochinese Communist Party (ICP) under Ho Chi Minh launched its bid for power the moment Japan surrendered to the Allies. It instigated the "August Revolution," an effort to rouse the masses and secure complete control of state institutions. On 24 August, the ICP and the military united front it had set up in 1941, the Vietminh (abbreviated from *Viet Nam Doc lap Dong minh*, or League for the Independence of Vietnam), compelled Bao Dai to abdicate. The revolution culminated on 2 September 1945, when Ho Chi Minh proclaimed the independence of Vietnam and the founding of the Democratic Republic of Vietnam (DRVN). Ho claimed the new government represented all major political currents in Vietnam. In reality, committed communists held most cabinet positions. That was not lost on noncommunist nationalists and the Allies.

The Revolution Turns Violent

No sooner had independence been declared in Vietnam and Indonesia than violence ensued. That violence was at first largely internecine and fratricidal. Within days after Sukarno declared Indonesia's independence, young militant revolutionaries formed local militias, or *badan perdjuangan* (fighting units), in many cities and smaller towns in Java. Most of these groups were autonomous and operated beyond the control of the Republican leadership. These groups were a new phenomenon, with membership consisting largely of young men who had been members of Japanese militias. They were driven by a new revolutionary spirit (although existing criminal gangs also started to operate under the banner of the revolution). Most *badan perdjuangan* distrusted institutionalized authorities and clustered around charismatic, fatherlike leaders. Their drive for political independence was closely linked to a desire for individual freedom. Their role models were a mix of traditional Javanese strongmen (*jago*), Japanese samurai, and the cowboys (*koboi*) from American western movies. Living dangerously was a core feature of their outlook, and "blood" a key word in their vocabulary. Taken together these militias embodied a new revolutionary vitality characterized by impatience and action, best summarized in the famous phrase by the poet Chairil Anwar: "I want to live another thousand years." The militias took possession of public spaces, controlled neighborhoods, and considered a free ride in public transport as their natural right.⁷

The violent operations initiated by these militias showed a similar pattern in the cities Jakarta, Bandung, Semarang, and Surabaya. They first clashed with Eurasian youths from within the part of the Eurasian community that had not been interned in Japanese camps and had felt humiliated by nationalist Indonesian youngsters. Soon after the Japanese surrendered, these Eurasians formed groups that took to the streets and celebrated in provocative ways the anticipated restoration of the former colonial order. They were often joined by small sections of colonial soldiers just returned from Japanese POW camps in Siam. This led to skirmishes and gang-like violence. The first colonial administrators of the Netherlands Indies Civil Administration (NICA) arriving in the wake of the British troops in late September exacerbated existing tensions. These uniformed NICA officers were accompanied by a small contingent of metropolitan Dutch troops, who were soon strengthened by newly formed military units made up of additional released prisoners of war. These European, Eurasian, Moluccan, and Menadonese troops would form the nucleus of the reemerging Royal Netherlands East Indies Army.⁸ Partly in response to these developments, *pemuda* militias started to kidnap, murder, and mutilate Eurasians and Europeans, and intimidated their indigenous servants, warning them to stay away. They insisted that shopkeepers bar European customers. The militias also attacked Indonesians they suspected of cooperating with the NICA. Europeans and Eurasians later labeled this bloody period in late 1945 and early 1946 the *bersiap*, a term derived from the prewar Boy Scout call "be prepared" used by young nationalists as a battle cry.⁹

From the start, the nature of this violence was deeply embedded in the former colonial order structured by racial differences. By deliberately attacking Europeans and Eurasians, as well as Chinese accused of collaborating with both the Dutch and Japanese for material gain, the militias sent a clear message that there was no place for these populations in an independent Indonesia. While Moluccan and Menadonese elite colonial soldiers were driven mainly by a growing fear of losing their privileges in a postcolonial order, Eurasian gangs also wanted to defend their precarious racial superiority vis-à-vis the "native" revolutionaries. The Chinese, for their part, realized that they were no longer embedded in a colonial structure which had offered them economic privileges and protection.

The level of violence increased as the reemerging colonial forces in cities like Jakarta and Surabaya started to assert their authority beyond the control of the British occupation forces. Like the actions of Eurasian youth gangs, their intimidating displays of violence, which were reminiscent of the colonial past, further provoked violent *pemuda* responses. *Pemuda* in turn managed to obtain large quantities of Japanese weapons, which also heightened the level of violence. An American liaison officer to the British forces complained about "roving patrols of trigger-happy Ambonese [Moluccan] and Dutch soldiers" driving around Batavia in open trucks shooting at anything suspicious, abducting, and torturing. Units of often-vengeful ex–prisoners of war made many Indonesian victims. They even attempted to kill moderate Indonesian prime minister Sutan Sjahrir and his foreign secretary, Mohammed Roem. The British authorities decided to disarm some of these units because of their undisciplined behavior. They also barred what were feared to be poorly trained and undisciplined Dutch troops from deploying on Java and Sumatra for several months. This concerned both units of former POWs and battalions of the metropolitan army.[10]

While large parts of Java thus fell into lawlessness and chaos, Ho Chi Minh's new regime endeavored to avoid a similar plunge into anarchy in Vietnam. Proclaiming independence had been easy; consolidating the authority of the new government proved far more challenging. Though it claimed jurisdiction over all of Vietnam, the DRVN struggled to assert its authority in the southern half of the country. There were two reasons for this. First, the communist footprint there remained very light, even after Ho proclaimed independence. Second, and perhaps most important, a number of noncommunist nationalist factions, abundant in southern Vietnam, actively resisted the new government because they saw it for what it was, an ICP front. In northern Vietnam, the DRVN's staunchest opponents were members of the Nationalist Party of Vietnam (Viet Nam Quoc dan Dang, or VNQDD), modeled after the Chinese Guomindang (GMD). That party had had successfully reconstituted itself and developed a respectable following since its decimation by the French in the early 1930s.[11] Based in Yunnan, China, during the Second World War, it enjoyed close ties to, as well as support from, Chiang Kai-shek's government. The Vietnamese Revolutionary League (Viet Nam Cach menh Dong minh Hoi, or Viet Cach), a loose coalition of political organizations and united fronts formed in 1942 and formally allied with the GMD, also opposed the DRVN, as did the Cao Dai and Hoa Hao, both fiercely independent religious sects with their own militias based in the deep South.[12]

Limiting the influence and activities of these and other opponents while preparing for the possible return of the French was the strategic priority of Ho's government after 2 September 1945. Following lengthy deliberations, Ho and other ICP leaders resolved to liquidate leaders of "reactionary" organizations and movements and other "traitors" (*Viet gian*). They sanctioned the formation of specialized counterrevolutionary units, or "killers' committees" as the French labeled them, to that end. At first, the units targeted mostly former ranking officials in the Nguyen court and the Bao Dai government, Trotskyists, members of the Viet Cach, and leaders of religious factions snubbing the DRVN.[13] Pro-French scholar and former imperial minister of education Pham Quynh, pro-Japanese civil servant Ngo Dinh Khoi (future Republic of Vietnam president Ngo Dinh Diem's older brother), and Khoi's son Ngo Dinh Huan were among the first victims of post-independence communist violence. Trotskyite leader Ta Thu Thau met his demise in Quang Ngai shortly after. "He was a patriot and we mourn him," Ho allegedly affirmed later, "but all those who don't follow the course I chart will be broken."[14] Communist agents murdered moderate political figure Bui Quang Chieu on 29 September.

For effect, some ICP/DRVN executions were public. Following an anticommunist demonstration organized in early September by the Hoa Hao, DRVN "policemen" tracked down and arrested the organizers, plus thousands of adherents. A month later, the regime executed publicly four Hoa Hao leaders at a soccer stadium. The same fate awaited the sect's founder and spiritual guide, Huynh Phu So, but he escaped (he was captured and executed two years later). The ICP dispatched in the name of the DRVN several thousand "enemies" in September 1945 alone.[15] Public terror effectively became a normal part of the Vietnamese communist struggle against domestic rivals.[16] ICP-sponsored extreme violence against these and other noncombatants did little to improve the DRVN's prospects. On the contrary, it undermined its legitimacy domestically and abroad and prompted calls for the resumption of French colonial control from both Europeans in Vietnam and Vietnamese themselves. Within weeks after its creation, the DRVN was a state in name only as civil war ensued.[17]

The British Factor

The British occupations of Indonesia and Indochina had been envisaged along more or less similar lines, but they evolved in a very different ways. British-Indian units landed on Java and Sumatra with the assignment to evacuate and secure all European civilian internees and Allied POWs and supervise the repatriation of over 250,000 Japanese troops, 73,000 of whom were stationed on Java. In the end, they needed three divisions (amounting to 65,000 men in February 1946) to fulfill this mission. The British acted as temporary Western caretakers with a limited assignment. Given the clear signs of a massive nationalist movement opposing the return of Dutch rule and the limited means they had at their disposal, the British decided to seize only the "key areas" of Jakarta-Bandung, Semarang, Surabaya, and Medan on Sumatra. Upon his arrival in Jakarta on 29 September, British force commander Lieutenant General Philip Christison announced that he had no intention to occupy the rest of Java and Sumatra. He added that he hoped for negotiations to start between the Dutch and Indonesians and that he expected the Japanese as well as the Indonesian authorities to maintain peace and order. This de facto recognition of the new Indonesian Republic gave local revolutionaries a boost and infuriated the Dutch.

The institutional weakness of the Republic, the retreat of the Japanese, the absence of the Dutch, and the late arrival and reluctant presence of the British initiated a period of statelessness in much of Java and Sumatra, which would last until April/May 1946, when Dutch troops started to arrive. This enabled young militant leaders to initiate violent local revolutions beyond the control of the Republican leadership in Jakarta and the British forces, as related earlier. After the arrival of the British, the Japanese started to retreat to their barracks. In early October, Japanese army leaders in Surabaya handed over almost all their military equipment to the *pemuda*. In Bandung and Semarang, however, Japanese troops followed British orders to maintain "peace and order," which led to violent confrontations with *pemuda* militias. Japanese violence in one place inspired *pemuda* in others to take revenge, claiming hundreds of lives on both sides. Later, this pattern of escalation was repeated when British troops clashed with *pemuda* militias. Observing the heated atmosphere in Java, President Sukarno warned British commander Christison on 9 October: "When mob psychology replaces ideological arguments, who is going to guarantee the safety of Dutch and Eurasian noncombatants?"[18] He was right. Over the next few days, dozens of Eurasians were killed in Depok, just south of Jakarta. British troops arrived just in time to prevent a bigger massacre. Republican leaders were anxious to contain the local violence, which seriously damaged their international reputation. Although they failed to prevent outbreaks of violence, they did succeed in organizing a mass detention of forty-six thousand Eurasians, primarily men and boys, in the second part of October, thus preventing more bloodshed.[19]

Two weeks before Christison's arrival on Java, British forces under Major General Douglas Gracey landed in Saigon to manage the repatriation of Japanese forces in Vietnam below the sixteenth parallel. The British contingent of eighteen hundred Indian and Gurkha troops would eventually grow to a force of more than sixteen thousand. Two days after the arrival of the first British troops, a detachment of the French 5th RIC (*régiment d'infanterie coloniale*) landed in Saigon. Gracey welcomed the detachment because he and his superiors believed the claim by French intelligence services that the Vietnamese were eager for the resumption of colonial control. Besides, Admiral Mountbatten, the Supreme Allied Commander in Southeast Asia, had promised the French that he would do his best to look after their interests in the region, and Gracey had no intention of letting him down.[20]

Although his mandate was the same as Christison's on Java, Gracey took a different approach in practice. He refused to recognize the authority of the DRVN, which he saw as a Japanese creation and puppet, and made no effort to arrange talks between Ho's regime and the French after his arrival.[21] Conversely, he recognized the jurisdiction of and met regularly with the new local commissioner appointed by Paris, Jean Cédile. Gracey also released approximately five thousand French colonial troops of the Cochinchina-Cambodia Division previously interned by the Japanese, and proceeded to rearm as many of them as he could because he was desperate for reinforcements.[22] On Java and Sumatra, the British only started to allow Dutch reinforcements in from March 1946, after the Dutch-Indonesian negotiations with the Republic got under way. Essentially, Gracey fulfilled his mandate of repatriating Japanese troops while enabling the French to resume colonial control. Gracey's refusal to engage Ho's government and recognize the authority of the DRVN dismayed ICP loyalists. For others, however, namely noncommunist nationalists, the British position vis-à-vis the DRVN was heartening. Chinese Nationalist general Lu Han, responsible for managing the repatriation of Japanese forces in Vietnam above the sixteenth parallel, not only adopted the same obstructionist stance as Gracey toward Ho and the DRVN; he actively supported their detractors, the VNQDD in particular, and leaned on Ho to welcome noncommunists into his government. GMD support for enemies of the DRVN compounded the problems faced by Ho's government and amplified political cleavages among Vietnamese.

France Returns to Vietnam

By the time Ho declared Vietnamese independence, Charles de Gaulle, leader of the Provisional Government of the French Republic, had already started enacting his plan to recolonize Vietnam and the rest of Indochina.[23] De Gaulle appointed two loyal servants with staunch colonial attitudes to serve his aims: Admiral Thierry d'Argenlieu as high commissioner for French Indochina, and General Philippe Leclerc as supreme commander of French forces in the Far East (Corps expéditionnaire français en Extrême-Orient, CEFEO).[24] As Gracey's actions indicated, the Allies were behind de Gaulle, including the United States. Franklin Roosevelt had been opposed to the resumption of both French and Dutch colonial rule, but Washington sang to a different tune by the time the Second World War ended. President Harry Truman fully approved the continuation of French sovereignty to ensure postwar regional stability.

As Vietnam sank deeper into lawlessness, anarchy, and civil war, unknown perpetrators loosely affiliated with the ICP assassinated French residents in Saigon and elsewhere. That created "an almost hysterical fear of the Vietnamese," as well as "an intense hatred and desire for revenge" among Europeans, who until then had nervously and passively observed events.²⁵ Heeding the pleas for intervention from the local settler population, Paris kicked its recolonization campaign into high gear during the last week of September 1945. "We must demonstrate our might and our resolve to use it" to convince "indigenous public opinion that France has no intent to renounce either its obligations or its rights," French military authorities noted. Displays of military strength were deemed essential in the countryside, since peasants were "gullible, easy to manipulate, and always ready to cower before those they judge to be mightiest."²⁶ Independence was not an option, because it was deemed that, for the time being, Vietnamese lacked the maturity to rule themselves.²⁷ Beyond these considerations, the use of force was vital "for the sake of our prestige," French military authorities concluded.²⁸

FIGURE 4.1 Security forces in French service guard a bridge over the Saigon River during the early revolutionary period in Indochina, October 1945. (© Imperial War Museum [SE 5170])

The 5th RIC and newly liberated, rearmed, and indignant colonial troops of the 11th RIC spurred into action on 23 September, staging a *coup de force* in Saigon. They took over administrative buildings and posts, effectively ousting the DRVN as presiding authority. Gracey, convinced that restoration of French rule was necessary to implement occupation tasks, did nothing to stop them.[29] By the official French account, the coup was really a "police action" sanctioned by Allied authorities.[30] Coming as it did shortly after savage retaliation against protesters and insurgents in Syria and Algeria in May, the 23 September coup in Saigon marked the third time in 1945 that France initiated a war of recolonization. As in Damascus and Sétif/Guelma, French colonial troops and settlers, finally freed from the fear and uncertainty that had plagued them for months, sought payback. They lashed out at the Vietnamese, by many accounts taking pleasure in mistreating the most helpless among them.[31] Armed European gangs ran "amok" in some neighborhoods, brutally beating innocent Vietnamese.[32] A mob even attacked a French woman supportive of Vietnamese independence, shaving off her hair as had been done after the liberation of France to females who had collaborated or cavorted with Germans.[33] This "outbreak of serious violence" perpetrated by "poorly-disciplined" Europeans was a harbinger of the systemic extreme violence against innocent civilians that was to come.[34] The French abided humiliation by the Germans during the Second World War; they could not, however, accept the same from Asians, and thus responded in kind the moment conditions permitted. "Primitively" detained in barracks after the 9 March coup, white colonial troops sought to erase their moral inferiority vis-à-vis counterparts newly arrived from France the moment they were released and rearmed.[35]

In the early morning hours of 25 September, armed bands of Vietnamese sneaked past Japanese guards and entered the tiny French enclave called Cité Hérault, located in a suburb of Saigon, and kidnapped dozens of Europeans.[36] According to survivors' testimonies, the captors thereafter subjected their victims to "incredible sadism," "unspeakable tortures," and "sickening cruelty."[37] Among the victims was an eight-month pregnant young woman who was allegedly "raped repeatedly, disemboweled (her fetus served as a football), and finished off in atrocious fashion."[38] In one particularly disturbing instance, "human sacrifices were consumed."[39]

The incident riled Europeans against the Vietnamese. Even teachers and professors turned against the local population, threatening to go on strike if they were entrusted Vietnamese students.[40] French military authorities resolved that a dramatic "display of force" was essential to "calm the Annamites."[41] The need to demonstrate resolve, on the one hand, and the desire to avenge compatriots killed in Vietnamese mob violence, on the other, encouraged French troops to show little mercy toward Vietnamese, including noncombatants, thereafter. Indeed, massacres of innocent civilians, "disgraceful scenes of vengeance against helpless Annamites," became defining features of the French recolonization effort long before the actual onset of the so-called Franco-Vietminh War in December 1946. Burning and confiscating personal property, beating and humiliating men, raping women and girls, bombarding villages, and executing prisoners à l'improviste were among the more odious acts perpetrated regularly and frequently by French troops after September 1945.[42]

On 5 October, reinforcements under General Leclerc arrived in Saigon. Within weeks, forces under his command grew to seventeen thousand. With a military force the size the Dutch could only dream of in this phase, Leclerc was able to reclaim all of Saigon and its periphery. The rapid pace of events heartened the general. In light of its "unfortunate experience" under DRVN authority, the Vietnamese population would surely understand that despite certain inconveniences French imperialism was "above all synonymous with order and peace."[43] Reports from Tonkin (northern Vietnam) that indigenous colonial troops were reintegrating their units as civil servants resumed their duties and shopkeepers once again sold to French clients prompted French military intelligence to conclude that the mere rumor that France was still powerful in the South was enough to initiate this reversal in Tonkin. Once France demonstrated this same power in the North, "submission of the Tonkinese will become reality."[44]

D'Argenlieu arrived in Saigon on 30 October 1945 intent on promptly reasserting French sovereignty over the rest of Indochina. Success in that endeavor hinged on "demonstrating force," he believed.[45] Leclerc fully agree. "Everyone who knows Indochina agrees that the presence of well-trained and armed troops will cause a swift change of attitude among all hostile elements," the CEFEO commander thought. "Everything in this Indochinese affair could be solved by French forces with adequate French means," he noted.[46]

For both d'Argenlieu and Leclerc, diplomacy was not an option until France achieved a position of absolute strength—that is, until it militarily dominated the situation.[47] Negotiating before French forces had a chance to demonstrate their strength and determination, both men believed, was counterproductive to their strategy. Besides, d'Argenlieu and Leclerc considered the DRVN an illegitimate puppet regime beholden not to Japan, as Gracey thought, but to Moscow and the socialist camp.[48] Even if France attempted negotiating with Ho's government, it could not hope to reach any agreement because Ho and his comrades "have always been our enemies."[49] Creating a loyal indigenous government to rival Ho's own, an idea floated by politicians in Paris, was equally unpalatable to d'Argenlieu and Leclerc because it would signal a lack of resolve and undermine if not derail entirely the recolonization project as they envisioned it.[50] "Negotiations with Yellows are a pure illusion," d'Argenlieu surmised.[51] At the limit, d'Argenlieu and Leclerc were prepared to consider the Philippine model of the Americans, consisting of a gradual transfer of power to indigenous authorities culminating in independence at the end of thirty years.[52] "The last absurdity would be to consider Indochina today as a country [*pays*] ripe for independence," Leclerc explained.[53] French military authorities were so convinced of the impossibility of negotiations with Ho that they tried to assassinate him.[54] Luckily for d'Argenlieu and Leclerc, Gracey never stood in their way nor insist that France engage in talks with Ho and his government, unlike Christison, who demanded the Dutch do just that with Sukarno and Hatta.

By the start of 1946 the French forces had successfully "pacified" much of southern Vietnam. There remained pockets of resistance, but the authority of Ho's government, shaky to begin with, had for all intents and purposes been erased.[55] Thereafter, d'Argenlieu and Leclerc set their sight on northern Vietnam. The first obstacle they had to overcome was Chinese Nationalist forces occupying Vietnam above the sixteenth parallel. Unlike the British, the Chinese were not amenable to the resumption of French colonial control. After lengthy negotiations, the two sides arrived at a solution. By the terms of a 28 February 1946 agreement, Paris surrendered all concessions in China in exchange for the right to deploy its armies in northern Vietnam as China's own withdrew. Despite some tensions, including one major altercation between French and Chinese Nationalist forces in Haiphong, the two sides honored the agreement. That, plus a separate agreement on 6 March between Ho's government and the French, negotiated under pressure from Chinese military authorities, paved the way for French forces to enter northern Vietnam.

No sooner had the last of Chiang Kai-shek's troops departed and Leclerc's forces moved in in early spring 1946 than French troops displayed the same aggressiveness and brutality toward noncombatants in northern Vietnam as they had in the South. As they took position in and around Hanoi, French troops ransacked the homes of and savagely beat Vietnamese known to harbor pro-independence sentiments. This was not a case of soldiers gone rogue. To the contrary, such behavior was entirely consistent with orders issued by military authorities in Indochina. Military Directive No. 1, dated 6 April 1946, consisting of a code of conduct for CEFEO forces in Tonkin, sanctioned violence against noncombatants as a means of deterring attacks against French nationals and interests, on the one hand, and progressively reestablishing "the prestige and authority of the French army," on the other.[56] The directive and subsequent instructions that were similarly worded caused excessive violence against civilians to accrue over time. According to Vietnamese testimonies, during a French sweep in Hon Gay on 8 July 1946 entire neighborhoods were "systematically reduced to ashes," and hundreds of innocent civilians were beaten, tortured, shot, "beheaded, drowned or burned alive." Several women were raped, some repeatedly, as children were thrown alive into burning fires.[57]

The French propensity for using extreme violence against civilians reached a culmination of sorts in Haiphong in the fall of 1946. Concerned about the infiltration of Chinese contrabands, including weapons, into Vietnam, d'Argenlieu ordered a naval blockade of northern ports. The blockade angered DRVN authorities, responsible for managing ports under the terms of the 6 March 1946 agreement. Tensions escalated rapidly thereafter. As troops and paramilitary forces loyal to Ho Chi Minh and his government clashed with the French with increased frequency, French general Jean-Étienne Valluy decided to take forceful and, above all, symbolic action. Valluy, who replaced Leclerc as CEFEO commander in July 1946 after the latter angered d'Argenlieu by revising his stance on negotiations and supporting diplomatic engagement of the DRVN, was as tough, single-minded, and racist as French officers came. The time had come to "teach a tough lesson" to those refusing to submit to French authority, he instructed his subordinates from his Saigon headquarters. The CEFEO must at once take control of Haiphong "by all means at your disposal," he instructed.[58] In a series of separate instructions, Valluy specified that the conquest of Haiphong must be "brutal" and the fight against those who resisted "without mercy."[59]

Colonel Pierre-Louis Debès commanded French troops in Haiphong. Debès was an "extremist" who hated the Vietnamese and loved using excessive force against them, Division Commander Louis Morlière confessed later. Like Valluy, Debès was convinced the Vietnamese understood only the language of force. He was a "brawler," according to Morlière, "a friend of disorder to reprehensible ends."[60] Following previous patterns of behavior and Debès's own instructions, the CEFEO set out to resolve the Haiphong crisis by targeting civilians. Between 23 and 28 November 1946, French forces acting on orders from Debès approved by Valluy indiscriminately and callously bombarded and strafed sections of Haiphong populated by Vietnamese in an operation tellingly called "Enfer" (hell).[61] As they did so, they carefully avoided damage and offered assistance to neighborhoods inhabited by European, Chinese, and other non-Vietnamese residents. Estimates on the number of Vietnamese civilians killed during Enfer range between five hundred and twenty thousand. French sociologist and antiwar activist Paul Mus claimed, based on an official report he saw, that six thousand civilians died in the attack. Historian Stein Tønnesson, who has conducted the most exhaustive study of the matter, concluded without providing numbers that "the casualties must be counted in the thousands, and most of them were civilians." In hindsight, he writes, it is reasonable to call the attack on Haiphong a massacre that served its purposes, as it enabled French forces to take control of the main gateway into Tonkin in five days with minimal losses.[62]

The carnage did not end there. No sooner had Haiphong fallen to the French than Valluy issued orders for the taking of Hanoi, the last urban bastion of DRVN authority. "To seize HANOI do not hesitate to hit hard by the barrel and the bomb," Valluy directed; "we must finish quickly by proving to our adversary the overwhelming superiority of our means."[63]

In its bid for mastery of Vietnam, the ICP/DRVN instigated violence and conflict against its domestic rivals. The French dramatically increased the volatility of the situation in their effort to crush Ho Chi Minh's government and reassert their jurisdiction over the entire Indochinese peninsula. Their use of extreme forms of violence as a central and declared element of strategy served their ends well. The violence was not an "unfortunate by-product" of circumstances. It was part of a purposely designed policy to make the civilian population bleed. French weapons and methods made civilian casualties unavoidable. French military strategy was predicated on hurting civilians to demonstrate strength and resolve while deterring resistance. This use of exemplary force was clearly instigated by French military leaders.

The British Stay in Indonesia

Events in Indonesia, after the early weeks of the revolution, took a very different course from those we have just seen in Vietnam, where British and Chinese Nationalist forces had withdrawn by March 1946. British authorities on Java initially hoped to stay aloof from any conflict, but over the months of September and October 1945 they were gradually drawn into the escalating violence by *pemuda* militias and gangs of Eurasians and returning colonial troops. Violence further increased from November 1945 until March 1946, when British-Indian troops confronted *pemuda* militias in Jakarta, Semarang, Bandung, and Surabaya in an attempt to restore "order" and safeguard the evacuation of European civilian internees. In January 1946, British-Indian forces drove out *pemuda* militias from Jakarta's various neighborhoods during a protracted campaign. In Semarang, the British arrived on 20 October in a city that was already in ruins because of heavy fighting between *pemuda* militias and Japanese elite troops. In reaction to the British offensive in Surabaya (see below), Indonesian fighters attacked British-Indian troops in Semarang when they started to evacuate European internees. Timely interference by Republican leaders from Jakarta facilitated the evacuation, but after a brief cease-fire, *pemuda* resumed their attacks. The British-Indian troops again faced fierce opposition, and their departure, immediately after the evacuation of internees, was nothing less than a narrow escape. Whereas the *pemuda* were driven out of Jakarta, in Semarang they reentered a devastated city.[64]

Confrontations between the British and *pemuda* militias also resulted in the devastation of a large part of Bandung and nearly the whole city of Surabaya. Similar to what happened in Semarang, the arrival of British troops in Bandung during mid-October was preceded by violent confrontations between *pemuda* and the widespread kidnappings and killings of Eurasians. Also here, former colonial army POWs formed a battalion. They appropriated the name "Andjing NICA" (NICA Dogs) that Indonesians had despairingly given them, probably as a result of their reputation for abuse against their opponents. Operating in support of Eurasian gangs and Chinese militias that tried to protect European and Chinese neighborhoods, they also contributed to an escalation of tensions and violence. The British occupied the northern, European part of Bandung, while the southern part remained under *pemuda* control. On 23 March 1946 the British set an ultimatum demanding the departure of the *pemuda* militias within forty-eight hours. The *pemuda* did in fact leave, but the night before they left they set large parts of southern Bandung—including the Chinese quarter—on fire. "Bandung lautan api" (sea of fire) became an iconic moment in the history of the Indonesian Revolution, but it was actually a setback resulting in the destruction of a large part of the city.[65]

A similar defeat *cum* destruction occurred in November 1945 in Surabaya. Here, *pemuda* had controlled the city from early October onward, when Japanese commanders handed over most of their military equipment, including twenty thousand firearms as well as trucks, tanks, armored cars, and artillery. In mid-October, *pemuda* groups rounded up large numbers of mostly Eurasian civilians and killed hundreds. When a British-Indian brigade landed in Surabaya on 25 October, its four thousand troops were outnumbered by tens of thousands of heavily armed Republican forces, *pemuda* militias, and armed groups of the population. Unaware of the extremely threatening situation in Surabaya, British headquarters demanded the immediate surrender of all weapons. This was ignored by both Republican and *pemuda* leaders. Fighting started immediately when the British tried to evacuate European POWs and Eurasian women and children. Thanks to a cease-fire mediated on 29 October by President Sukarno and Vice President Hatta—who tried to prevent another blow to the Republic's international reputation—the evacuation started. As it unfolded, British commander A. W. S. Mallaby was killed, probably by an Indonesian sniper. The evacuation continued because President Sukarno offered the British his apologies and ordered the *pemuda* to maintain the cease-fire.

When the evacuation was over, the British sought revenge. With the arrival of the complete 5th Indian Division, their forces in Surabaya amounted to twenty-four thousand troops, supported by tanks and airplanes. Another ultimatum was set and ignored. And so started the battle of Surabaya on 10 November, which

FIGURE 4.2 The burned-out car of British brigadier A. W. S. Mallaby on the spot where he was killed in Surabaya during the partial British occupation of Java, 30 October 1945. This incident further escalated the urban battle between British troops and Indonesian forces in the key city. (Collection of the Netherlands Institute of Military History)

would last for three weeks. British determination to punish and destroy the enemy met revolutionary fury and the determination to defend Surabaya at all costs. The battle took the lives of thousands of Indonesian fighters and noncombatants, destroyed most of their military equipment, and devastated the city of Surabaya. Ninety percent of the population fled the city.[66] The battle of Surabaya showed similarities to the French attack on Haiphong one year later. Both cities were destroyed, but the French and British had different motives and drew different conclusions. Whereas the French decided to regain colonial control and saw Haiphong as an example to be replicated, the British had their revenge and were even more eager to leave Java and Sumatra as soon as possible. The restoration of Dutch colonial authority was never a priority to them. The British were only able to leave Java in November 1946 owing to the cumbersome Dutch-Indonesian negotiations and the slow arrival of Dutch troops after they were allowed back starting in March 1946.

For the Republic, 10 November became Heroes Day, celebrating the biggest battle of the entire revolution. This celebration conceals the reality of a bitter defeat and an irreparable strategic mistake in the loss of almost all military equipment, which the Republic would need so badly when the Dutch arrived in force on Java and Sumatra in the course of the next year and a half. To the Dutch, the battle of Surabaya gave the first indication that the Indonesian Revolution was not a plot of a small group of Japanese-indoctrinated men while the vast majority of the population was still loyal to their former colonial masters. However, still very few Dutchmen began to realize that the Indonesian Revolution might be too big to defeat.

Internecine violence among Indonesians did not cease after October 1945. Among the groups that had been closely associated with the former colonial order and had cooperated with the Japanese military regime were the indigenous administrative elites. Feelings of revenge were widespread in Java and northern Sumatra, where these elites had enriched themselves while the population had suffered from forced labor recruitment and malnutrition and starvation, as previously noted. All over Java, many administrators at the district and village levels had lost their legitimacy and became the target of so-called *daulat* actions. *Daulat* stands for "popular sovereignty," and *mendaulat* was the verb that indicated that people took into their own hands the right to kick corrupt administrators out of their offices. To demonstrate their fall from power, these men were paraded around by an angry mob (*dombreng*). But kidnappings and killings of "corrupt" officials occurred as well. Many administrators had already left their position before the mobs reached their doorstep. Most *daulat* and *dombreng* actions occurred soon after the proclamation of independence, but they were not restricted to the period September 1945–1946. Depending on the extent to which administrators were forced to cooperate with the Dutch, violent *daulat* actions continued until the end of the revolution.[67]

In Banten, in West Java, and in Pekalongan, on the north coast of Java, short-lived leftist revolutions took place at the end of 1945. Here, leftist leaders tried to establish soviet-like people's councils, abolished taxes, and distributed food and textiles confiscated from Japanese warehouses. However, they made the strategic mistake of excluding Muslim leaders from their movement and were soon faced with Islamic opponents and Republican security forces, which put an end to their socialist revolutions.[68]

Daulat actions were not restricted to Java. In Aceh and in the colonial plantation belt on the east coast of northern Sumatra, mass killings by local revolutionary militias put an end to aristocratic rule between December 1945 and March 1946. The aristocratic elites in Aceh and the northeast coast of Sumatra had played a key role in the system of indirect colonial rule and had been loyal to the Japanese military as well. Revenge was the motor of the *pemuda* movements.

Aceh was the first liberated region of Indonesia because the Dutch never tried to reoccupy the area.[69]

In the colonial plantation belt on the east coast of Sumatra, the ruling aristocratic elite had expected a return of colonial rule and their privileged position under Dutch protection. In September 1945, a small group of Dutch special forces headed by Lieutenant Raymond Westerling landed in Medan, to locate and assist Allied POWs and civilian internees and to prepare the return of colonial rule. Westerling rapidly recruited a local paramilitary police force manned by several hundred Moluccan ex-KNIL troops and started to impose Dutch authority in the midst of the emerging national revolution. Seemingly unknown to the Dutch authorities in Batavia, Westerling waged a local private war, hunting down *pemuda* leaders and criminal bands, all the while relying on torture and highly performative acts of intimidating violence. In early October 1945, a small contingent of British-Indian troops occupied the city of Medan. The British soon concluded that Westerling's actions contributed to a spiral of violence. They disarmed his men but continued to rely on his services and his extensive intelligence network until Westerling was called back to Jakarta, where the Dutch asked him in July 1946 to create the notorious commando unit known as Depot Speciale Troepen (DST).[70] Westerling's actions represent another example of bottom-up escalations of violence in the early days of the Indonesian Revolution.

The East Sumatran countryside was in the hands of revolutionary militias with different ethnic origins (various Karo groups, Javanese migrant workers) and diverging ideological orientations (nationalist, communist, Muslim), and various gangs led by local warlords who exported tobacco and rubber to Singapore in exchange for weapons. Because of the collapse of state control, the early days of the revolution were extremely violent there. Revolts against aristocratic rule but also conflicts among militias and criminal gangs threatened the countryside. In March, a violent revolutionary fury put an end to aristocratic rule, killing hundreds of aristocrats in a bloody revenge for collaborating with colonial and Japanese power holders. When the fighting was over, Republican leaders from Java managed to calm down the heated atmosphere of death and destruction. By then, many people wanted the Republic to reestablish order.[71]

It is difficult to estimate the precise number of victims of the violence initiated by Indonesian, British, and Dutch forces between September 1945 and April/May 1946. Contrary to Bussemaker, Cribb, and Frederick, who mention a number of twenty to thirty thousand Eurasian victims, Bart Immerzeel has convincingly calculated that five to six thousand Eurasians were killed. Mary Somers-Heidhues estimated that approximately ten thousand Chinese lost their lives during the revolution.[72] There are no precise figures of victims among the local administrative aristocracies. In Java, most of the targeted administrators were *didombreng* (paraded around) or abandoned their posts themselves; but in northern Sumatra, a few hundred members of the aristocratic elite were killed. In confrontations with British and Japanese forces, an estimated twenty-five thousand Indonesians were killed, while more than 650 British-Indian soldiers and hundreds of Japanese lost their lives.[73] We may conclude that in total, approximately forty thousand people died in Java and northern Sumatra at the beginning of the Indonesian Revolution.

The local revolutionary forces in Java and northern Sumatra were strong, and the violence they produced was primarily driven by revenge against representatives of the old colonial order (Eurasians and former colonial soldiers) and those who had collaborated with the Japanese (administrative aristocrats and Chinese traders). Violence was primarily destructive and often self-defeating. In stark contrast to the internecine violence perpetrated by ICP/DRVN death squads in Vietnam, Republican leaders had little to no control over these violent manifestations of *pemuda* revenge. The Republic did manage to organize the internment of Eurasian men and boys in order to prevent further bloodshed, and did intervene in Semarang and Surabaya to secure the evacuation of European civilian internees. However, it could not prevent the destruction of a large part of Bandung and the city of Surabaya. Republican forces put an end to small-scale socialist revolts in Java but came too late to prevent the mass killings on the east coast of Sumatra.

Dutch Decolonization: Federalism and Violence

In contrast to the French who tried to reoccupy Vietnam by force, the British forced the returning Dutch to negotiate an agreement with the Republic. This implied a de facto recognition of Republican authority over a large part of Java and Sumatra. Meanwhile, the Republic managed to establish its own army, which gradually incorporated various militias and eventually got a better grip on local administration. In Java and Sumatra, violence started to recede from society while the revolution turned into a more regular confrontation between Dutch and Republican troops. Newly emerging and competing states (Dutch, Republican, and federal), although fragile and fraught with internal frictions, managed to end the large-scale local violence that had characterized the early days of the revolution.

Inspired by the French approach in Indochina, the Dutch tried to impose a federal structure in order to contain the influence and power of the Republic. The Dutch design for federalism in Indonesia was characterized by a patronizing attitude. Because Indonesians were not yet considered to be able to run their own country, a gradual process of decolonization was planned under strict Dutch control. Lieutenant Governor-General Hubertus van Mook (1945–1948) personified this policy.[74] Federalism had to guarantee cultural diversity in the archipelago while also serving to isolate the Republic, to be surrounded by federal states willing to cooperate with the Dutch. "Good governance" was given as a precondition for independence—as if the Dutch were still in a position to set preconditions to independence.

The flagship of federal Indonesia was the State of Eastern Indonesia (Negara Indonesia Timur), which covered the eastern part of the archipelago, including the islands of Bali and Sulawesi. In March 1946, Bali was more or less brought under Dutch control by three KNIL-battalions made up of ex-POWs who had been released from prison camps in Siam and Burma. With often undisciplined violence, nationalist militias were attacked, and hundreds of freedom fighters killed. In November 1946 Dutch troops destroyed the main nationalist guerrilla force of about one hundred men in Bali. All were killed.[75] The next month, Van Mook convened a constitutive conference in Bali attended by representatives of the future state of Eastern Indonesia. During the conference he dictated the structure and the political layout of the new state and tolerated no criticism. The conference was closed on 24 December after the delegates had elected a pro-Dutch president while the administration of the new state was basically in Dutch hands.

The capital of the state of Eastern Indonesia was Makassar in South Sulawesi. In September 1945, Australian troops had landed there and facilitated the restoration of Dutch rule. The Australians were accompanied by five hundred mainly Moluccan and Menadonese colonial troops. As in Java, clashes soon ensued with nationalist forces, until the militias were disarmed by the Australian military. In January 1946 the Australians were replaced by British troops, who in turn left in June. At that moment Dutch civil administration was restored but faced serious problems, as South Sulawesi was in a permanent state of turmoil. The conservative Dutch resident Carel Lion Cachet tried to co-opt the local aristocracy but failed to persuade the most prominent leaders.[76] Meanwhile, nationalist militias gained ground and terrorized groups and officials who cooperated with the Dutch.

When Lion Cachet asked for extra military support to "pacify" the area, the Dutch military commander Lieutenant General Simon Spoor sent in the newly formed special forces unit Depot Speciale Troepen led by Westerling. This small unit of some 130 men was allowed to operate outside the regular military chain of command and practically received carte blanche to "restore order" under ill-defined emergency law. Westerling, who had been promoted to captain, arrived in early December 1946 and immediately started his cleansing operation (see also

Bennett and Romijn in this volume). Villages were surrounded, after which all males were assembled and houses searched for weapons. Based on often unreliable intelligence from local informants, "terrorists" were identified and demonstratively executed on the spot. Houses containing weapons, but also entire villages, were set on fire. The "Westerling method" was also practiced and even further perverted in the following months as subordinate special forces commanders and regular KNIL support units started to practice it in the northern part of South Sulawesi. A state of terror and fear was deliberately created for strategic ends, which increased distrust and hatred among the population.[77] Both the Dutch military and the civilian leadership were quite well informed of the methods used in South Sulawesi. Lieutenant Governor-General Van Mook would even compare them to recent Japanese practices. He nevertheless stated on 4 January 1947 that the military violence was unavoidable in order to facilitate the establishment of the State of Eastern Indonesia. At the same time, prime minister of the Dutch-initiated Negara Indonesia Timur, Deang Malewa, confessed that he feared Westerling's men more than nationalist militias.[78]

FIGURE 4.3 Indonesian villagers are forced to watch as commandos from Captain Raymond Westerling's Depot Speciale Troepen (DST) execute approximately twenty men from Salomoni and surrounding villages on South Sulawesi. The Dutch captain, who had a leading role in fighting the local insurgency, was not personally in command of this action on 12 February 1947. (Collection of the Netherlands Institute of Military History)

When nationalist militias retreated into the mountains, the Dutch authorities saw this as proof that the method worked. However, eventually Dutch civilian and military leaders in Jakarta realized that the mass killings in South Sulawesi had gotten out of control. In late February 1947, General Spoor revoked emergency law and ordered Westerling to return to Java. He and his special forces and regular colonial forces had murdered at least thirty-five hundred people between December 1946 and February 1947. In the wider period between July 1946 and July 1947, over six thousand people, but probably more, lost their lives during the struggle in South Sulawesi. Regular colonial army, police, and auxiliaries accounted for close to one thousand victims, while nationalist militias murdered sixteen hundred persons.[79] Westerling would not be brought to justice for his role in the massacre, suggesting the method was approved by the military leadership. The "Westerling method," although never practiced on a similar scale, would become an example for some other Dutch units elsewhere in Java and Sumatra.[80]

Republican leaders initially had to accept the federal structure imposed by the Dutch. The agreement of November 1946 between the Dutch and the Republic created new tensions on both the Dutch and Indonesian sides between politicians who aimed for a diplomatic compromise and military hard-liners who wanted to reach their goals with military means. Dutch army commanders urged the "reestablishment of order" by force, meaning the elimination of the Republic, after which negotiations could start with "moderate" Indonesians. This never materialized. The Dutch assembled 120,000 troops by mid-1947 and launched two major offensives against the Republic in July 1947 and December 1948, framing them as "police actions," just like the French. However, the Dutch failed to develop a successful counterinsurgency approach while being confronted with an increasingly effective Indonesian guerrilla strategy. Unlike in Indochina, where the United States stepped up support for the French, the Americans pressured the Netherlands to give up what they saw as a hopeless and—in light of mounting Cold War tension in Asia—counterproductive fight to reestablish control of the former colony.[81] The fragility of Dutch policy became apparent when the most important federal states turned against the colonial power and sided with the Republic. Despite this shift of loyalty, soon after the formal transfer of sovereignty in December 1949, the Republican government abandoned the federal structure and installed a unitary state.

The outburst of violence in Indonesia immediately after independence resulted largely from anger and frustration among young radicals acting in defiance of the new, ostensibly sovereign state under leaders Sukarno and Hatta. By contrast, in Vietnam, the violence ensuing right after independence was essentially state sponsored, a product of Ho Chi Minh and other communist leaders' effort to consolidate DRVN authority by liquidating domestic opponents and detractors. British occupation forces did not end the violence in either Indonesia or Vietnam, but changed its nature. In abetting the return of and resumption of colonial control by the French, the British contributed to the onset of hostilities and the systematic victimization of noncombatants by French forces. After the signing of the February 1946 agreement with the Chinese Nationalists, the French implemented in the North the same policies and tactics, including systematic violence against civilians, that they had employed in the South. Conversely, British forces deployed on Java and Sumatra mostly kept the Dutch at bay through 1945 and much of 1946. However, unlike their compatriots in Vietnam, the British themselves unwillingly became directly implicated in the violence in Indonesia—and on a massive scale.

While some of the parallels are striking, the processes in Indonesia and Vietnam were each unique, owing to radically different styles of revolutionary governance, international contexts, and colonial potentials. The ICP's effort to eliminate domestic rivals, ruthless as it was, exacerbated existing political cleavages in Vietnam and turned the Vietnamese revolution into a nasty civil war. Local violence in Java in 1945–1946, for its part, was primarily directed toward pillars of the old colonial regime, namely Eurasians, Ambonese, and Menadonese with ties to the colonial army, Chinese *peranakan*, and local administrative elites. In this context, noncombatants were deliberately attacked by revolutionary groups. This would strain relations between these groups and the Indonesian nation-state after 1950. In contrast to Vietnam, the revolution in Indonesia was, immediately after the proclamation of independence in Jakarta, driven primarily by local forces that often operated beyond the control of the Republican leadership. Vietnam and Java both experienced interventions by Allied forces, but owing to the initial absence and weakness of the Dutch—in contrast to early French reoccupation efforts—the British unexpectedly faced much more violent resistance, which made them de facto recognize the Republic and decide to leave Java as soon as possible. Extreme violence toward and by colonial associates in 1945–1946 in Indonesia was connected to the long-established characteristic of co-option in the colonial system. This may explain why *bersiap* violence against Dutch and pro-Dutch groups in Indonesia far exceeded Vietnamese violence against French nationals. In turn, this gave an early impetus for more spontaneous, locally driven escalations. Combined with Dutch weakness in military terms, as well as a lack of state control, this contributed to a pattern whereby—on both sides—extreme violence in this phase was driven bottom-up rather than directed top-down, as in Vietnam.

Two important sources of Dutch weakness—the lack of strategic potential of the metropole and British constraints imposed on Dutch actions—were not at play for the French in Vietnam. The CEFEO had carte blanche to do as its leaders wished there. Assuming as they did that demonstrating strength and resolve was essential for compelling the Vietnamese to accept the resumption of colonial control, French military authorities sanctioned and even encouraged the use of extreme violence against both belligerents and non-belligerents by troops under their command. The suffering endured by Vietnamese civilians after the French returned in the fall of 1945 was also the product of military leaders' obsession with their own and France's prestige, on the one hand, and their reliance on exemplary force to assert it, on the other. Dutch commanders were only gradually enabled to display similar traits once they came in possession of more military means from late 1946. Nevertheless, the outcomes of these differing processes—either bottom-up or top-down—were surprisingly similar in both cases: widespread campaigns of extreme and exemplary violence.

5

THE PLACES, TRACES, AND POLITICS OF RAPE IN THE INDONESIAN AND THE ALGERIAN WARS OF INDEPENDENCE

Stef Scagliola and Natalya Vince (in collaboration with Khedidja Adel and Galuh Ambar)

Rape stands out, compared with other acts of violence in wartime—even other acts of extreme violence—as it is never officially sanctioned and in theory should always be punished. While it is not an inevitable feature of war,[1] it is nevertheless a persistent problem, as civilian and combatant women have been seen as "sexual booty" for conquering soldiers since time immemorial.[2] Some cases of systematic and/or mass rape have become iconic, often because they are seen to embody the "barbarity" of (former) enemies. In other cases, endemic sexual violence in wartime barely registers on wider public consciousness. The vast theoretical literature on why soldiers rape in wartime contrasts sharply with the scarce, fragmented, and scattered nature of specific accounts of rape that one can find in cursory court cases, passing references in soldiers' memoirs, and the often hesitantly spoken testimony of victims.

Through the two case studies examined here, the Indonesian War of Independence (1945–1949) and the Algerian War of Independence (1954–1962), we seek to demonstrate the dynamics at play that increase the risk of rape, and at the same time explore how knowledge about rape is silenced, transmitted, or documented. From the outset, it is important to underline that there is little we can quantitatively affirm about the relative occurrence of rape in the two wars.[3] A superficial comparison between available French and Dutch court records might suggest that proportionally more cases of rape and sexual violence were prosecuted through Dutch military courts than through their French counterpart. For a total 220,000 military personnel who served in Indonesia over four years, Dutch Military Justice records that were preserved yield seventy-two cases in which Dutch military personnel were accused of sexual violence, fifty-three of which cases resulted in guilty verdicts.[4] In the French records, the historian Marius Loris-Rodionoff found thirteen rape cases, out of a total of 636 cases for charges ranging across desertion, manslaughter, theft, and disobedience, that were prosecuted through the Constantine Permanent Tribunal of the Armed Forces. This tribunal was one of three of its type in Algeria that disciplined some of the two million soldiers deployed by the French army in Algeria.[5]

Statistically, this kind of comparison is largely meaningless. Rape has always been underreported and under-prosecuted, both in civilian societies and in theaters of war. In wartime, bystanders, mostly fellow soldiers, rarely break the code of silence about offenses they have witnessed. The silence on the side of the victims can be attributed to societal norms and pressure not to undermine the "honor" of the family.[6] A comparison between the Indonesian and Algerian context becomes meaningful if we focus on the visibility of rape as a form of violence committed by the French and Dutch armies. One of the biggest scandals

FIGURE 5.1 Djamila Boupacha, a member of the FLN and victim of rape during the Algerian War of Independence, visits the Labour Party headquarters in London in the company of other Algerian functionaries, March 14, 1963. (Keystone-France / Gamma-Rapho via Getty Images)

of the Algerian War of Independence was the torture and rape, while in French army custody, of Djamila Boupacha, a member of the Algerian National Liberation Front (FLN).[7] A wide range of French intellectuals, politicians, and artists denounced her treatment, while Spanish artist Pablo Picasso painted her portrait. The scandal became emblematic of the broader treatment of Algerians by the French state. A similar cause célèbre is absent from contemporary accounts of the Indonesian War of Independence a decade earlier. In his war diaries, Indonesian general Abdul Haris Nasution does refer to the rape of Indonesian women by Dutch soldiers, but it features almost in passing.[8] This contrast is mirrored in the historiography: the significant body of literature on sexual violence committed by French troops in Algeria[9] has no equivalent in the Dutch-Indonesian context.

Thinking about the relative visibility/invisibility of rape, and the nature of the sources that we have, and do not have, at our disposal, is central to understanding the dynamics of rape in wartime. Not only does it enable us to examine why rape happens—that is, whether it functions as a weapon of war and how it is facilitated by certain types of warfare—but it also gives us insight into how victims might seek redress and how the act of condemning rape was politically weaponized. This chapter begins by delineating the places and contexts in which Indonesian and Algerian women were especially vulnerable to rape. We quote at some length from sources such as judicial records, contemporary published accounts, memoirs, and oral histories, because their very existence is at the core of the analysis in parts two, three, and four of the chapter, in which we address attributed motivations, politicization, and redress.

The Dynamics of Rape in Guerrilla Warfare and Counterinsurgency

Both the Indonesian and the Algerian wars of independence were colonial conflicts conducted through a similar kind of guerrilla/counterinsurgency warfare that created specific contexts which made particular kinds of violence and sexual violence more likely. Compared to each other, both of these conflicts also had their own specificities.

Rape in the Village

In both Indonesia and Algeria, a common moment for rapes to be committed was in the aftermaths of "sweeps" or "mopping up" actions, searches meant to comb out villages where—according to (often outdated) intelligence—enemy forces were active. Defining "enemy forces" was not clear-cut, however, as the spaces in which nationalist combatants and civilians operated were the same. Indeed, the distinction between combatant and civilian was blurred by both guerrillas and conventional European armies. In addition to sweeps, rural populations were subjected to collective punishments, summary executions, and, in the Algerian case, mass population displacement into camps by European armies. Simultaneously the very same armies might sustain a discourse about wanting to protect "the people" from "the outlaws." Troops involved in sweeps were often strangers to the village (i.e., not locally stationed) and were able to move on after attacks without being easily traceable or identifiable. Rapes could often be part of a series of violent acts directed against civilian populations, including burning down homes, tainting foodstuffs, and stealing. For example, between 2 and 7 April 1949, the special forces of the Dutch colonial army (the "red berets") committed a series of crimes in the region of Sukabumi in Indonesia. In the course of five days, they raped a twelve-year-old girl and four married women, sexually assaulted twelve other women, killed seventy-seven Indonesian civilians, wounded one, committed 177 acts of theft, and burned down a house.[10]

Unarmed villagers were extremely vulnerable, as an account documented in a field court-martial following the rape of a child during a patrol in Soekowirjo reveals: "All the men were brought together. The perpetrator took the opportunity and abused K.: M. pointed his gun at 10-year old K., after which he laid it away, and raped her."[11] The number of soldiers involved in a case of rape made it even harder for women and girls to fight back, and reduced the likelihood of reporting by fellow soldiers, as they were collectively implicated. A case that did make it into the Dutch military records describes a gang rape in the following terms: "One of the three who deliberately grabbed I. in a violent way, picked her up and brought or rather dragged her to the guard post while she was unwilling and resisted, pulled her to the floor, so that she lay on her back, while the suspect pulled her sarong [cloth used as skirt] off, and held her ankles to the floor, G. held her arms to the floor. When she could no longer defend herself, V., K. and G. raped her."[12]

An often-cited description of rape against rural Algerian women comes from a diary entry of Algerian teacher and author Mouloud Feraoun. On 8 January 1957 he describes the systematic mass rape of women in the region of the Ouadhias, in Kabylia. While the men were locked up or shot, "women remained in the villages, at home. They were given orders to leave the doors open and to stay isolated in the different rooms of each house. The village was thus transformed into a populous BMC [military brothel], into which the mountain infantry and other legionnaire companies were unleashed."[13]

In Algeria, the process of a search typically began with a series of violations of Algerian social space, which step by step could culminate in rape. First, by entering into the home, as men not related to the women who lived there, soldiers were breaking with the principle of the *horma* (the sacredness of domestic space and of the separation of the sexes outside the family). Second, body searches involved stripping women naked. This was highly sexualized and often based on claimed knowledge about local cultural practices, such as women shaving their pubic hair—which supposedly pointed to their having had recent sexual relations with a husband who was suspected of having joined the rural guerrillas.[14] Women were also considered to have "more places to hide things," supposedly necessitating searches of the vagina and anus.[15] In a number of women's accounts, rape is presented—or implied—as the culmination of this incremental process of increasingly exposing and making women's bodies vulnerable.

In other cases, soldiers stationed in a rural area acted outside of a military operation. A soldier in South Sumatra wrote about a new member of his unit in his diary, a remarkably daunting character, who would "break out, take the car and gun of the desk sergeant, drive to a village, summon the village head to provide him with a woman, and come back the next morning."[16] In this case, the village head was likely coerced into the position of recruiter; in other cases, women were simply snatched by the military personnel themselves. This is described by a member of an intelligence unit in Central Java, in his covert coverage of how his unit operated: "The members of the intelligence service do not engage in long-lasting sexual relationships with Indonesian women. Yet, according to Tuminah (a woman who operates in this unit) at night sometimes women are taken from the village by force. Apparently, there are sexual needs, but this is not accommodated through assimilation [i.e., by building local relations]."[17]

Whether committed outside or within the context of military operations, rapes often unfolded in similar ways. In the following case, an errand of three Dutch military personnel who left their camp to trade chickens for clothes turned into "a raiding party of a number of villages." According to the court-martial, "They intruded into a house. S. admitted to having grabbed the lady of the house with the intention of sexually assaulting her, after which the woman began to scream and ran out of the house."[18]

Similar circumstances are documented by Loris-Rodionoff in his summary of the rare cases of rape that made it to the Constantine Tribunal of the Armed Forces: "These rapes are premeditated, they happen at night, while on leave, sometimes under the influence of alcohol."[19] A case in point is that of three parachutists charged with rape in 1957, who sneaked out of their camp at night:

> They walked until 23.00 [11 p.m.] and arrived at Ben Hamdani. They entered a first gourbi [makeshift home] where they carried out an

identity check. Then they knocked on the door of a second gourbi shouting "Patrol!" The door opened, and they entered. They found a young Algerian woman called KK, her husband MM and the mother of the young woman. The three men made the girl leave and took her into another room. RR and TG "abused her," in the language of the indictment. They raped her. Then they went into another gourbi without finding any women. They came back to the gourbi of the K family. They made the parents of K, who was 15, leave. They were guarded by RR. TG and CP "tried to abuse her." They hit her, ripped her clothes, and stripped her naked. They laid her on the ground. The father of the young girl managed to intervene and challenged their behavior. He reminded them that he was a veteran and a former soldier. After this, they gave up.[20]

The men then left and went on to sexually abuse and rape two other women in the village. What is striking is how they deliberately abuse their authority by presenting themselves as operating as part of a military action (knocking on the door and shouting "Patrol!"), knowing that this is strictly against orders.

The Domestic Context of the Army Barracks— Typical for Indonesia

One feature of the Dutch army in Indonesia that did not have an equivalent in the French army in Algeria was the figure of the *baboe*. *Baboe* is a word of Indonesian origin, used by the Dutch to refer to female domestic cleaners or housekeepers. The presence of subordinate Indonesian women as concubines who were expected to take care of the household and offer comfort and sex to their Dutch masters had been a well-established feature within the colonial civilian and military context. In the post–Second World War military context, with the majority of troops deployed from the Netherlands, it was adopted in a slightly different form. There was approximately one *baboe* for every five to eight men in the barracks, employed to cook, clean, and wash clothes. This constant presence of Indonesian young women was in some cases the context for durable relationships, but also for harassment and coercion. The opportunities to abuse these women were numerous, as they were present in all the spaces of "intimacy"—the washing rooms, dormitories, and kitchens. In one field court-martial judgment, for example, "soldier T.B. in M. has had intercourse under threat of a weapon [i.e., rape], with a woman of Indonesian origin, named D. The perpetrator has, after getting drunk, and going to bed, soiled his bed, after which he called for a *baboe* to clean the room, and then grabbed her."[21] For this rapist, sexual relations with the *baboe* are apparently part of the "services" she provides. In another account, produced by former members of a Dutch army unit in 1996, one veteran recalls being encouraged by fellow soldiers to have sex with a clearly non-consenting *baboe*: "At a certain moment, they were getting me drunk or half drunk, and started to offer me one of their many *baboes*, who luckily said, Tida mau, toean (which means, I don't want to, sir)."[22] In both these accounts, *baboes* are not considered individual women with agency, but rather as part of the services of a barracks. In fact, *baboes* often had the additional informal "task" of providing "sexual relief" to the unit. Local commanders would make such arrangements to prevent their men from contracting venereal diseases when visiting prostitutes (in Algeria, the French army formally created military brothels for the same purpose of "sexual release"). In a diary account, H. van Hoorn describes traveling a long way with a group of men and lodging as guests at an army logistical base in Banjoewangi: "[We] went to town to have some food and went to bed early. We had traveled for 270 miles. At night we were woken by a lot of noise and ado. It turned out to be R. who was after the *baboes* of our hosts. This is really impolite; one should not behave this way as guest."[23] This is not to say that all sexual contacts between *baboes* and Dutch military personnel could be characterized as

FIGURE 5.2 Four "*baboes*" wash uniforms inside a military encampment in 1949. In Indonesia, unlike in Algeria, such local female workers were common on military bases and smaller posts during colonial times. Dutch military personnel often had intimate relations with these women, but sexual abuse also occurred in this setting. (Collection Netherlands Institute of Military History)

nonconsensual, or even that all came down to exploitation. There is evidence of "love affairs" and caring relationships developing between soldiers and *baboes*, yet even then we have to keep in mind the structural power difference between Dutch military and Indonesian women. Moreover, relationships between Dutch soldiers and Indonesian women were not static; they could develop over time and transform from a relation of coercion and exploitation into one in which mutual profit and consent was the basis.[24]

The Prison or "Regrouping" Camp—Typical for the Algerian Context

Two aspects of the Algerian War of Independence were distinct from its Indonesian counterpart: first, the visibility of women recruited into the FLN and its National Liberation Army (ALN), and, second, the *camp de regroupement* ("regrouping camp"). The majority of women contributed to the struggle by cooking, healing, and washing for ALN guerrilla units hiding in the countryside, as well as in urban areas. The best-known women, however—foregrounded by both the FLN and the French media—were smaller in number and joined rural guerrilla units, notably as nurses, or became members of urban bomb networks. Accustomed to representations of Algerian women as passive and cloistered from the outside world, the French army was taken by surprise by this new role, but very rapidly Algerian women would be treated in the same way as Algerian men. They were arrested, interrogated, and tortured as suspects. This is in contrast to the Indonesian context. A few Indonesian women's fighter units were formed, but Indonesian nationalist leaders primarily envisioned a caring role for Indonesian women during the revolution. By joining forces in women's federations, they were expected to provide first aid and food to male combatants and civil servants, and to support displaced refugee families.[25]

Just as in the rural setting, the violence committed against Algerian women in custody reveals a pattern. First, they were made to strip, then they were insulted, often in highly sexualized terms, after which they were tortured—again in sexualized ways—with electric shocks applied to the genitals. The final act of degradation was being raped, either with an object and/or by one or more men. The ways in which women use a far less explicit language than this to describe such horrific experiences is illustrated by Djamila Boupacha's account of her treatment in prison, conveyed to her lawyer Gisèle Halimi. She had been arrested on suspicion of being a member of the Algiers bomb network in 1960:

> They spat on me. . . . I was naked, they were spitting the beer that they were drinking. . . . The electrical wires, they stuck them . . . do you know

how? With strips of tape . . . on my nipples . . . on . . . I can't tell you. . . . Everywhere, do you understand? . . . It's a terrible thing. The bottle, they forced it in. . . . My parents don't know. I mean, they know but they don't know everything. I didn't say anything. It's too serious for us. I don't know if I'm a young girl [i.e., a virgin]. Do you understand? I fainted, there was blood, when they took me back down to the cell.[26]

This hesitantly conveyed account became world news. Less well known and publicized is the rape of the Indonesian activist Sitti Hasanah Nu'mang. Based in Pare Pare, South Sulawesi, as a member of an underground organization, she was arrested along with her father and brother in February 1947, had to witness their execution, and was later drugged and raped. This story was told in her memoirs, which were published in 1995.[27] The fact that we possess Boupacha's contemporary account prompts reflection. While the vast majority of Algerians were illiterate, a number of those in the ALN's urban network in Algiers—including Boupacha—came from middle-class backgrounds and were educated in French, and therefore able to articulate to European audiences what had happened to them, however difficult this still was. For Boupacha's account then to become public knowledge, it had to be publicized by the team of FLN lawyers and supporters and find resonance in the French press.

The overwhelming majority of women's stories of rape in Algeria did not reach this level of visibility. Around a third of the Algerian rural population was forcibly displaced into *camps de regroupement* that were created with the aim of dismantling FLN support networks and were under the control of the army.[28] This meant that families were displaced from their homes and uprooted from their usual forms of social organization. These camps differed from internment camps—which existed in both Indonesia and Algeria as a form of preventive detention—in that they specifically targeted civilian populations. Accounts of rape in *camps de regroupement* only emerged from the 2000s onward. In 2001, Mohamed Garne, born in such a camp in April 1960, won a thirteen-year-long legal battle to be recognized by the French state as a war victim. His sixteen-year-old mother, Kheira Garne, had been gang-raped by French soldiers, and Mohamed's disabilities were the result of these same soldiers beating the pregnant teenager in a failed attempt to provoke a miscarriage. Mohamed Garne was awarded 30 percent of an invalidity pension for three years as a compensation for his "psychological problems."[29]

Prisons or camps could also be improvised. Khedidja Adel has been carrying out painstaking work on the "women's prison of Tifelfel" in the Aurès Mountains that was set up in 1955 and consisted of two requisitioned houses. Twenty-two women were imprisoned there from August 1955 to October 1956, with their newborn babies and young children, to isolate them from the male members of their families who had joined the guerrillas. According to memories shared by Adel, women, and notably young women without children, were brutally tortured and frequently subjected to sexual violence and rape by their guards—Algerians, Moroccans, and Frenchmen.[30] At the same time, being imprisoned for more than one year with often the same guards created a certain kind of familiarity. While they explicitly feared particular guards, there were others who expressed sympathy for them, and cried at seeing the violence inflicted on them.

The cases of rape presented here seem to point to two distinct contexts. They are either committed during an operation in the field or an interrogation in custody, or outside a military operation in "leisure" time. But the contrast is only superficial, as both dynamics of rape are the product of guerrilla/counterinsurgency warfare. Besides the lack of clear distinction between fighting forces and civilian populations, there is also the problem of constant "flux."[31] Counterinsurgency warfare means that the spaces and times of frontline combat and off-duty "leisure" are not fixed but change continuously, depending on the movement of troops. To fight nationalist guerrilla warfare, European armies developed small, highly mobile units that tracked insurgents across large rural areas, with no obvious rear base, operating relatively independently of main command structures. Ordinary troops that were deployed in rural areas a great distance from central command could also "afford" such behavior with little risk of being caught. The opportunities to engage in rape or sexual harassment were a product of the kind of warfare these troops were engaged in: rural, remote, and with no obvious front line. This means that in both wars of independence, circumstances were created in which troops could easily come into contact with local women, in a context of relative autonomy, and thus relative impunity.

Motivations for Rape in Wartime

Feminist scholar Cynthia Enloe, who has worked extensively on gender and militarism, classifies rape in wartime into three main types: "recreational rape," "national security rape," and "systematic mass rape."[32] Similar kinds of classifications are used by other scholars.[33] Cases that take place in villages, in *camps de regroupement*, or in army barracks might fall into the category of "recreational rape." They are enabled because commanders—either at the local or national level—are unable or unwilling to enforce discipline. In the words of Dominique Olivier, a French army veteran of Algeria, "If there is a very bad captain, or second lieutenant who's no better, you're heading for a disaster, a catastrophe. First of all, lots of people will be killed, and then as the second lieutenant doesn't control his men and the captain doesn't control his second lieutenant, you can be sure that *mechtas* [villages] are going to burn, girls will be raped, and the few possessions that they [rural civilians] have in their homes will be robbed, etc."³⁴

Implicit in many contemporary accounts and memoirs is the notion that combat heightens men's uncontrollable "need" for sexual gratification. Dutch veteran Sikke Galama recalls such a mood after combat: "The urge for female flesh, you may even call it lust, increases after fear has waned."³⁵ Viewed from this perspective, rape could be seen by some as the consequence of a failure to secure sexual relations through consensual or monetized forms. This kind of thinking underpinned Western armies' role in actively organizing prostitution to channel this "need." Yet besides the fact that it is highly questionable whether organized prostitution reduces incidences of rape,³⁶ we must also treat the idea of an "uncontrollable urge" with suspicion. Other men subject to the same dynamics of war be it in the barracks surrounded by *baboes*, or guarding women in the makeshift prison of Tifelfel—did not rape. Occasionally, as a Dutch soldier writes in his diary, some even intervened to stop rapes happening: "When we came nearer we heard two soldiers on patrol inside and a woman's voice say 'tida toean,' 'no sir.' After a second I recognized the voice of one of the sentries, flung the door open, and held the startled fellow soldiers to task about their behavior."³⁷ Similarly, in an Algiers torture center, FLN militant Louisette Ighilahriz was saved from repeated torture and rape by a French military doctor.³⁸

The rapes that victimized Louisette Ighilahriz and Djamila Boupacha in Algeria, and Sitti Hasanah Nu'mang in Indonesia,³⁹ fall into Enloe's category of "national security rape." This is rape deployed as a tool of terror to punish women who are labeled subversive and perceived as a threat to the nation and/or state. But here again there is ambiguity. In their witness accounts these women state that they are being targeted for who they are—nationalist activists—but the acts of violence to which they are subjected also reflect a loss of discipline of their captors, blurring the lines between "recreational" and "national security" rape. This is shown in the case of H. G. Esméralda (the pseudonym of Huguette Akkache, member of the Algerian Communist Party). Her account of being held by elite paratroopers at a torture center in Algiers tells of women being raped by paratroopers who are drunk, who clumsily grope, and whose appearance is disheveled: "It was extremely messy everywhere, paras came and went carelessly dressed: gray underwear, barefoot, topless or in a vest. When they saw me they made vulgar jokes."⁴⁰

Based in urban centers and staffed by senior officers, interrogation centers were under much closer central control than rural units. The fact that torture, rape, and murder of suspects routinely took place at these centers indicates complicity in such forms of violence at the highest levels of power and that they were part of a system, as Raphaëlle Branche has demonstrated in her pathbreaking work on torture during the Algerian War of Independence.[41] Yet, there is no evidence that rape resulted from top-down orders in the course of the Algerian war. Similarly, in his seminal study of Dutch military violence in Indonesia from 1945 to 1949, Rémy Limpach concludes that while in some cases clear orders to carry out summary executions and burn down villages can be traced back to higher command, this is not the case with regard to the act of rape.[42] This by no means exculpates French and Dutch army commanders from complicity or responsibility in the incidence of rape, despite the fact that many would fall back on the "few bad apples" analogy to explain "unacceptable" acts of violence committed against local populations, if these became public. Nevertheless, while it is clear that the type of conflict created circumstances that enabled and thus facilitated rape, this does not mean that "systematic mass rape," to adopt Enloe's term, was part of French or Dutch military policy in Algeria or Indonesia.

It remains much debated, notably in the Algerian case, whether or not rape was ideologically motivated, a key aspect of the definition of systematic mass rape. Scholars who examine rape by the French army in Algeria argue that possessing and degrading Algerian women was a way to humiliate enemy men, to undermine their family and by extension the nation.[43] To quote Branche, "Rape is an act of violence in which the penis of a man is the means—but another object could be used—and the vagina of the woman is not the ultimate goal. . . . The desire is less sexual than the urge for possession and humiliation. . . . Through the woman, shaken up, beaten up, raped, the soldier attacks her family, her village and all the circles to which she belongs, including the last one: the Algerian people."[44]

This hypothesis is plausible, but hard to prove. When looking back beyond the time frame of the conflicts in both Indonesia and Algeria, we can see how "possessing colonized women" was a recurrent theme. One of the ways in which colonial rule was exercised was through the sexualized objectification of the bodies of the colonized. As Elizabeth Wood has argued, armed groups who reinforce cultural taboos about sex with target populations will have relatively low levels of sexual violence against those populations, while in the absence of such cultural taboos, sexual violence will be high.[45] There were certainly no cultural taboos about Dutch men having sex with Indonesian women, nor French men having sex with Algerian women; on the contrary. Colonial exhibitions in which colonized people were the exhibits, sex tourism, and the extensive production of pornographic images of colonized women divided into "types" such as "young Arab woman," "Moorish woman," or "young Kabyle woman" are but a few manifestations of this.[46] The sexualized imagery of North African women encouraged white men to peek beneath the "mysterious" veil to discover "primitive" and "wild" women.⁴⁷ In the Southeast Asian context women were stereotyped as precociously promiscuous.⁴⁸ In fact, in many of the Dutch diaries of Indies veterans, local Indonesian women are referred to as "mysterious" and prone to seduce innocent conscripts.⁴⁹ The inferior legal, political, economic, and social position of colonized people gave them only limited room for maneuver to avoid the images and roles assigned to them, and the margins were even narrower for women.

For Ann Laura Stoler, the asymmetry in the sexual relationships in the colonies between European men and local women was a metaphor for a broad range of power structures. On the one hand, there was the urge to set strict boundaries between the realm of the colonized and colonizer, to decrease the risk of "racial degeneracy." On the other hand, Dutch colonial authorities actively encouraged cohabitation with local women because of the lack of European women. Born out of an enterprise of commercial exploitation primarily driven by men, the Netherlands Indies evolved into a society in which employing local women—often young teenage girls—as servants and mistresses of male administrators or as concubines of local colonial troops became a common practice until around the 1920s.⁵⁰ Susie Protschky situates the *baboe* in the barracks during the war of independence in the continuity of these practices: "Their domestic labours were provided in a context of militarised violence and built on colonial class and racial hierarchies developed in civilian as well as wartime practices."⁵¹

Algeria was a settler colony where very rapidly there was a balance of European men and women. However, the social space of the European nuclear family coexisted with a state- and military-organized prostitution of Algerian women on a significant scale. In anticolonial resistance from the late nineteenth century onward, we can observe the figure of the Algerian woman as the embodiment of autochthonous "authenticity" that needed to be defended from the colonial male gaze. A key figure in reinforcing this discourse during the Algerian War of Independence was the Martiniquais psychiatrist and author Frantz Fanon, who had worked in a psychiatric hospital in Algeria. As an active supporter of the FLN, he published an essay in the FLN newspaper *Résistance Algérienne* in 1957, depicting European men's rape of Algerian women as the logical consequence of colonial domination.⁵² He presented the bodies of Algerian women, hidden behind the veil and thus "unknown" to the colonial gaze, as the symbol of an unfinished conquest. In the eyes of the European man, he argued, the Algerian woman "has an aura of rape about her."⁵³

The argument that the colonial legacies of the subordinate position of colonized women and decades of objectifying imagery were disinhibiting factors in regard to sexual violence during the wars of independence is convincing. The evidence also suggests that the lack of prosecution of cases of rape by the French and Dutch armies reflects a widely held view that the victims—colonized women—were not considered important enough to risk damaging soldier morale. However, arguing that Algerian or Indonesian women literally and metaphorically represented an unconquered territory and as such were vulnerable to rape is much, much harder to prove. One of the complicating factors is that rapes were also carried out by Algerian and Indonesian men serving in the French and Dutch armed forces. Recruitment among local men was extensive, in part to save money and limit metropolitan loss of life, in part because their knowledge of local languages, terrain, communities, and power relations was extremely useful.[54] In oral histories in Algeria, one of the groups that rural populations single out as particularly feared were the *commandos de chasse* (literally "hunting commandos"). These were highly mobile, relatively small troop units created to hunt down ALN rural guerrilla units by mimicking their tactics. They often had a large percentage of Algerians in them—in the words of French general Maurice Challe, "The best *fellagha* [pejorative term for a member of the ALN] hunter is the Frenchman of North African descent."[55] This relatively high presence of Algerian men participating in patrols and sweeps explains why in women's accounts of sexual violence, Algerian and not French soldiers are sometimes presented as more brutal, and more likely to rape. In the words of Chérifa Akache, who offered logistical support to the ALN in the region of Kabylia, "When it was the French [soldiers], it was OK. But as soon as they brought in the *harkis* [Algerian auxiliaries in the French army], they knew the population and the problems began [a euphemism for rape]."[56]

The significance of the *roles* that military personnel carried out (where they were and what they were doing) rather their *identities* (their ethnicity) when determining the types of offenses soldiers were likely to commit is reflected in the work of Christiaan Harinck. In his study of how Dutch military theory was translated on the ground during the Dutch-Indonesian conflict, he points to the need for a "safe" environment for potential offenders. Rape was more likely to happen in areas with low levels of insurgent action, by groups of men in small patrols who would rapidly move on to another area.[57] One subgroup among the Dutch armed forces is overrepresented in the judiciary records for acts of violence against civilians: the Korps Speciale Troepen (special forces). Like the *commandos de chasse*, they had a significant proportion of local soldiers (in particular coming from the Moluccan islands), were able to operate autonomously, and were accountable only to the highest level of command.

Given the very similar dynamics of rape in the Indonesian and Algerian context, the contrast in the politicization of the topic is striking. It demands taking a closer look at how rape has been theorized and politicized—or not—by both anticolonial movements.

Winning the War through Reputation Damage: Politicizing Rape by the Enemy

To legitimize their claims to statehood, the Indonesian and Algerian nationalist movements drew in their discourse on the principle of the right of all peoples to self-determination,[58] a well-established notion since World War I. Another common feature in their propaganda and that of their liberal and left-wing supporters was comparing the colonizer's violence to Nazi practices.[59] A new point of reference, that of human rights, started to gain ground after 1948 and the publication of the Universal Declaration of Human Rights—mostly too late to feature in discourses around the Indonesian war. The complete absence in the Indonesian context of the rape of Indonesian women by the colonizer as a symbol of colonial oppression shows that Indonesia's international campaign against the former colonizer was primarily focused on the illegitimacy of Dutch recolonization. Indonesian women as victims of sexual violence simply did not feature. Even Indonesian women's organizations, who in 1952 discussed societal problems affecting women such as polygamy, child marriage, and poverty leading to prostitution, did not address the issue of sexual violence.[60] The topic did resonate, much later, in the world of fiction, through the popular 1982 novel *Wanita Lima Nama* by Kawar Wati.[61] In contrast, in Algerian campaigning against French colonial rule, the rape of Algerian women was a key tool in discrediting France's claims to legitimacy. This theme was woven through the contemporary academic frameworks and political discourses on the war—and in many ways still is. Fanon's work has played a powerful role in shaping how subsequent scholars have framed the motivations of French military to rape Algerian woman.[62] Rape is not only talked about more often in the Algerian case—it has become a fundamental frame through which the war is characterized.[63] In short, while Indonesian propaganda efforts to discredit the Dutch focused on extolling Indonesia's rights *as a nation*, Algerian denunciations of the French additionally condemned violations of *human* rights.

Geography as well as chronology account for the different ways in which the sexual abuse of Indonesian and Algerian women by European armies was treated by nationalist movements. In 1945, Indonesia had just emerged from a period of mass forced prostitution of European, Eurasian, and Indonesian women under Japanese occupation (1942–1945). At the time the problem was silenced, but even when in the 1990s the taboo was broken, the public discussions revolved around the suffering of Dutch and Eurasian women, not that of Indonesian women, despite their numerical overrepresentation as victims of this war crime.[64]

By the early 1960s, attitudes toward sexual violence were very slowly beginning to shift. Zohra Drif, a member of the FLN's urban bomb network in Algiers, was asked to write a pamphlet for *Les Temps Modernes*, the literary magazine of French philosopher and political activist Jean-Paul Sartre. In *La mort de mes frères*, Drif presents a narrative of Algerian women as victims of death, violence, and rape, and Algerian men as emasculated by this French assault on "their" women.[65] In an interview decades later, she explained her intent to delve into some of the worst aspects of the war to "have an impact on a certain section of the [metropolitan French] population."[66] The prostitution of Algerian women as a form of colonial attack on the Algerian family was addressed in a book cowritten by Algerian nationalist Salima Bouaziz, who belonged to the FLN's French network.[67]

Women and men in the FLN were aware of what kinds of accounts of violence were most effective in turning international opinion against the French. The women who brought Djamila Boupacha's account of rape to the French public were her lawyer Gisèle Halimi, a member of the FLN's collective of lawyers, and the feminist Simone de Beauvoir, an influential supporter of the anticolonial struggle. For the nationalist movement, the fate of the young, French-educated Boupacha embodied the barbarity of the French army in Algeria and the vacuousness of its claims that it was pursuing a "civilising mission." For an early 1960s French public, she was the most "sympathetic" kind of rape victim—young, attractive, and sexually inexperienced.[68] For Halimi and Beauvoir, Boupacha's case would also represent a key step in the later campaigns in France pressing for women's bodily autonomy. Halimi and Beauvoir would challenge France's restrictive abortion law in the 1970s. Halimi would play a key role in challenging lenient sentences given to rapists and restrictive definitions of what constituted "rape," culminating in the 1980 revision of French legislation on rape (which dated from 1810). In the case of Indonesia, the rape of Indonesian women during their struggle for independence would be given political meaning only decades later.

Dealing with Rape: Recognition and Redress

At the time of the Indonesian and Algerian conflicts, few women who were victims of rape were able to obtain redress, or even have their stories recorded. Boupacha's story was told because it was politicized by the FLN. A judicial investigation was begun, brought against "X" (unidentified suspects), for "arbitrary detention and willful injury" but ran into difficulties when the commander in chief in Algeria, General Ailleret, refused to provide photographs of soldiers serving in the barracks where Boupacha had been attacked so that she might identify them.[69] Women who had some kind of positive relationship with some members of the French or Dutch armies were perhaps more likely to prompt some form of official response. In Algeria, there is at least one case in the archives of local women in one village complaining to the Specialized Administrative Section (SAS, a civilian-military unit established to administrate and control rural populations)[70] about a mobile unit that had committed rapes in their village. In November 1961, the head of the Aghribs SAS declared that thirty women had come to see him to complain about the behavior of the *commandos de chasse* of Akfadou. Seven of the women had filed complaints for rape, but these do not seem to have led to any trials, only to the reassurance from the head of the SAS weeks later that the perpetrators had been "severely punished."[71]

In the case of the Ben Hamdani rapes in 1957, it seems very likely that the three parachutists charged by a French military tribunal with attempted rape were eventually disciplined only because one of their victims was the daughter of a former Algerian soldier in the French army, who persisted in seeking to bring the men to justice. For the French army, it was the victim's father who merited the perpetrators being sanctioned. Their punishment was very light. Two of the men, "TG" and "RR," received a suspended sentence of three years, while the third, "CP," was acquitted. What is telling is that TG and RR, unlike CP, already had a history of undisciplined behavior and were therefore punished more for insubordination than for rape.

The evidence on redress is not always easy to interpret. One possible explanation for why many of the rape cases prosecuted through Dutch military courts were rapes of *baboes* is that there was more empathy for them as victims, as they were part of the social circle of the military camp. Another explanation is that they were more likely to be raped, as they lived in the barracks. Rather than giving a witness statement condemning a rape, or intervening to stop an assault taking place, troops could just as easily close ranks and get a *baboe* dismissed from her job, with no chance of getting her case heard in a military court. In this situation, *baboes* could have more to lose by complaining than women from the local village. And all of these explanations could also be true at the same time, varying from barracks to barracks.

What is undeniable is that the vast majority or Indonesian and Algerian women had no mechanisms and no leverage to report rape at the time. In both colonies, rape in times of war and peace was barely recognized as a crime. The colonial legal code in place in Indonesia since 1918 did not consider rape a crime against the person, but rather a crime against public morality. Therefore, if the woman who was raped was considered to be a prostitute or of "loose morals," in the eyes of the law and military justice she was not a rape victim, as public morality was not offended.[72] This explains why a notable number of rape cases in the archives are of girls under the age of fifteen, which was the age of consent. These cases were easier to prosecute, as the offenses were most obviously illegal, and the victims fit the profile of a rape victim (i.e., virgins) according to the morality codes of the time. Similarly, in France, rape was not a crime that was taken seriously either by society or the law in the late 1950s and 1960s, unless the victim fitted similar criteria.

Extensive research has shown that the consequences of rape can impact the rest of a woman's life, leading to infertility, damage to genitals, incontinence, family rejection, psychological trauma, aversion to sex, sexually transmitted diseases, unwanted pregnancy, and the complications of abortion. The children born of rape and their mothers have to confront the shame often heaped on them by their own societies. These consequences undoubtedly will have affected the lives of many Indonesian and Algerian women. To a certain extent, we can only speculate about this, given the scarcity of sources and the social taboos that continue to be attached to rape. At the same time, these fragments and taboos underscore the importance of valuing and historicizing other kinds of sources, such as poems, novels, and anthropological and linguistic studies, which enable women's voices to emerge, as well as reading court records "against the grain" and conducting oral histories. Through this, small references to how women endured sexual violence and how they, and their communities, coped with the consequences emerge. An illustration of such a coping mechanism is offered by ethnographer Camille Lacoste-Dujardin, who conducted research in the region of Iflissen in Kabylia in 1969. She states, "They have chosen to forget. Not only have husbands not divorced, and the young girls rapidly married, but they also tried to get the victims to abort, so that no child would be born of these rapes."[73] Women also employ euphemisms and strategic silences. Expressions such as *ksen fellacent esser* (they took her intimacy from her) in Kabylia and *l'monqer* (deliberate badness/evil) employed by women in the Aurès to refer to rape illustrate ways of articulating one's experiences without being explicit. Sitti Hasanah Nu'mang's reference to how she was raped while unconscious employs similar kinds of euphemisms: "In solitude I lamented my fate. Father was shot, I was polluted and helpless, only God knows why."[74]

Women also have a language of resistance. In the Aurès, M'barka, who provided logistical support for the ALN, describes how at the outbreak of war women in the village were instructed by members of the FLN on how to protect themselves from the risk of being raped. They had to make themselves ugly, take off their jewelry, avoid brightly colored clothes, and smear themselves with dirt and animal excrement.[75] Women held in the women's prison of Tifelfel describe giving their babies to young unmarried women to hold in an attempt to protect them when soldiers came into their space looking for a woman to rape. Though it is uncertain whether these strategies worked, their historical relevance lies not in their efficacy, but rather in the way women tried to achieve a sense of control over their own lives and, later, life stories. In Kabylia, rural women also composed and transmitted oral poetry that included references to rape and made it part of the story of their community, less about specific women. Among those collected by historian Souhila Benkhellat we find, "Forgive the Senegalese who killed my father, but there will be no forgiveness for the Frenchman or the *harki* who dirtied my daughter and my sister."[76]

For Djamila Boupacha, who had actively chosen to publicize her story of torture and rape in custody to advance the cause of independence during the war, taking (back) control of her painful history after the war also involved generalizing it to embody all Algerian women. In the 1990s, the portrait that Picasso had painted of her after she became a cause célèbre came to Algiers. At the opening exhibition, a fellow attendee (who did not recognize her) asked, "Is that Djamila Boupacha?" to which she replied, "No, it's the woman at war."[77]

New opportunities for formal redress can arise when the social agency of victims of war changes. From the 1990s onward, after the wars in Rwanda and Yugoslavia, when rape was used as a tool of ethnic cleansing, a much greater understanding of and political sensitivity to rape as a weapon of war emerged. In both the French-Algerian and the Dutch-Indonesian contexts, this facilitated the revisiting of wartime cases of rape, and other forms of wartime violence, through court cases. In France, there were several legal attempts, but a series of amnesty laws passed after 1962 limited the possibilities of bringing legal cases against the French state for crimes committed during the war in Algeria. Mohamed Garne, the abovementioned child born after the rape and beating of his mother by French soldiers, had to fight for recognition as a war victim throughout the 1990s. When in 2001 he won his case, this was in a societal context in which French torture of Algerians during the war of independence had dramatically returned to the attention of the French media, prompting the collection and dissemination of testimonies from French army perpetrators, bystanders, and victims. Illustrative was the publication, in 2000, of the testimony of a former member of the Algiers bomb network, Louisette Ighilahriz, on the front page of *Le Monde*. Ighilahriz described the terrible torture she had endured in French army custody. She subsequently revealed, little by little, and then explicitly in a prime-time documentary on French television, that she had been repeatedly raped by French army officers.[78] This prompted a series of investigations in the French media into torture and rape. Ighilahriz successfully took French army general Maurice Schmitt to court for defamation after he accused her of lying. She won a symbolic one euro, which she then lost on appeal.

In the Netherlands, it was through the activities of the human rights activist organization KUKB, led by Jeffrey Pondaag,[79] which for years had pushed for apologies and compensation from the Dutch state to Indonesian victims of

Dutch violence, that a case of rape was successfully brought to court. On 27 January 2016, Mrs. Tremini, an Indonesian woman eighty-five years old at the time of the trial, who in February 1949 was raped in the city of Peniwen by five members of a Dutch special forces unit, won her law case against the Dutch state and received 7,500 euros in compensation. The severity of the crime, gang rape under threat of a weapon, convinced the judge to overrule the statute of limitation of thirty years. Human rights lawyer Liesbeth Zegveld recorded Mrs. Tremini's testimony:[80]

> It was Saturday 16.00 [4 p.m.], we heard Dutch soldiers enter our village, together with my niece, we hid under my bed, suddenly they entered my house screaming "get out, get out" so we got out of the house, I saw five soldiers, who were looking for my husband, who had already fled to hide, because they could not find him I was dragged into a room by one soldier, my niece was not allowed inside, he undressed me while laughing until I was completely naked, he entered my vagina with his hands, I begged, "Sampunndoro—I beg you don't do it sir"—but because I was held at gunpoint I was afraid to do anything. Under threat I was forced to have intercourse with all five soldiers, one by one.[81]

Mrs. Tremini had to wait until the turn of the century, when public discussion about the right of victims of war to reparations had gained traction, before her case could be brought to the fore in the Netherlands. Rape during the Algerian War of Independence had already mobilized public opinion in France in the late 1950s and early 1960s because of the interplay between French left-wing intellectuals and Algerian activists who had a keen sense of how to frame their message in order to become politically relevant.

In a 2020 article, Susie Protschky argued that "the recent Dutch endorsement of an independent historical inquiry [of which this edited volume is an outcome] into the military actions of the late 1940s would not have happened had historians not persisted with the problem of how to frame questions about and find evidence for atrocities."[82] This framing and reframing is, of course, a multi-directional process, with new political and legal frames also shaping historians' reinterpretations.[83] Protschky's article is a case in point. She analyzes Dutch soldiers' collections of amateur photographs of the apparently banal domesticity of barracks life, notably photographs of *baboes* and of soldiers with *baboes*. Seeking to give space to silences, Protschky argues that women's facial expressions and the unrequited touching in images can be read as an "evidence base positing the likelihood of women servants having experienced sexual coercion and violence in this context."[84] At the same time, into these silences, we also place our own subjectivities and the dominant frameworks of our times. In 1981, Malek

FIGURE 5.3 The eighty-five-year-old Mrs. Tremini (*right*) won a civil court case and 7,500 euro compensation from the Dutch state for being a victim of rape by five Royal Netherlands East Indies Army special forces personnel in February 1949 in Peniwen. Her daughter and a witness are sitting next to her. (Yvonne Rieger-Rompas, private collection)

Alloula published his influential analysis of nineteenth-century Orientalist photography of Algerian women. In an analysis echoing that of Fanon, he argued that "possessing" Algerian women's bodies was both a metaphor and a mechanism of imperial rule.[85] As Cynthia Enloe pithily analyzed Alloula's analysis, "Becoming a nationalist requires a man to resist the foreigner's use and abuse of *his* women. But what about women themselves? . . . Malek Alloula and other male nationalists seem remarkably *in*curious about the abused women's own thoughts—and about the meaning they might have assigned to foreign conquest."[86]

Much of our analysis confirms arguments already made in the literature about the specific dynamics of guerrilla warfare and counterinsurgency, and the factors likely to contribute to a higher incidence of rape: a relatively small group, only loosely under central command, often with a high degree of mobility, is more likely to commit rape. Like perpetrators of other acts of extreme violence, rapists will have taken into account that the risk of getting caught and punished was very low. Impunity reigned, as the system for monitoring, reporting, researching, prosecuting, and punishing abuse was challenged by constant movement of troops and the often covert nature of operations. The dynamics of rape in custody are also familiar, with rape used as a means of torture and humiliation. That rape in custody did not take place to the same extent in Indonesia as in Algeria and that Dutch equivalents of the French *camps de regroupement* were not established is not a matter of ethics, but of counterinsurgency strategy and of scale. That the figure of the *baboe* as servant and potential sexual partner in all army barracks is missing in the Algerian context is related to the difference in colonizing strategy: Algeria was a settler colony, whereas Indonesia, for the Dutch, was a commercial enterprise led primarily by men.

When taking a closer look at the different nature of the sources that we have at our disposal to study rape in the two conflicts, we are compelled to think carefully about who is more likely to get heard, if women get heard at all. Only women who had some degree of trust in the judicial system of the colonizer, and were exceptionally brave, would file a complaint themselves. But the vast majority of victims were doubly silenced as colonized women. This immense silence in contemporary records is mirrored in the historiography. What the comparison has shown is how "getting heard" in the Algerian case was established through the politicization of rape as a propaganda tool of anticolonial struggle. For historians, this necessitates exercising caution when articulating rape as a colonial attack on the family and the nation, as this is first and foremost political discourse of the time, with a long afterlife. It succeeds in mobilizing attention to challenge colonial domination and abuse, but at the same time sidelines elements of the story (such as, for example, the role of autochthonous troops in committing rape) that do not neatly fit the colonizer/colonized dichotomy.

Women's accounts often hint at messier histories of motivation, opportunity, resistance, and remembrance than can be found in literature that is more theoretical, or focused on the national level. Obtaining these personal accounts requires in many cases a slow and painstaking process of building trust and deep knowledge of local contexts and culture-bound codes for talking about rape and sexual violence. Two stories collected by Galuh Ambar in Indonesia and Khedidja Adel in Algeria in the course of their ongoing projects are deeply suggestive of the value of trying to untangle these entangled histories. In the first case Ambar is confronted with two strongly divergent accounts about a number of rapes that took place in late December 1948 in Yogyakarta, in the aftermath of the Dutch occupation of the city. In a contemporary report from Indonesian local authorities estimating Dutch damage and violence in the neighborhood of Godean, six rapes are recorded.[87] Yet during a seminar that Ambar attended, meant to review the history of the Indonesian Revolution, historian Darto Harnoko claimed that according to an Indonesian veteran deployed in the area, thousands of Indonesian women had been raped.[88] This massive discrepancy is in itself worthy of investigation: What are the processes of transmission or non-transmission between the moment in which the acts of violence took place and the two radically different assessments of the numbers of victims? How do these figures map onto women's stories? What are the political and social interests at stake that might explain a (possibly) artificially low figure in the earlier period, or a (possibly) much inflated figure later on?

The second story is that of Laâtra, a woman from the Aurès Mountains in Algeria, in an oral history interview she gave in 2019. Laâtra is euphemistically referred to by some of her neighbors as "the wife of the sergeant." In a fragmented account, spoken in front of her visibly shocked daughter, Laâtra described being kidnapped from her village of Roufi (Ghoufi) and forced to live in the local barracks between 1956/57 and 1960/61. Laâtra had initially been arrested as the wife of a member of the rural guerrillas, and for her own activities in providing food for the nationalists. She describes being beaten and insulted, but promised that she would be released in a few days. One of the members of the local *harka* (regiment of Algerian auxiliaries in the French army) then decided that she would be "reserved" for a noncommissioned officer—the "sergeant" to whom her neighbors refer. Laâtra thus remained locked up in the barracks alongside some other young women who, like her, had been designated as "girls for the soldiers." One of the *harkis*, who was from the same small village as she was, tried to inform her father of what had happened, but when her father came to the barracks to try to free Laâtra, he was sent away with the false message that she was there of her own volition.[89]

Laâtra's story is striking, as it reveals a "type" of rape hitherto not discussed in the extensive literature on rape in the Algerian War of Independence—informal "brothels" created by groups of troops through kidnapping women who were not remunerated—in other words, sexual slavery. The first question, then, is why is so little known about this? Was it extremely rare? Or have historians not been asking the right questions using the right language? The use of the euphemizing expression "the wife of the sergeant" by Laâtra's neighbors is striking—it even implies a certain status, far removed from the term "sex slave." In a wartime situation of extreme poverty and violence, her kidnapping perversely provided her with improved material conditions—she was better fed and, as the sergeant's "wife," had her own accommodation. She was also extremely lonely, and at one point tried to climb a wall, injuring herself in the process. She was not seeking to reach the outside world, but trying to join the kidnapped women kept by less highly ranked troops and who were housed together, with a group of *harkis*. Because she had been kidnapped and raped, Laâtra later was also in many ways as trapped in her village as she was in the barracks—upon her release her husband refused to take her back, although she did later remarry. Finally, what happened to Laâtra's story between her release in 1960/61 and telling it to the interviewer in 2019? In a small village where clearly many people—possibly everyone at the time—knew what had happened to her in the barracks, how is it that her daughter did not know, and why had Laâtra decided to tell her now?

In sum, taking the Algerian and Indonesian cases together highlights the importance of going beyond, on the one hand, questions about why soldiers rape and how they get away with it and, on the other hand, discussions of the psychological and physical impact of rape on its victims—without denying the burning importance of these issues in a global context in which rape continues to be used as a weapon of war. The process of seeking to establish a historical comparison pushes us to shift the focus toward analyzing how rape is given meaning, or non-meaning, and by whom, and for what purposes, at the local, national, and transnational levels. It demands that we pay attention to how these different scales of meaning interact, and how they change over time.

6

"THE NORMAL ORDER OF THINGS"
Contextualizing "Technical Violence" in the Netherlands-Indonesia War

Azarja Harmanny and Brian McAllister Linn

In 1963, two years before the United States committed its armed forces to large-scale "search and destroy" operations in Vietnam, one journalist recalled Lieutenant Colonel John Paul Vann explaining "the essentials of guerrilla war." Among the most important of Vann's principles was to recognize "this is a political war and it calls for discrimination in killing. The best weapon would be a knife.... The worst is an airplane. The next is artillery. Barring a knife, the best is a rifle—you know who you are killing."[1] Vann's views on guerrilla warfare and his dismissal of conventional military methods are echoed in the memoirs of the controversial Dutch special forces captain Raymond "Turk" Westerling a decade earlier. In a stinging retort to those outraged by his summary execution of four prisoners during the Indonesian struggle for independence, Westerling claimed that had he followed "the normal order of things" of European "professional military men," he would have pulverized the village with artillery or aerial bombardment.[2] He insisted that his own counterinsurgency tactics, which emphasized the face-to-face killing of those he deemed guilty, were both more effective and more moral. During a campaign of less than three months on South Sulawesi, the so-called Westerling method resulted in the execution of many hundreds of noncombatants. The Vann-Westerling critique of the misapplication of Western technology in unconventional conflicts has long been a truism among counterinsurgency theorists. Like the two veterans, they maintain that "heavy" weapons such as artillery and aviation that employ "indirect fire" in which the "shooter" does not see the target not only are ineffective against mobile, dispersed guerrilla bands, but also inflict disproportionate destruction and death on the civilian population that the government is legally and morally obligated to protect.[3]

In Dutch historiography of the Netherlands-Indonesia War of 1945–1949, this issue has centered on the term *technisch geweld* (technical violence). Coined by Van Doorn and Hendrix in their 1970 study on a general "derailment of violence," *technisch geweld* was loosely defined but mainly referenced the use of indirect-fire weapons such as artillery and aviation.[4] Later authors have suggested a strong link between *technisch geweld* and excessive violence, arguing that almost by definition it victimized noncombatants. Many have suggested that *technisch geweld*, especially artillery bombardment, caused the majority of Indonesian civilian casualties.[5] Yet as historian Bart Luttikhuis recently noted, those scholars who write on *technisch geweld* have so far failed to provide either a clear definition of the term or an analytical framework to distinguish between extreme/excessive and normal/legitimate violence.[6] This distinction often proves to be more complex for the use of indirect-fire weapons than for direct forms of violence such as execution, torture, and rape. Moreover, they have provided little empirical substantiation of their claims.

This chapter seeks to provide a preliminary response to the challenge by Rémy Limpach, reiterated by Luttikhuis, that a study of *technisch geweld* in the Indonesian archipelago is long overdue.[7] We apply this term in a comparative and contemporary context, including not only concurrent decolonization struggles such as Indochina (1945–1953) and Malaya (1948–1950), but such contemporary irregular conflicts as Korea (1945–1953), the Greek Civil War (1947–1949), and the Hukbalahap Rebellion (1946–1954). By not treating the Indonesian case in isolation, we achieve a more nuanced understanding of its relative scale and—even more difficult to establish—its impact on those at the receiving end of violence. Including these conflicts not only avoids restrictions imposed by "decolonization" but corroborates the "greater" Second World War interpetive framework outlined by Roel Frakking and Martin Thomas in this volume.

As a first step to what we anticipate will be an extended and informed scholarly debate, we ask three questions. First, we examine whether the Netherlands armed forces' use of indirect-fire heavy weapons between 1945 and 1949 was exceptional when seen in the context of historical developments and compared to other contemporaneous conflicts. Second, we address the question of the effectiveness of the use of these weapons in irregular wars like the Netherlands-Indonesia War. Third, we will discuss the use of heavy weapons in Indonesia and critically assess the frequently repeated assumption that heavy weapons rather than "direct" forms of violence caused the bulk of military and civilian casualties in that conflict.

"Heavy Indirect Weapons" in a Historical Perspective

The historiography of the Netherlands-Indonesia War has tended toward studying Dutch military practices in isolation, and nowhere is this more apparent than the treatment of indirect weapons. But the Dutch forces were the inheritors of a firepower revolution that occurred between 1860 and 1945 and that witnessed massive changes in weapons technology, doctrine, and military organization.[8] In barely eight decades ordnance evolved from the smoothbore cannon to the atomic bomb. The increased range, accuracy, and lethality of infantry rifles drove artillery from the front lines and into concealed or protected firing positions. Near simultaneous developments in steel construction, recoil systems, explosives, and optics greatly increased artillery's range and destructive effect. Over time, armies developed sophisticated methods of "indirect fire" based on forward observers and directed by a centralized control system to identify and destroy targets far beyond human sight. Artillery was divided between guns fired directly at enemy positions and howitzers and mortars, which fired at an angle, their shells arcing over obstructions before exploding. A further division was between fortress artillery—some of forty-centimeter caliber firing a one-ton shell fifty kilometers—and mobile, light, or medium-caliber field artillery that accompanied armies on campaign. The destructive power of the latter was manifest in the Franco-Prussian War, when in a few hours the massed fire of some 540 field guns shattered French infantry, killing ten thousand and wounding twice that many. Ominously, the Germans later turned their artillery on Paris, a late addition to other efforts to end irregular resistance through food denial, property destruction, and extrajudicial killings.[9]

The cumulative effects of the firepower revolution were apparent in the First World War, when artillery repeatedly slaughtered attacking infantry and imposed the stasis of trench warfare. It became a military commonplace that artillery conquered and infantry occupied. For their March 1918 offensive the Germans concentrated some 6,500 artillery pieces and 3,500 trench mortars to overwhelm 2,686 British artillery.[10] Firepower escalated not only upward to include larger and larger caliber guns, a multitude of shells (including gas), and tanks, but also downward as riflemen went into battle carrying mortars, machine guns, grenades, and flamethrowers. For frontline soldiers, distinctions between direct and indirect fire were often meaningless: they shot blindly to suppress enemy fire more than at individuals. To concentrate and control such copious firepower required the construction of a vast logistical infrastructure, hundreds of staff officers, a sophisticated observation and reporting system, and fire plans that extended into the thousands of pages. Aviation became an essential asset for artillery, first to identify enemy batteries and observe their own artillery's fire, then to drive away the enemy's observation aircraft, and finally as flying artillery to strafe and bomb.

The Second World War continued the trend toward greater and greater application of firepower, and further blurred differences between direct and indirect heavy weapons as well as the distinction between combatants and noncombatants. The fascist powers may have initiated "total war"—and gloried applying it on civilians from Warsaw to Nanking. And in many instances the worst incidents of extreme violence—the German soldiers who murdered Jews, prisoners, and civilians, and the wholesale Japanese butchery of Chinese and Filipinos—were conducted with supposedly more discriminate pistols, rifles, bayonets, and even swords. But the extent of the Axis military triumphs ultimately forced their opponents to embrace total war, and ultimately to practice it with far more devastating results. Even more than in the First World War, to produce, distribute, and apply such firepower required the mobilization of the personal, economic, and social resources of the nation-state, blurring any lines between civilians and military. During the Normandy campaign of June and July 1944, Allied bombers dropped over fifty thousand tons of ordnance, destroying much of France's transportation system and killing thousands of civilians.[11] Even in more isolated areas in the Second World War, firepower reigned: a British commander in Burma grimly noted that a recent artillery barrage had reduced one ridgeline's height by one thousand feet and added "two feet of dead Japs."[12] Although comparisons are both misleading and insensitive, it is evident that during the war there were many instances when the expenditure of ammunition in a single day exceeded the sum total of the Dutch armed forces in four years of fighting in Indonesia.

The increase in weapons' range and lethality revolutionized how Western armies conducted warfare in several ways. In what Stephen Biddle termed the "modern system," soldiers were organized into integrated "combined arms" forces that augmented strengths and shielded weaknesses.[13] Modern armies could no more disaggregate their component parts than a professional football team would play only goalkeepers. To post–Second World War professional officers, Vann's call to throw aside modern weapons and return to knives would have been worse than impractical romanticism—it would have required the unnecessary sacrifice of their soldiers' lives.

This firepower revolution and the modern system also impacted colonial warfare. From a 1940s perspective, firepower in the Netherlands-Indonesia War was limited both technically—since most of the airplanes, artillery, and tanks used by the Dutch were classified as "medium" or even "light"—and in quantity. This was in keeping with prior experience with colonial warfare, when the use of both artillery and aviation was often limited by terrain, cost, objective, and the nature of the enemy. Artillery was most effective when indigenous opponents either sought battle against large colonial forces or allowed themselves to be besieged. But almost as important as its destructiveness was what colonial theorist Charles Callwell termed the cannons' "terrifying moral effect" on enemy warriors and populations.[14] Aviation had similar effects on matériel and morale. In 1911, less than a decade after the first powered flight, aircraft were incorporated into colonial warfare when an Italian pilot dropped grenades on Arab tribesmen at a Libyan oasis. After the First World War the British relied on "aerial policing" to pacify the empire from Afghanistan to Somalia. With conscious irony, British poet Hilaire Belloc summarized the importance of modern weaponry in the acquisition of empire with the couplet, "Whatever happens, we have got / The Maxim Gun, and they have not."[15]

Those military theorists who fought against imperial domination also accepted the firepower revolution and the modern system. Indeed, much of their focus was on how to obviate both, at least until their own sides were ready to apply them. The analogy ascribed to Mao Tse-tung of the populace being the "sea" through which the guerrilla "fish" swam illustrates a ruthless acceptance that civilians must not only support the insurgency politically but shield its agents even at the cost of government retaliation. There were no neutrals; the populace had to be fully committed in what Indonesian theorist Abdul Haris Nasution termed "total people's war."[16] But for both Mao and Nasution the ultimate objective was to create professional, conventional armies. Indeed, revolutionary forces soon proved every bit as willing to use indirect-fire weapons—at times more effectively than did their "imperialist" opponents. At the decisive battle of Dien Bien Phu, the North Vietnamese concentrated 490 mortars, howitzers, and cannon against the French, at one point delivering some fifteen thousand shells in a single day. The North Koreans had a dominant advantage in heavy weapons when they invaded the South in 1950, and the copious use of firepower increased with the intervention of the Chinese. In a single month in 1953, communist forces fired 220,000 shells against United Nations forces, prompting one witness to assert, "In Korea our troops have encountered enemy artillery fires of an intensity few veterans of World War II ever experienced."[17]

Firepower in the Era of the Netherlands-Indonesia War

Many of what Christopher Bayly and Tim Harper term the "forgotten wars" of the "greater" Second World War were simultaneously continuations of prewar struggles, decolonization conflicts, and manifestations of the Cold War.[18] They often pitted religious, nationalist, and/or communist insurgents against allegedly "colonial" or "imperialist" forces, but all were complicated by ethnic, sectarian, communal, regional, class, and civil dissension. In most conflicts both government and antigovernment forces employed heavy indirect weapons. But with the exception of a few incidents, artillery and aviation remained secondary to more traditional small-war tactics such as patrolling, offensive operations, and protecting key towns and installations. Blurring the line between combatant and noncombatant, military and civil operations were often combined in coercive measures to separate guerrillas from the populace and extend government control: resettlement and ethnic expulsions; social engineering through compulsory education, civic associations, and loyalty programs; social and economic reforms; prison camps; food control; curfews; mass arrests; extrajudicial punishments; and so forth. Their cumulative effects forced the guerrillas into depopulated, isolated regions where they could be more easily targeted by artillery and aviation. Firepower—in the form of indirect heavy weapons—thus augmented military operations, but it was not the primary means of enforcing control over the population or inflicting casualties on the enemy.[19]

The Greek Civil War serves as an informative introduction to the post–Second World War conflicts if for no other reason than it complicates arguments that Western forces were more willing to use heavy weapons against Asians. As with other contemporary conflicts, Greece's was a complex internal conflict internationalized by the Cold War. The communist Democratic Army of Greece (GDA) initially fought as small gangs of guerrillas, but increasingly sought to control territory, requiring it to adopt the weapons and methods of conventional forces. The Greek National Army (GNA) underwent a similar evolution from right-wing vigilantes and demoralized reservists to a professional, combined-arms force. In what was to be a common aspect of postwar conflicts, both sides were equipped, trained, and supported by communist or capitalist powers.

The use of heavy weapons on both sides was impressive. In one 1949 operation, the Greek National Army captured 14 artillery pieces, almost 200 mortars, and over 600 machine guns. By that time, the GNA itself possessed 175 medium field guns, almost 600 tanks and armored cars, and a growing air force. But if the quantity of ordnance grew, so did the quality of its application. Initially both sides used artillery with little military skill, and even less concern for civilian casualties. Observers repeatedly criticized the tendency of GNA commanders to rely on air strikes and artillery barrages rather than engage the enemy with their infantry at close quarters. By mid-1948, American and British aid led to a rapid increase in military efficiency against the communist forces. The government's air force underwent a similar revival, and by 1949 its fighters and bombers were an integral part of ground assaults. As important as military reforms were the Greek government's policies of relocating civilians—perhaps 10 percent of Greece's population was moved—and denying food and shelter to the guerrillas. The effectiveness of these measures was augmented by the communist leadership's disastrous decision to concentrate their forces and establish fortifications in the northern mountains, further removing them from the population. With the enemy now stationary, the GNA was able to use firepower freely to shatter the opponent's defenses and drive the remnants of the communist forces across the border. Indirect heavy weapons thus proved decisive, but only after a combination of government population-control measures, GNA improvement, and communist mistakes had provided the optimum conditions for using them.[20]

The contemporary conflict in South Korea reveals many similarities to Greece. Until the North Korean invasion in June 1950, the Republic of Korea's (ROK) security forces' primary mission was establishing government authority in a country torn by rebellions, paramilitary violence, banditry, and guerrillas. One American witness criticized what he termed "Oriental methods of criminal investigation," but these practices—mass incarceration, resettlement, food denial, torture, and summary executions—had been, and were being applied by Western military forces.[21] Although brutal, by early 1950 these had been so effective that the North Korean leadership concluded it would have to invade the South. The North Korean forces possessed an overwhelming advantage in tanks, aviation, and artillery, outnumbering their ROK opponents in the latter by three to one. During the war's mobile operations of 1950—when the front shifted from the southern tip to the Yalu River—both sides used firepower with little regard for civilian casualties. Although initially limited to industrial and transportation targets, after the Chinese intervention American bombers were ordered to "destroy every means of communication and every installation, city, and village" in North Korea, excepting only electrical plants.[22] With the establishment of a fixed front in 1951, South Korea's armed forces were reorganized to fight a high-firepower conventional war. The number of artillery batteries increased by 500 percent in barely a year. The results of this shift were apparent between April 1951 and April 1952, when Republic of Korea and United Nations forces fired over eleven million shells. The North Korean and Chinese forces also increased their artillery from 852 in January 1952 to 1,246 by July. As in Greece, the increased reliance on firepower reflected a shift in the military situation from small bands of guerrillas to conventional forces holding fixed positions. And, as in Greece, this led to separating combatants from the populace and allowing government forces to increase their level of firepower and target enemy combatants rather than civilians.[23]

The use of artillery and aviation by the Armed Forces of the Philippines (AFP) against the communist Hukbalahap insurgency showed many similarities with the Greek and Korean cases. Under the government's "mailed fist policy," between

1946 and 1950 the army, police, and paramilitaries conducted a brutal repression campaign that included forced resettlement, mass arrests, looting, arson, and summary executions. Unfortunately, the government forces were also guilty of corruption, brutality, rape, extrajudicial killings, and numerous other abuses. Artillery and air strikes were freely employed in much-publicized "ring of steel" operations against alleged Huk strongholds. Both at the time and later, these martial spectacles were criticized by participants, foreign observers, and the Huks themselves, though the latter benefited greatly from the increased popular hatred of the government.

The appointment of Ramon Magsaysay as secretary of defense in 1950 reversed this dire situation. As one veteran explained, "Magsaysay had a very clear understanding of the war's objective, to win the people away from the other side over to the Philippine government's side. You don't do that by killing people's innocent relatives. You don't make war where it will hurt the people you are trying to win over; you try to strike at an identified enemy."[24] One of Magsaysay's more successful initiatives was to bolster the AFP's demoralized conscripts and police with elite Battalion Combat Teams (BCTs)—expert at patrolling, night movement, ambushes, and skirmishing. Once infantry had located a guerrilla band, the BCT could swiftly bring down fire from its organic artillery company or from air bases only a few minutes' flight from the theater. More important than bombers and fighters were military reconnaissance aircraft used to spot guerrilla bands, sometimes calling in air strikes, sometimes harassing them with improvised bombs, and sometimes vectoring in BCT units. They also flew agricultural experts over the mountains and jungles to chart clandestine Huk farms to destroy a few weeks before the harvest. Airplanes also dropped leaflets inscribed with a large pharaonic eye to convey the impression of being under incessant surveillance. A more ruthless tactic was flying an airplane with a loudspeaker thanking a fictional informer over an area known to contain a guerrilla band. This not only demoralized the guerrillas, but it also occasionally prompted purges, so that the Huks executed some leaders and caused others to defect. Such military adaptations were made more effective by other programs that relocated thousands and destroyed villages and crops. Separated from their information and supply network, the Huks had to disperse to survive and were reduced to spending much of their time attempting to grow food in the inhospitable jungles and mountains. With guerrillas segregated from their civilian supporters, the AFP shifted to more firepower-intensive military tactics. Such measures effectively ended the conflict within three years, though self-styled Huks ranging from vigilantes to vice lords continue to this day.[25]

The British senior command in Malaya was initially skeptical about the utility of mid-spectrum firepower in what they misperceived as a race war between

Chinese and Malays. From 1947 to 1950 members of the Royal Artillery in theater were often detached to infantry duty, and as the government forces were undermanned and much of the territory was contested, naval and land artillery and aviation targeted guerrilla concentrations. The decision to remove much of the rural Chinese population to protected camps gradually separated the guerrillas from their logistical, informational, and recruiting support. As the government forces began clearing the more populated areas and the guerrilla bands were broken up and driven into the depopulated jungle fringe, there was more emphasis on indirect fire for harassment and interdiction. In Operation Nassau, field and naval guns fired over sixty thousand rounds, and in one month in 1953 a single battery fired over seventeen thousand shells from thirty separate locations, moving its guns over sixteen hundred miles. Most of these missions were to destroy guerrilla camps located by infantry patrols and "flush" guerrillas into ambushes. But aviation's contribution to observation, reconnaissance, and resupply were equally important to the success of the counterinsurgency campaign. To obviate the danger of "friendly fire," the British ruled that artillery and aviation could not be used within five hundred yards of troops or civilians.[26]

Preliminary Conclusions

These brief summaries provide a framework for establishing "standard operating military procedure" for indirect firepower at the time of the Indonesian-Netherlands conflict. Perhaps the most important commonality is that in all cases indirect firepower was what modern military nomenclature terms a "force multiplier." It augmented the capacity of the military forces, providing lethal or destructive effects that would have been otherwise impossible. It extended the range and effectiveness of government forces and allowed them to stage offensive operations against an enemy already weakened by food control and population removal measures. These conflicts became increasingly military-versus-military encounters between small patrols in which "the support of the indirect fire," as one veteran of the Huk campaign maintained, was "the most important consideration."[27] Artillery drove guerrillas into ambushes, smashed their camps, and harassed them day and night. Aviation provided an offensive capacity that extended far beyond the infantry patrols and artillery range, though its effects were often hard to ascertain. One Philippine officer recalled the most successful air strike he knew of was on a Huk mountain camp that killed twenty-seven guerrillas. But he noted that the bombs had missed the camp completely: only by luck had they fallen on the fleeing guerrillas. And it required an infantry patrol to march for two days through the jungles and hills to ascertain the damage.[28] Based on this and other anecdotal evidence, most casualty figures ascribed to artillery or air strikes are unverified "guesstimates."

A second commonality was that the use of "heavy weapons" was limited by a variety of factors, from environmental to economic. These were conflicts fought in terrain that ranged from jungle to grassland to mountains (in some cases all three), characterized by unpredictable weather (inimical to both gunnery and flying), and by a lack of surveying or mapping that so reduced accuracy that several missions were canceled. The lack of visibility and accurate maps made "friendly fire" or amicide a persistent concern, especially when supporting unseen troops in close combat. To these environmental factors were added such logistical problems as building and maintaining fire bases or airfields in areas with primitive roads and little infrastructure. For forces fighting on an economic shoestring—as these were—artillery, tanks, and airplanes were prohibitively expensive. In many cases cannons, tanks, and even personal weapons were salvaged from wartime battlefields and maintained through improvised supply systems. In 1950 the combined field artillery of the French forces in Indochina was some four hundred guns, with almost a quarter of them unusable owing to age or disrepair. Shortages in munitions, fuel, warehousing, and spare parts were common. And for those using artillery or aviation, the cost was not simply the weapons and ordnance themselves, but the skilled personnel needed for their use and maintenance. Artillery training required far more time than infantry training, especially for officers, and pilot training was even lengthier. And dispersing artillery and aviation near to infantry for combined-arms operations also required dozens of soldiers to act as cooks, mechanics, drivers, security, and other support.[29]

A more contested attribute of artillery and aviation was what Callwell termed its "moral effect." The evidence for this is somewhat contradictory and anecdotal. The dramatic visual effects of artillery or aviation strikes were terrifying, although Huk leader Luis Taruc claimed his guerrillas were indifferent to them. But the diary of the Huk who ghostwrote Taruc's autobiography contains many entries on the demoralization caused by the constant presence of observation aircraft, and the ensuing air, artillery, or infantry attack.[30]

The lessons drawn by military officers who participated in or studied these campaigns reached a consensus about the role of firepower in counterguerrilla operations. They concluded, as did Stephen Paget about naval gunfire in Malaya, that its military effectiveness was "situationally dependent."[31] Unless the enemy concentrated to defend territory, the majority of air and gunfire was expended on harassment, the interdiction of supply routes and trails, and "flushing" the guerrillas into infantry ambushes. In Malaya one flight crew assigned to an infantry unit was credited with inflicting more casualties than the rest of the squadron's air missions combined. However, as in the Philippines, British veterans of this campaign did not view "body counts" as the measure of aviation's success. They gave equal credit to reconnaissance, intelligence gathering, psychological operations, transport, and logistics.[32]

The crucial factor in the Philippines, Greece, and Malaya was the government's ability to segregate guerrillas from the civilian support base. Once that was achieved, there was both a greater likelihood that artillery and aviation would be militarily effective and a corresponding effort to avoid collateral damage against property and people. In both cases, Western forces sought a balance of ensuring that their heavy weapons had maximum effect without causing excessive and counterproductive destruction. For some counterinsurgency theorists, it led to a significant reappraisal of how to evaluate the effectiveness of their firepower. One example of this reappraisal appeared in the US Army's 1963 counterinsurgency manual. The manual, which drew explicitly on the Hukbalahap campaign, broke with the army's conventional warfare doctrine and insisted "the psychological impact of artillery in support of counterguerrilla operations will probably be out of proportion to the damage that the fire has actually accomplished." Indeed, damage was almost secondary to artillery's importance as "a two-prong morale factor; it is both devastating to the guerrilla and reassuring to the counterguerrilla."[33] In another break with conventional doctrine, the manual emphasized the vital importance of careful planning and discrimination, so that "the resulting artillery fires will not cause ill effects or perhaps alienate the population and cause them to support the insurgents."[34] Whatever their army's later practices in Vietnam, American counterinsurgents both acknowledged their debt to earlier irregular conflicts and sought to incorporate their perceived lessons of firepower discrimination and restraint.

Netherlands-Indonesia War

As in most independence struggles in this period, the Indonesian National Army (TNI) never acquired the amount of heavy weaponry and trained personnel necessary to match the colonial power.[35] Dutch forces remained tactically superior to the TNI in all but a few minor regular combat situations.[36] As a result, the TNI leadership's adoption of guerrilla strategy in 1947 was the only way to expel the Dutch armed forces without risking self-destruction. As the First Indochina War shows, this level of asymmetry was not inevitable. With Chinese support, the Vietminh gradually succeeded in creating conventional forces with a sizable arsenal of support weapons after 1949. Its massed artillery and level of training and organization played a decisive role in the crucial battle of Dien Bien Phu in 1954.

FIGURE 6.1 Vietminh troops move Chinese-built artillery in preparation for the battle of Dien Bien Phu, 1954. The Indochina War was the only war of decolonization in which Western forces were locally matched or trumped in heavy military equipment on the ground. (Collection Jean-Claude Labbe / Gamma-Rapho via Getty Images)

In Indonesia, the battle of Surabaya taught the belligerents important lessons early in the conflict and paved the way for a different outcome. After the Japanese capitulation on 15 August 1945, followed two days later by the Indonesian Proclamation of Independence, British-Indian troops temporarily occupied several so-called key areas in the archipelago. In Surabaya in November 1945 the heaviest battle of the entire war would take place, in which artillery, air power, tanks, and naval gunfire all played an important part. During the initial stages of the fighting, inadequately armed British-Indian units were overrun by numerically superior Indonesian fighters. British losses ran into the hundreds. After Brigadier Mallaby, commander of the 49th Indian Infantry Brigade, was killed by insurgents on October 30, General Sir Philip Christison (commander of the Indonesian theater) famously threatened "to bring the whole weight of my sea, land and air forces and all the weapons of modern war against them until they are crushed," a warning that was acted on ten days later, on November 10.[37] The British opened with a naval bombardment by three destroyers, followed by a bombing campaign from the air by RAF Thunderbolts and Mosquitos and from land by the Royal Artillery. After weeks of heavy fighting and thousands of Indonesian casualties, the British regained control over the city, whose inhabitants had by then mostly fled to the surrounding countryside.

The fight taught the belligerents important lessons early in the conflict. The Indonesians experienced that conventional battles, fought largely with confiscated Japanese war matériel supplemented by a range of improvised weapons, produced unacceptably high casualties among their own troops. Although after Surabaya Indonesian forces waged several other conventional-style battles in regions where the Dutch sought to expand their presence after taking over control from the British, eventually the TNI leadership felt forced to fully adopt guerrilla tactics.[38]

The British occupational forces on their part drew the lesson from Surabaya to resort more to firepower in order to prevent a repetition of the early stages of the fighting. According to Major General D. C. Hawthorn, commander of the 23rd Indian Division, indirect-fire support weapons had proven their worth during the battle. In a training instruction issued afterward, drawing lessons from Surabaya, he concluded, "Should we again be involved in this type of fighting the maximum use of all weapons must be made from the outset."[39] Equally, the Dutch concluded, after a report from a General Staff colonel who toured Indonesia when the fighting in Surabaya was still going on, they should augment their troops with more support weapons. With those they would be able to deal the Indonesian forces a "decisive blow" during a large-scale operation.[40] Five months after the battle, when Dutch units were still fighting under British command, the commander of the Netherlands Marines Brigade again stressed the need for heavier firepower: "Contrary to what many people think (presumably by deliberately wanting to keep hidden the actual state of war), there is heavy fighting for Surabaya going on. The nature of the opposition is such that it cannot be broken without artillery, tanks and other heavy auxiliary weapons. The English commander General Mansergh will, after 5 years of war experience in Burma etc., be the first to confirm this."[41]

A final way in which the battle of Surabaya set the stage was in how the use of force by both sides was framed. Although the British had won the battle, they would remember it as the "Hell of Surabaya," while to Indonesians November 10 became known as the opposite: Heroes Day, a national holiday to this date. This can be partly explained by the disparity in armament. In British literature one finds many accounts of horrified Indian Army soldiers appalled by the fanaticism of the *pemuda* fighters ("drunk and half crazed at the sight of blood"), who stormed Sherman tanks with bamboo spears and knives and employed suicide squads with explosives against British armor. British accounts of Indonesian use of tanks, artillery, and other heavy weapons during the battle are plentiful, but stress the lack of expertise among the newly formed Indonesian troops in handling them.[42]

In Indonesian historiography, by contrast, the use of heavy weapons by the nationalist fighters was downplayed in favor especially of the bamboo spear (*bambu runcing*), which came to symbolize not only the David-versus-Goliath-like heroism of the battle, but also the revolutionary spirit of the Indonesian freedom fighter.[43] The British offensive was on the other hand portrayed as brutal, barbarous, causing excessive civilian casualties, and being in violation of international conventions on the conduct of war.[44] This pattern repeated itself during the rest of the conflict between the Indonesians and the Dutch, in which each party would accuse the other of fighting cowardly and utilizing the wrong methods. The Indonesian fighters were criticized for not fighting "properly" in European eyes and hiding among civilians, the Dutch for using conventional weapons against both fighters and civilians (a variant of the Vann-Westerling argument).

The Dutch army commander in the Netherlands East Indies General Simon Spoor was a strong advocate of a conventional strategy to defeat the Indonesian Republic. But a large-scale offensive operation had to be postponed until mid-1947, when the troop buildup had reached the minimal required level. When Operation Product (also called the "First Police Action" by the Dutch, or the "First Dutch Military Aggression" by Indonesians), from 21 July to 4 August 1947, got under way, General Spoor had at his disposal around one hundred thousand troops, supported by twenty-two field artillery batteries and a total of eleven air force squadrons, seven of which were bomber and/or fighter squadrons—the same as the number of Royal Air Force combat squadrons used against a much smaller insurgent movement in Malaya. Dutch combat capacity consisted of B-25 medium bomber and strafer planes, and Spitfire Mark IX, P-51 Mustang, and P-40 Kitty Hawk fighter planes, all belonging to the Royal Netherlands East Indies Army Air Force (ML-KNIL). These were supplemented by Fairey Firefly Mk I fighter-bombers and Consolidated FBY Catalina flying boats employed by the Netherlands Naval Aviation Service (MLD) for fire support. This amounted to 150–175 planes for bombing, fighting, and strafing (machine-gunning ground targets) missions, but in reality only one-third of those were actually available, because of continuous shortages of crews and spare parts.[45] Even when fully operational, these forces were still limited means when compared to, for example, those of the French in Algeria, who had three to four hundred attack aircraft at their disposal in a country with only one-sixth of the population of Indonesia.[46]

The field artillery batteries consisted of two sections, both equipped with four QF twenty-five-pounder field guns. According to one of the Dutch artillery instructors, this light field gun had been "one of the miracles of the war," superior to the 105 millimeter howitzers, mounted on Sherman tanks, to be used as artillery by the five-thousand-strong Marine Brigade sent to East Java.[47] Later, a separate artillery battalion was created for the Marine Brigade, as the Shermans proved to be too heavy and cumbersome in the Indonesian terrain. Additionally,

FIGURE 6.2 A formation of American-built B-25 medium bombers in service with the Royal Netherlands East Indies Army Air Force. The airplanes in this 1946 photo have been modified with extra heavy machine guns to strafe ground targets. (Collection Netherlands Institute of Military History)

some infantry battalions, laying hands on prewar KNIL guns, constructed three "illegal artillery" units on their own, which supported their battalions during Operation Product. When the troop buildup was complete, the Dutch forces in Indonesia had a total of around 150 field guns.

Initially the artillery units were organized on the divisional level, but as soon as they arrived in Indonesia, the batteries were divided among the brigades, as the likelihood for divisional operations was deemed low. During Operation Product, many batteries were included in offensive columns into which the infantry brigades had been divided.[48] In addition to field artillery, the Dutch forces were also equipped with antitank guns and grenade and rocket launchers, as well as antiaircraft guns, which turned out to be superfluous and thus, in some rare cases, were trained on ground targets instead.[49] In sum, the Dutch had considerable means to use *technisch geweld*. However, like the French in Indochina and some other cases described above, the Dutch armed forces—military aviation in particular—were operated on a shoestring and had to be spread over vast areas. Finding spare parts, ammunition, and skilled personnel was a continuous limitation to actual combat power. In the course of time, this became more problematic for the

Netherlands than, for example, the French in Indochina, as heavy US equipment started to flow more freely to Indochina from 1949, while both the US and the British government put increasingly tight restrictions on arms sales to the Dutch East Indies after the 1947 military offensive.

During the operation, some artillery units initially carried out a preplanned creeping barrage (*vuurwals*) to clear out possible resistance on parts of the route the combat columns would follow on the first day of the offensive. In the days after, artillery provided fire support for infantry units that occupied cities and carried out mopping-up operations in their vicinity. For the ML-KNIL, their most important task during Operation Product was to destroy the Indonesian Air Force (AURI), mainly consisting of Japanese warplanes. The operation was carried out successfully, after which the AURI was unable to play a significant role during the rest of the conflict, apart from some minor raids.[50] In one such attack, on the city of Semarang during Operation Product, bombs were dropped from a Japanese "Nate," killing seven Indonesians.[51] In search of this plane, Dutch pilots later that day shot down an Indian DC-3 Dakota carrying medicine and supplies to Yogyakarta, killing eight passengers, among whom were several founding fathers of Indonesian aviation. While the event is still widely commemorated in Indonesia, it is largely absent in Dutch historiography on air operations during the First Police Action, which in most cases focus on the military success of the operation.[52]

The incident was also an example of the political sensitivity of the use of air power in an asymmetric conflict like the Netherlands-Indonesia War. As the owner of the Dakota was a wealthy Indian businessman, the incident led to a diplomatic falling out with India, which was not solved until 1950, when the Dutch government supplied India with a replacement plane. India immediately transferred the plane to Indonesia, which by then had already gained its independence.[53] While the Indonesians, in consultative bodies like the United Nations, willingly used incidents like these to stress the barbaric nature of Dutch aggression, the Netherlands made a concerted effort to cover up and downplay the use of its own air force and point to its restrictive nature.[54]

At first glance, it might seem obvious to see the artillery and air force as having the highest military value in their classic roles during the two large-scale Dutch offensives. (The second offensive, after Product, was Operation Kraai, or Crow, which began in December 1948 and was also known as the Second Police Action or Second Dutch Military Aggression.) According to Van Doorn and Hendrix, the violent guerrilla phases that followed "offered far fewer options for these weapons; the continuing sweep operations in the occupied territory were a less rewarding project." The authors conclude that "the limited value of these weapons in the counter-guerrilla has not prevented them from being used extensively."⁵⁵ However, while artillery was important during the two major offensives, it was never decisive.

Artillery's main contribution was in support of infantry sweeps and mopping-up operations in the months after the offensives, during which a close tactical cooperation was developed.⁵⁶ Artillery helped infantry dominate their ground with the least possible risk. Compensating for continual shortages of troops and protecting the infantry, artillery clearly performed the abovementioned role of a force multiplier. Moral effect, that other attribute of heavy weapons, was also frequently mentioned in the Indonesian context. The official war diary of one artillery regiment acknowledged both elements: "3–6 R.V.A. participated several times in support action of Infantry V. . . . These actions with artillery bombardments aimed to break the morale of the opposing party and thereby make it possible for the own infantry to achieve the set goals with as few losses as possible!"⁵⁷ Indeed we find many examples, particularly from the years 1946–1947, of infantry sweeps where the textbook procedure is followed: a preliminary artillery bombardment is called in to lessen the enemy's fighting spirit and ability before the infantry moves in to clear the area.⁵⁸ However, in regions with very low troop density, this picture did not always hold up. In 1949, after the Second Police Action, the Dutch army controlled such large swaths of land that there was a troop shortage practically everywhere where fighting was going on. Indeed, in that same year, two high-ranking artillery officers warned against the practice of requesting artillery for targets without any accompanying infantry action. A result, as the officers established, was that the enemy would leave its positions as soon as the first shells started coming in, only to regroup practically unscathed after the shelling had finished: "The wrong method thus followed only had the result that the enemy became accustomed to artillery fire and learned to successfully evade it, and then continue his activity elsewhere. Moreover, this led to a pointless waste of ammunition."⁵⁹

This underlines the situationally dependent effectiveness of indirect-fire weapons. In all the asymmetric conflicts discussed in this chapter, artillery and air forces operated in service of infantry, and worked most effectively in that regard. In Indonesia, this was widely recognized both by soldiers on the ground and officials at higher levels. Dutch military leaders, for example, explicitly prohibited the use of offensive air power without cooperation with or a follow-up by ground troops. Although this directive was not always followed, it is a clear indication that the military was aware of the limited use of air power in and by itself in the Indonesian conflict. Indeed, restrictions on the use of offensive air power were already in place from the moment the first Dutch troops arrived on Java under British command and remained so for much of the war.⁶⁰

As we have seen above, the effectiveness of the use of indirect-fire weapons is to a large degree dependent on and tied to measures to control the population and separate it from insurgents. However, much like the French in Indochina, Dutch security forces never made an integrated effort to segregate the Indonesian civilian population from the guerrillas. This may have contributed to a less targeted use of both indirect- and direct-fire weapons than in the course of the other conflicts analyzed in this chapter. While the use of artillery and air power increased dramatically in the first half of 1949, the last year of the war, it brought the Netherlands' forces no nearer to a military victory. Guerrilla units operating from pockets all over Java and Sumatra intensified their attacks on convoys, bridges, and military outposts, making 1949 the deadliest year for the Dutch military in Indonesia.

One of the most effective ways the Indonesian troops managed to inflict enemy casualties was the large-scale employment of mines and improvised explosives. In Indonesia the latter mostly took the form of *trekbommen* ("pull bombs"), mostly former Japanese ordnance dug into the ground, making road travel a Russian roulette for many Dutch convoys. These weapons, which can be viewed as an Indonesian form of *technisch geweld*, took an increasing toll on Dutch units, further affecting their already falling morale in the course of the conflict. In the seven months between the end of the second military offensive and the official cease-fire agreement of 10 August 1949, almost six hundred Dutch vehicles were struck by mine blasts, inflicting the majority of the more than one thousand fatal Dutch military casualties in the same period.[61] As the following paragraphs clarify, casualty figures are much harder to establish on the Indonesian side.

The Wonosari "Operetta"

As mentioned in the introduction, the suggestion that heavy weapons caused the majority of Indonesian military and civilian casualties has never been substantiated nor assessed critically. Dutch historians have referred to the works of Republican military leaders T. B. Simatupang and A. H. Nasution, but the examples provided in these two standard works hardly support this claim. Whereas both officers regularly mention civilian casualties as a result of air raids or shellings, Nasution lists equally high or higher casualty figures for infantry actions and summary executions.[62] In his book *Report from Banaran: Experiences during the People's War*, Simatupang writes that in Dutch air raids like that on Wonosari, "it was mainly the common people who suffered."[63]

However, it remains questionable if air attacks caused the bulk of the casualties in this particular case. On March 10, 1949, the Dutch unleashed a large-scale offensive against the city of Wonosari in Central Java in response to the Republican *serangan umum* (general attack) on Dutch-occupied Yogyakarta nine days earlier.[64] The Dutch sent over thirty planes to Wonosari, where they expected the commander in chief of the TNI, General Sudirman, to reside. The air force bombed and strafed Wonosari before airborne troops descended at the airstrip northwest of town. For the Dutch, it was one of the largest combined operations outside of the two so-called police actions, but by contemporaneous standards it would have been seen as a small-scale offensive action. As it turned out, Republican troops had already left the area, possibly as a result of an aerial raid some two weeks earlier, which was not followed by infantry action.[65] According to one veteran, the operation had "a certain operetta character," which was "a typical feature of major actions."[66]

Ten days later, the Indonesian delegation to the United Nations picked up on the news of the attack and formally requested an investigation by the UN Commission for Indonesia (UNCI). In a communiqué issued by Nico Palar, the head of the Indonesian delegation to the Security Council, it was stated that the attack resulted in "one hundred people killed" and "five hundred houses" burned down.[67] The local team of UNCI observers subsequently investigated the matter. As it found little evidence to support the Indonesian allegations—according to locals one civilian had been killed and ten had been wounded by aircraft fire—the UNCI concluded that "the importance of the incident has been exaggerated by the Republican circles."[68]

Although the Wonosari incident has been portrayed as a prime example of disproportionate *technisch geweld*,[69] these findings question the suggestion that indirect-fire weapons caused large numbers of civilian casualties there. What arises from the sources is a mixed picture. In Wonosari itself, the air attack does not seem to have caused many victims. It is possible that in some of the outlying villages in the region, which were also attacked by the ML-KNIL on the same day and were not inspected by the UNCI observers, there were more casualties. A clearer picture, meanwhile, is derived from the actions of the airborne infantry, who reported forty enemy casualties during their operations in and around Wonosari.[70] In addition, a field artillery unit that fired 974 shells in the area over the course of six days seems to have caused mainly material damage, as the unit found the region largely abandoned.[71] Finally, a radio report from the TNI Java Command Headquarters mentioned (although the reliability of the broadcast is hard to assess) that in a related retaliation for the Indonesian *serangan umum* on 1 March, some two hundred inhabitants of villages surrounding Yogyakarta were rounded up and summarily executed by the Dutch as punishment for harboring guerrillas.[72]

After societal unrest in 1969 concerning allegations of Dutch war crimes in Indonesia, the government of the Netherlands had a memorandum drawn up with excesses committed by the Dutch military.[73] It is striking that this so-called *Excessennota* contained not a single case of *technisch geweld*. Rémy Limpach has convincingly shown that multiple cases could have been included.[74] Nonetheless, the majority of known examples of Dutch atrocities during the war still consists of "direct" killing of noncombatants by infantry units or intelligence personnel. This is likely to have been similar in other decolonization conflicts. It is hard to assess whether this reflects the actual situation or merely shows the limited availability of sources on the nature of casualties. However, considering that Dutch troops were fighting an enemy often described as "invisible," as well as the many unofficial reports that infantry patrols were told to "fire at everything that moves," the distinction becomes increasingly blurred, making broad generalizations on casualty figures and their causes problematic—as the case of Wonosari shows.[75] But it is precisely the indiscriminate nature of much of this infantry violence that challenges the assertion that "direct methods" lead to fewer innocent victims.

Our research leads us to three conclusions. Our first is that the isolated study of the war in Indonesia had led Dutch historians to speculate on the impact of *technisch geweld* on the population. This has resulted in a propensity to cite specific incidents as demonstrating the excessive nature of the Dutch application of heavy weapons, such as the attack on Wonosari. But primary research into this case indicates that not only was the incident exceptional, but it is also highly uncertain that indirect gunfire caused the majority of civilian casualties there. As was the case in other armed clashes in Indonesia, and in other irregular conflicts, the effectiveness of the application of *technisch geweld* was situationally dependent. More research into other controversial incidents is needed to achieve a more balanced appraisal of *technisch geweld*. Our second point is that expanding the perspective to include other contemporary conflicts allows the placing of Dutch military methods into a better historical context. Apart from the definitional vagueness surrounding the term *technisch geweld*, we can draw the following interrelated conclusions from this explorative comparison. Studying the use of indirect-fire weapons in the context of the "greater" Second World War shows that they were applied far more promiscuously, and with far greater destructive effects, in intra-European, intra-Asian, and conventional wars than they were in Indonesia. When compared to contemporaneous irregular conflicts, the Dutch use of *technisch geweld* was similar to that of other government forces in Greece, South Korea, Malaya, and the Philippines. Like other conventional armies of the period, the Netherlands troops recognized that artillery and air power were a force multiplier, augmenting ground operations and compensating for troop shortages. As with other contemporary armies, the Dutch valued *technisch geweld* both for its destructive effects and its perceived psychological impact. Whether it validated these expectations was due less to the inherent capabilities of *technisch geweld* than to situational variables, of which the most important was often the effectiveness of the armed opposition. That the Dutch were probably less discriminate in their use of heavy weapons in the later stages of their war was also situationally dependent. Like the French in Indochina, the Dutch failed to segregate the guerrillas from the population that supported them. Our third point is that researchers should avoid a simplistic cause-effect assumption that indirect-fire weapons are not only counterproductive but by definition more inhumane in irregular conflicts. An outright dismissal of *technisch geweld* for its "indirect" destruction runs the risk of glorifying "direct methods" such as those practiced and advocated by Captain Westerling.

7

"BLOODSHED ON A RATHER LARGE SCALE"

Tactical Conduct and Noncombatant Casualties in Dutch, French, and British Colonial Counterinsurgency

Christiaan Harinck

Over the past three decades, historians have paid ample attention to the extremely violent nature of the wars during the first wave of decolonization. The dominant perspective has been the violence visited by the colonizer on the colonized, with torture, executions, and forced displacement standing out as the most prominent topics. Somewhat surprisingly, one major group of casualties of colonial violence has hardly been studied in depth: noncombatants killed or wounded on the battlefield. Civilian casualties as "collateral damage" of military operations are ubiquitous in wars past and present and arguably especially so in guerrilla war, where the distinction between combatants and noncombatants, as well as between the battlefield and the rear, is opaque to say the least.

While exploring and explaining civilian casualties for the wars of decolonization, this chapter attempts to merge two strands of historiography. On the one hand, there is the abovementioned literature on the violent nature of decolonization, which centers on the victims of targeted violence and policies, while the context of war and the battlefield dynamics remain largely out of focus.[1] On the other hand, there is a vast literature that considers the decolonization wars and colonial counterinsurgencies from the perspective of the development of warfare in general and counterinsurgency theory in particular. Casualties figure primarily as an element in assessing the strengths and weaknesses of the tactics and strategies chosen by the insurgents and counterinsurgents.[2] The comparative approach taken in this chapter, based on an in-depth study of (Dutch) military doctrine and practice in Indonesia juxtaposed with a broad reading on military theory and practice in other wars, inevitably leads us to the realization that understanding extreme violence in war cannot be separated from understanding the tactical context and internal military logics that spawn it.

The main wars analyzed and compared in this chapter are those in Indonesia (1945–1949), Indochina (1945–1954), Malaya (1948–1960), and Algeria (1954–1962), as these stand out for their prolonged fighting and casualty tally. Like elsewhere in this book, Indonesia will feature as the central case, but will not be dominant. To a lesser extent, the French campaign in Madagascar (1947–1949) and British operations in Kenya (1952–1960) are also taken into consideration. Compared to the wars mentioned above, these last two wars were—militarily speaking—low in intensity when viewed from the counterinsurgents' perspective. However, they resulted in enormous casualties on the insurgents' side.

Regardless of the differences in scale, combat intensity, and political context addressed in the introduction to this book, the abovementioned wars were similar in various respects. Two important similarities are central to this chapter. First, all these wars saw a vast discrepancy between the fatal casualties suffered by counterinsurgents and those they were able to inflict. Second, for the insurgents, the share of noncombatant casualties as compared to combatant casualties was significant in all these wars. These two phenomena are often mentioned in the literature, but seldom are they explained.

Explanations for these phenomena can be found in three categories: the conduct of the counterinsurgent forces, the conduct of the insurgents, and external factors. As this chapter is focused on counterinsurgency warfare, the first category of explanations takes center stage. Specifically, this chapter offers an explanation of the discrepancies in casualty numbers and makeup in counterinsurgencies between 1945 and 1962 by highlighting three elements of colonial counterinsurgency warfare during this period: the continuation of prewar discourses on (colonial) public order and counterinsurgency warfare, the use of modern weaponry, and the (often conventional) types of tactics that were used.

Counterinsurgent military conduct certainly is not the only possible explanation for the large numbers of noncombatant fatalities in the wars under consideration, nor are noncombatant casualties the only explanation for the discrepancies in casualty numbers and ratios. Insurgents knowingly fought among the people, while sometimes limited tactical proficiency or inadequate equipment could make them unequal adversaries for counterinsurgents, resulting in higher insurgent casualties. The role of insurgent capability and conduct in this regard fully deserves further research, but falls out of the scope of this chapter.

The two decades that followed the Second World War saw the emergence of the classic theoretical concept of "counterinsurgency" (often abbreviated as COIN), mainly as a result of reflection on the wars in Malaya and Algeria.[3] In this classical Western concept of COIN, the focus is on protecting, winning over, and/or coercing the local population, as opposed to a mainly enemy-focused approach. In practice, COIN resulted in attempts to use population-centered methods (ranging from guarded villages, provision of foodstuffs and medical aid via improving infrastructure, to support of government and policy reform) in addition to military action against the insurgents, which was also in the first place focused on weakening the enemy's grip on the local population. However, the wars during this period were largely fought without such a coherent theoretical counterinsurgency framework, and it would be ahistorical to impose it on them. Therefore, "insurgency" and "counterinsurgency" are used as general categories for uprisings and the military effort to put them down, with "COIN" being reserved for the later theoretical approach and doctrine.

Casualty Numbers in Perspective

Before turning to those explanations, it is imperative to provide some sense of the casualty discrepancies in the conflicts under consideration. As already addressed in the introductory chapter, casualty numbers are notoriously difficult to come by. The numbers mentioned here are mostly rough estimates and should be treated with care and caution.[4] Wide discrepancies are all too apparent when one looks at the available numbers. Rather than trying to arrive at exact figures, the aim here is to discern trends within and relationships between them. In this chapter, "losses" and "casualties" refer to fatalities, unless otherwise stated.

Each conflict was quite costly for the colonial powers, with casualties running into the thousands. Only Kenya and to a lesser extent Madagascar could be seen as outliers. However, the losses of the colonial powers shrink and often pale in comparison with the casualties they inflicted. In Indochina between 1945 and 1954, the French and their local allies suffered 92,800 fatal casualties, roughly the same as the number of French soldiers killed in 1940. Meanwhile, the Vietnamese suffered some 300,000 to 500,000 dead, resulting in a ratio between 1:3.2 and 1:5.4.[5] While fighting the 1947 insurrection in southeast Madagascar, French forces lost around 350 men killed, against somewhere between 6,000 and 9,000 insurgents killed, according to official figures, for a ratio of between 1:17.1 and 1:25.7. The real butcher's bill of the Madagascan insurrection is likely much larger and more complex, however.[6] In Indonesia, the Netherlands armed forces suffered 4,751 fatal casualties.[7] Dutch military sources claim around 100,000 Indonesians were killed (most likely an underestimate), resulting in a ratio of more than 1:20.[8] It should be noted that the fatal losses of Dutch colonial police and paramilitary forces are not known. British forces active on Java and Sumatra in 1945 and 1946 suffered 620 men killed, while inflicting a reported 13,441 Indonesian enemies killed, again a ratio of around 1:20.[9]

British and Commonwealth operations in Malaya between 1948 and 1960 resulted in 1,865 soldiers killed, while 6,711 enemies were reported killed, a ratio of 1:3.5.[10] According to official British figures on the so-called Mau Mau rebellion, 63 British and 170 African soldiers and policemen, and 1,800 local militia troops, died in Kenya. At the same time, 11,500 insurgents were killed, according to official figures—today, historians consider 20,000 to be closer to the truth. This results in a ratio of 1:5.6 to 1:9.8.[11] The war in Algeria, perhaps numerically the most complex case, cost the French forces 25,064 men killed, although this excludes an unknown number of Algerian auxiliaries in French service. According to their own estimate, the French inflicted 141,000 fatal casualties on the insurgents. Algerian postwar estimates start at a total of 300,000 Algerian fatalities, resulting in a ratio of somewhere between 1:5.6 to around 1:12 and possibly beyond.[12]

It is clear, then, that the casualty ratios display discrepancies that range from large to enormous. It is also certain that these numbers must include (though to various degrees) many noncombatants killed. In Indochina, at the least, of the minimum of 300,000 Vietnamese killed, around 125,000 are believed to have been noncombatants—slightly over 40 percent of the total of fatal casualties inflicted.[13] Indonesian casualty numbers are a more intricate subject. Indonesian sources suggest 45,000 to 100,000 combatant, and 25,000 to 100,000 noncombatant fatal casualties—but this includes not only the casualties of the fighting against the British and the Dutch, but also the many casualties of intra-Indonesian political violence.[14] If these estimates are anything to go by, the percentage of noncombatants in the casualties of Dutch and British operations in Indonesia might range from around 25 percent to as high as over 55 percent.

France's war in Algeria, infamous for torture, extralegal killings, and large-scale disappearances of people, shows similar numerical problems. Between 35,000 and 65,000 Algerian civilians are believed to have been killed or wounded by French forces (2,788 French civilians were killed by the insurgents during the war). Besides these, many Algerians were killed in intra-Algerian violence.[15] Despite all uncertainties surrounding casualty numbers, the gaps between insurgent and counterinsurgent fatalities are clear and undeniable.

Discourse: The Will to Put Down

During the period under consideration, "collateral damage" was accepted to a high degree. This was true in a very general sense in Western thinking about warfare, as for example shown by the Allied bombing campaigns against Nazi Germany,[16] and also in the specific context of colonial policing and counterinsurgency. But "collateral damage" is not just a natural phenomenon of warfare. Rather, it can be considered "the calculated result of policy decisions," as Bruce Cronin writes. Therefore, it is useful to take a look at the notions underlying its widespread acceptance.[17]

Practices of colonial policing and "pacification" by military means before 1945 were often harsh. A colonial state's army was primarily used in crushing insurgencies when they arose, while its police forces were entrusted with controlling the local workforce to ensure the economic interest of the colonial and metropolitan political and business elites.[18] Yet ideas on the need for a (more) considerate treatment of the local population in combating insurgency and "unrest"—which might result in fewer noncombatant deaths—had been around for decades and were sometimes explicitly stated in doctrinal publications. From time to time, some officers and military thinkers pushed for the application of some of these ideas into practice.[19]

Unfortunately for many colonial subjects, the potential benign effects of these ideas were blunted by the realities of colonial rule and warfare. In general, population-friendly notions were often vague and abstract, and seem to have been of relatively little significance in actual military conduct, while narrowly defined tactical aims and colonial and racial prejudice often proved to be much more influential. Take the French colonial officer Hubert Lyautey, who was resurrected from obscurity by COIN theorists later on and praised for his foresight and wide-ranging approach to counterinsurgency. Yet in his own days, Lyautey's ideas were never very influential outside the circle of his own command and that of a few sympathetic fellow officers.[20] Or take the case of the British Army's notion of "minimum force." Some scholars have suggested that after a period of brutal repression of (mostly urban) unrest in India, the British Army developed the minimum-force approach during the second and third decade of the twentieth century. Commanders were instructed and inclined to use as little force as was feasible (minimum force) in order to avoid unnecessary bloodshed. How these orders were interpreted and to what extent they were adhered to have been hotly debated.[21] In the final analysis, minimum force was a fluid concept and could easily be dismissed by soldiers as irrelevant for an insurgency in the countryside, as opposed to the urban setting in which the concept originated.[22] The British Empire showed some unique features, but was no exception to the general trend.

The ethics on display in many other colonial counterinsurgency doctrines are to a large extent of the utilitarian variant.[23] Notions of a more humane treatment of the local population are almost never presented as a good in themselves, but rather are informed by their perceived effect. The "Precepts for the

Politico-Policing Task of the Army," the main Dutch tactical manual of the interwar years, for example, stated that "tactful" behavior toward the population "usually achieves more than using violence."[24] If the ethics underlying military conduct are primarily purpose- or consequence-driven, it means that their raison d'être dissolves if the intended consequence no longer seems to be obtainable. To put it in the practical terms of colonial counterinsurgency: what was the point in treating the local population more humanely when they were already (perceived to be) in open rebellion or supporting the insurgents? This might seem obvious, but it has important ramifications: parts of the doctrine could be used in a flexible way or even dispensed with, while the colonizer still remained within the doctrine's general framework—thereby also partly explaining the gap between colonial theory and practice.

This dynamic was not just a facet of colonialism, but part of a wider Western discourse on the use of (military) force to quell large-scale civil disturbances and rebellion. Christophe Wasinski summarizes the situation where such repression is considered socially, politically, and legally acceptable and technically feasible as "la volonté de réprimer."[25] This "will to put down," or "will to punish," came almost naturally to military men educated in the late nineteenth and early twentieth century. As one of the most famous nineteenth-century military theorists, Carl von Clausewitz, phrased it, war is in essence the violent struggle to impose one's will on the other and break his will to resist.[26] And most Western militaries considered that struggle to be the exclusive domain of armies. Insurgents fighting as guerrillas therefore did not only break the law, they also broke with the norms of the military, further strengthening the military's will to put down and lessening its consideration of the collateral costs. To the military minds, punishment was due in the case of insurrection or guerrilla warfare—a punishment that could easily end up being meted out to the innocent.[27]

Distinguishing between "the guilty" and "the innocent" while suppressing insurrection or fighting a guerrilla war was of course rather difficult. Up to a point, however, it was not considered to be of the utmost relevance. In the context of the ethical basis of military thinking that sees military repression as the last resort of the state, soldiers and politicians deemed "collateral damage" a sad but unavoidable aspect of use of military force to curb resistance. It should not be forgotten that collective punishment still had a basis in international law mid-century, albeit implicitly.[28] The colonial context in which such military impulses were generally given free rein, and where the population was often regarded in collectivist and racialized terms, only exacerbated these tendencies. This further blurred the distinction between the guilty and the innocent, and therefore between combatant and noncombatant.[29]

Discourse after 1945: A Brave New World?

The colonial world in 1945 was radically different from what it was before the Second World War. A combination of (international) political change, the advent of anticolonial ideologies, and the embarrassments suffered and promises made by colonial powers during the war made a return to most colonies' prewar situation impossible, while the call for independence was greatly strengthened and wildly embraced. At the same time, the experience of occupation, resistance, and nationalist mobilization and organization during the war, and the massive availability of surplus weaponry and ammunitions, as well as changes in military and communication technology, greatly increased the military potential of an anticolonial insurgency.[30]

Western militaries found it difficult to adapt in this context. These challenges were exacerbated not only by the fact that organized learning during a conflict is difficult in itself, but also because the post-1945 colonial "savage wars of peace" were often only one of many problems confronting the armed forces in question. During the war in Indonesia, the Dutch armed forces initially reissued their prewar colonial tactical manual, in addition to the normal tactical training publications (which were based on that of the British Army). Gradually, new training directives and tactical instructions were developed and issued. In content, these publications did not form a radical departure from the prewar past. These newer publications were more up to date in a narrow tactical sense, taking the enemy's possession of light machine guns and mortars into account, for example. But looking at the core principles and assumptions, these publications did not form a radical departure from the prewar past. No integrated counterinsurgency doctrine was produced by the Dutch armed forces during the war in Indonesia. As a decolonization war with various parties involved, the conflict was deeply political, but the Dutch armed forces were both unable and unwilling to let that knowledge influence the prescribed tactical conduct of its forces. Dutch counterinsurgency remained strongly enemy-centered. Only during the last months of the war, when the Dutch military strategy had clearly failed and diplomatic talks with the Indonesian nationalists were under way, did the military, or at least elements of it, start to appreciate the centrality of the political and civil dimension of the conflict. It was too little, too late.[31]

The French experience in Indochina was not dissimilar. The French forces in Asia had slightly more time to doctrinally adapt to the post-1945 style of insurgency, only yielding definitively in 1954. The adapting was made more difficult by the fact that the French were also confronted by forms of regular warfare as the conflict in Indochina wore on. Perhaps unavoidably, most of France's military

FIGURE 7.1 The original 1953 US Information Agency caption with this photo said, "The French Foreign Legion is playing the major combat role in the war against the Vietminh. Here a red-suspect has been found hiding in the jungle and is now being questioned by the advance patrol, who caught him." (National Archives photo no. 306-PS-55 [10516])

innovation involved technical and tactical military solutions, although there were some experiments with improved intelligence gathering and counterguerrilla operations through the use of local allies.[32]

After the humiliating loss in Indochina, French thinking took a turn of its own. On reflection, some officers called for bringing older colonial concepts such as those of Lyautey up to date by taking the enemy's communist ideological and organizational power into account.[33] Several went further. A group of officers had become so impressed with communist tactics and their success that they concluded that France had to copy such tactics in order to prevail in a future insurgency conflict. The result was the infamous *guerre révolutionnaire* concept, which basically stated that the army had to match the opponent's guerrilla mindset, propaganda capabilities, ruthlessness, and commitment. To a certain degree, this is what all early counterinsurgency theorists of the 1950s and 1960 stated.[34] Elements of the French military embraced it with zeal and vigor. It found its practical application in the Algerian war within the elite regular army units such as the paratroopers and the Foreign Legion. And it morphed naturally with the determination and tenacity of French Algeria's white settlers to resist any compromise with the Algerian nationalists (and the French government). Not all French units adhered to *guerre révolutionnaire*. As the alternative was a continuation of the standard French approach to combating insurgency, French efforts remained harsh along the line.[35]

During the late 1940s, the British military was on a similar course. After almost six years of bloody conventional warfare, the army had some difficulty in returning to prewar imperial policing after August 1945.[36] And even then, the pace of learning and adapting was slow. The first two versions of Britain's postwar manuals, "Imperial Policing and Duties in Aid of the Civil Power" of 1947 and 1949, remained traditional in context, content, and intent.[37] In British colonies, the police formed arguably a more important part of colonial law and order than was the case in the Netherlands East Indies or French Indochina. There were several attempts to change the organization and practices of colonial policing within the British Empire after 1945, but these were severely hampered by the decolonization process. In practice, colonial officials and officers often resorted to military means to quell the various "emergencies," the ideal of reform notwithstanding. In this respect, the British were more like their French and Dutch counterparts.[38] The ultimate success in Malaya was exceptional and based on an integrated civil-military counterinsurgency strategy, but some of its causes are still debated. What is clear is that the notion of "hearts and minds" involved far more coercion than has often been suggested. The limits of persuasion in British counterinsurgency were also clearly shown during the simultaneous Mau Mau rebellion in Kenya, where coercion, more than anything else, was the key.[39]

Overall, it remains safe to say that the dominant approach to counterinsurgency after 1945 remained heavily militarized and extremely violent. In practice, the emphasis remained on the military destruction of the enemy, with only Malaya as a partial exemption. As a French official reflection on the war in Indochina put it, "Only those operations whose aim is the extinction of the enemy dispersed within an area can be placed on the asset side of the balance sheet." Such "surgery," resulting in the removal of the "gangrenous tissue," was "the actual pacification."[40] As a result, counterinsurgents continued to accept relatively high levels of collateral damage and high numbers of noncombatant deaths, and sometimes even deliberately aimed for this with collective punishment and reprisals, as in the case of the French in Indochina in 1945–1946 (see also chapter 4).

Noncombatant fatal casualties in many antiguerrilla operations were unlikely to be reported as such. The almost complete absence of the subject of noncombatant casualties within the Dutch army's archival records, or in the French army's 411-page postwar tactical appraisal of the Indochina conflict, are cases in point.[41] Pieter Lieb describes the German approach during the Second World War as "few carrots and a lot of sticks." This categorization might be applied to most counterinsurgencies conducted up until the 1960s, given the "slowness to adapt to the new challenges posed by politically inspired insurgency after 1945" that most militaries displayed, as Ian Beckett notes.[42]

Weapons of "Collateral Damage"

Notions on how to combat insurrection and insurgency may have changed fairly little in the first two decades after 1945, but the military means available to counterinsurgents certainly did. Even when compared to the period just before the Second World War, military forces after 1945 were much faster and more mobile thanks to motor vehicles and airplanes and radio technology. They also had more access to both heavier weaponry and lighter and more effective automatic firearms. As a result, their lethal potential had greatly increased. Only in Indochina, the French were eventually increasingly matched by a foe that—predominantly as a result of Chinese communist support from 1949 onward—was equally equipped and armed. In all other cases, despite increased availability of small arms, disparity between insurgent and counterinsurgent weaponry and equipment remained vast. This technical superiority was not without effects. As Robert Cassidy concludes in his study on counterinsurgency warfare and military culture, there is a strong relationship between having military technical superiority and using it to excess.[43] This was especially fitting for an age holding so much faith in technological progress as the twentieth century.[44] In a twenty-first-century context, Bruce Cronin typifies this as "reckless endangerment warfare," meaning the "employing of overwhelming force against legal targets under conditions that are likely to produce high levels of collateral damage."[45] The decolonization wars of the 1940s and 1950s seem to match this description.

In spite of radical technological progress, counterinsurgency after 1945 remained primarily an infantryman's war. But the firepower that infantry units now possessed, and the quick access they had to heavy support weapons thanks to radios, was unprecedented. At this point, it is important to note that in this study "heavy weapons" refers to a broad category that includes all heavy infantry weapons and heavy support weapons. Heavy infantry weapons are crew-served heavy machine guns, mortars, and, eventually, also recoilless rifles that are available to infantry companies, battalions, and regiments. Heavy support weapons include all types of artillery, armored fighting vehicles, and aircraft (and occasionally naval guns) that were available at higher levels within the military organization. Within the framework of this book, it is essential to note that this category is much broader than that used by Azarja Harmanny and Brian Linn in their chapter, which consciously excludes heavy infantry weapons.

When evaluating the use of heavy weapons as defined in this chapter, it is necessary to consider their destructive power, their effectiveness, and, related, their relative tactical (or even strategic) importance. The destructive power is often impressive.[46] Such was their destructive power that it is tempting to attribute a large portion of the noncombatants killed to the (indiscriminate) use of heavy weapons. But on closer inspection, it turns out that the many heavy weapons are not as effective as it might appear at first glance. Mortars, artillery, and close air support often require prodigious amounts of ordnance to achieve the desired tactical effect. Such quantities were often not available or transportable in the context of colonial counterinsurgency. At the same time, heavy weapons were often dispersed instead of concentrated, further reducing their potential effect. As a result, there is an argument to be made that heavy weapons were not of major importance in post-1945 colonial counterinsurgency.[47]

However, when taking other factors into consideration, it becomes clear that heavy infantry weapons and heavy support weapons may have an outsize effect on counterinsurgency. First of all, insurgents seldom used trenches or fortifications, while mostly lacking the weapons needed to reply to the use of heavy weapons (exceptions existed, especially in Indochina and to a lesser extent in Indonesia). As a result, even heavy infantry weapons could have a devastating effect when they hit a concentration of insurgents. Guerrillas by nature shun concentrations, but they could not always be avoided: just before an attack on a counterinsurgent position/unit, when fleeing the scene of battle in a disordered manner, and when the counterinsurgents were not thought to be near. As a result, counterinsurgent use of heavy weapons could be deadly in both defensive and offensive operations, particularly when there was good intelligence on the enemy's whereabouts.

Second, heavy weapons are also often heavy in a literal sense, especially when road-bound mobility is limited and guns, ammunition, and supplies have to be carried by man or animal during offensive operations. In such cases, troops might increasingly use heavy infantry weapons in the tactical role of heavy support weapons, or, reversely, leave their own heavy infantry weapons in store and rely on artillery or armed aircraft for close fire support. Both tendencies blurred the distinction between heavy infantry and heavy support weapons, resulting in small infantry units with overpowered support, or support weapons being used extensively to perform the role of true heavy weapons.[48]

As far as noncombatant casualties are concerned, there is another important factor that increased the potential lethal effects of the use of heavy weapons. Guerrilla warfare is war without front lines, and fighting often occurred in and around villages or other places where people actually live and work. At least in Indochina and Indonesia, the areas of major confrontation were often densely populated.[49] Population patterns in Algeria were somewhat different, but part of the war was fought among and in inhabited areas. Generally speaking, while guerrillas often hid in faraway places, fighting often took place in or near population centers. Malaya stands out for the many clashes that occurred deep in the woods or at least in less-populated areas. This can be attributed to British successes in isolating the insurgents from the population (see also Harmanny and Linn in this volume). Kenya and Madagascar stand somewhere in between in this regard.[50]

With low visibility, chaos, and high chances of civilians being around, operations in built-up and inhabited areas came with an increased risk of wounding or killing noncombatants. This problem applied equally to both infantry and heavy weapons. As a Dutch platoon commander remembered, "When we opened fire, it was on the TNI [Indonesian National Army], and if they were in or near a village, too bad, but fire we did."[51] In such classic guerrilla situations, the "better safe than sorry" argument had always held a high risk of innocent bystanders getting hit; but new infantry weaponry, such as light mortars, submachine guns, and light machine guns, greatly increased the deadly effect of colonial forces.[52] This definitely also applied to the use of heavy support weapons. Artillery and air support may have used much less ordnance than during regular warfare, but could still have a physically devastating effect, with resulting casualties.[53]

The natural and architectural surroundings could also further increase the chances of people—combatants and noncombatants alike—getting hit. Not just bombs and grenades, but also modern full-powered cartridges used in most handheld weapons could rips through bamboo or a wooden structure with relative ease. In fact, the walls of Indonesian rural houses were often so loosely made that Dutch soldiers were encouraged to poke through them with their bayonets when conducting a search.[54]

During the dry season, the use of incendiary bullets or rounds entailed the threat of fire, with the French use of napalm in Indochina vastly increasing these chances. To a lesser extent, heavy infantry weapons could also have a devastating effect on some of the simpler stone and mud-constructed buildings in North Africa. Indochina saw a telling effect of all the violence visited upon the countryside: rapid urbanization as villagers increasingly sought shelter in the larger towns and cities.[55]

FIGURE 7.2 Dutch marines advance through a burning village while expanding the Dutch-held perimeter around Surabaya in June 1946. Both Dutch and Indonesian armed forces are known to have used arson on a vast scale as a deterrent, collective punishment, and as scorched-earth tactics. In this case, it is unclear who started the fire. (Collection Netherlands Institute of Military History)

The destructive power of heavy weapons was sometimes also amplified by the geographical circumstances. Broken terrain softens the effect of exploding shells,[56] except when there is lots of hard natural material. Artillery and mortar fire is especially lethal in rocky or wooded terrain: shells hit the treetops or rocks and explode, sending down and around deadly waves of shell fragments and razor-sharp bits of the natural material that was hit (to a lesser extent, sustained machine-gun fire can also achieve this).[57] Part of the fighting in the various Southeast Asian wars discussed, as well as the Mau Mau rebellion in Kenya and the uprising in Madagascar, took place in wooded areas, whether it was (semi-)jungle or the ordered and often tree-rich landscape of plantations. Guerrillas in North Africa often sought refuge in mountainous regions. Attacks with heavy weapons were only effective if enemy forces were in some numbers in the immediate vicinity of the place of impact. But when they were hit in that way, the results could be devastating.

Estimating the Effects of Heavy Weapons

Given the lack of attention to the issue of noncombatants in many of the primary sources, it is often hard to find concrete examples of the effects of the weapons used, let alone a detailed breakdown of the casualty figures. Some of the claims made in the preceding paragraph about the effects of heavy weapons in the conflicts under scrutiny here therefore remain somewhat speculative: there are good reasons to assume their destructive power—and thereby their lethal potential—but less actual evidence. Still, there is documentary and anecdotal evidence that confirms the argument made above.

One indication of the effects of heavy weapons comes from the appraisal of the enemy. Both the Vietminh and the Algerian FLN considered the French artillery fire effective. The FLN explicitly warned its members of the effects of French artillery strikes in rocky terrain.[58] Indirectly, the French themselves also did acknowledge the grave dangers that the use of heavy support weapons entailed for noncombatants. According to a French military memorandum on the lessons to be learned from the war in Indochina, political considerations sometimes forced the French "to avoid the destruction of civilian resources and local populations. This constraint forced us to deny our troops those supporting fires [artillery and close air support] which were most effective but also the most destructive."[59] Or, as a French artillery officer put it euphemistically, the use of artillery "makes it difficult to identify rebel elements from within peaceful populations."[60]

Sometimes an attempt was made to distinguish casualties in retrospect. An uncommonly detailed Dutch report from an action on 31 December 1946 sheds some light on the issue. The artillery of III AVA KNIL fired on six different Indonesian positions. The local population had been ordered to evacuate by the colonial authorities. Nevertheless, of at least fifty persons reported killed by the artillery fire, only twenty-seven were recorded as being members of an enemy organization—implying that the remaining twenty-three were civilians. Such a breakdown into types of casualties is extremely rare in Dutch military reporting.[61]

Anecdotal evidence from other sources also supports our suspicions.[62] In one major action, Dutch aircraft bombed Palembang in the closing days of 1946, killing more than a thousand inhabitants, according to Red Cross personnel present.[63] Although this number was likely an exaggeration made in good faith in the immediate aftermath of the air strike, the destruction to the town and the loss of life were significant. The scale of the bombing of Palembang was an extreme case during the war in Indonesia.

It might be more useful to follow the actions of one infantry unit and its use of heavy weapons over time, for example KNIL inf. I, a Dutch colonial infantry battalion that was at the forefront of operations against Indonesian nationalists.

As was the case throughout the Dutch colonial army, many of the enlisted men were Indonesians themselves. Along with others, this unit was especially active in the first few months of 1949, when the guerrilla fighting in Indonesia reached its peak. Such was their experience that the officers of the battalion produced a reflection on the recent fighting in March 1949, admitting that many of the enemies killed were in fact noncombatants, resulting in "bloodshed on a rather large scale."[64]

Between 1 January and 31 March 1949, KNIL inf. I and subordinate units were involved in eighty-five violent contacts, only a few of which were initiated by the enemy (those consisted mostly of ambushes and firing at Dutch convoys). In total, the unit recorded 880 enemy dead (93 in January, 407 in February, and 380 in March). KNIL inf. I and its subordinate units lost 20 men killed in this period, a ratio of 1:44. Of the 880 enemy dead, 383 (43.5 percent) fell in seven operations (8.2 percent) in which KNIL inf. I was supported by either artillery, aircraft, or armored vehicles, or a combination of these. More than 40 percent of the fatal casualties inflicted fell in the few actions where heavy support weapons were used.

If the numbers of KNIL inf. I are to be trusted, they must be considered the minimum, as the war diary records several actions for which the number of enemy personnel killed is given as "unknown." Moreover, the war diary mentions several instances of the use of aircraft or artillery without any infantry actions, for most of which no casualty numbers are given. Two of them resulted in respectively thirty and "many" enemy personnel killed.

This lack of numbers is a common occurrence in the reports of Dutch artillery units. The staff of 4 AVA, an artillery unit responsible for both fire support and patrolling, structurally reported all casualties of artillery fire as "unknown" between January and May 1949. The 2–12 RVA conducted sixty-eight fire support missions between January and September 1949. Only for nine of these actions are fatal casualties inflicted given (222 in total).[65] It is impossible to determine how many of the 880 enemy casualties KNIL inf. I reported for January–March 1949 were killed by small arms fire, heavy infantry weapons, or heavy support weapons. The 43.5 percent that fell in actions supported by heavy support weapons can be interpreted in subtly different ways, but its large share seems telling.[66]

As a final note, it should be stated that almost all the violent clashes of this unit took place in or directly near villages, and all the independent artillery and air strikes were directed at villages. Finally, how many of the 880 killed were actually enemy personnel, and how many were civilians caught in the crossfire or shot by Dutch soldiers unwilling and unable to make a distinction, it is impossible to tell precisely. Again, according to the memorandum on guerrilla warfare drafted by the unit itself, a large number of them probably were civilians.

Tactics of "Collateral Damage"

As discussed above, disregard for "collateral damage" remained enshrined in military theory of the era, and the use of modern (heavy) weaponry further increased the risks of civilian casualties. But how do noncombatant casualties fit in with actual tactical conduct during the various wars under consideration in this chapter?

While aggressive small-scale patrolling might have been the professed ideal, mid-twentieth-century counterinsurgency campaigns often witnessed various larger-scale tactics. As most armies soon found out, there was almost never enough manpower available to effectively patrol the entire area of operations. This could quickly turn into a vicious circle. As there were too few troops to effectively patrol the area, the enemy got the opportunity to infiltrate. Once there, it posed a threat to various military, political, and economic structures. This called for an increase in static guards, further reducing the available manpower pool for active patrol duty, making it again easier for the enemy to infiltrate, and so on.

In French Indochina, this problem was especially acute. Based on their experiences, the French calculated that a numerical superiority of at least 6:1 was necessary to successfully encircle and destroy an enemy unit. Unfortunately for the French, such a superiority was almost never available. By 1951, 80 percent of the available troops were used in guard duty and to man defensive positions.[67] In Indonesia after mid-1947, when the Dutch massively increased the size of the territory under their nominal control, Dutch troops were spread so thinly that many units simply had no tactical reserves. Many brigades collectively made do with only a platoon worth of reserves.[68] In Malaya, counterinsurgent success is often highlighted, but Commonwealth forces there faced no more than eight thousand insurgents at any one time, while having themselves at their disposal a force of eventually (as of 1953) forty thousand military personnel, thirty thousand police, and forty-one thousand special constables.[69] This was a force ratio the Dutch and French could not imagine even in their wildest dreams.

Large areas and difficult-to-find enemy forces called for larger-scale operations, of companies, battalions, and sometimes even parts of entire brigades trying to surround an area suspected of holding enemy troops and subsequently combing through it in order to catch the enemy. Various terms were employed for this activity, such as "cordon and search," "sweeping," "clearing," and "search and destroy," and their respective equivalents in French, Dutch, Vietnamese, Malay, and Arab. While the emphasis might differ between catching guerrillas or killing them, the essence of these operation remains the same: trying to force the enemy to stand and surrender or be destroyed.

Such actions aimed at destroying the enemy were seldom very effective. In Indochina, the French army tried to address this problem by large-scale experimenting with airborne and mobile troops. But tactical innovation proved inadequate to address the structural problems. The main problem was lack of manpower (along with lack of time) to thoroughly search an area.[70] In Algeria, where the force ratios and the terrain were more favorable to the French, tactical innovation, including helicopter-borne special forces, did reap some results.[71] Owing to a lack of troops and a lack of success, Dutch forces in Indonesia also increased the scale and scope of offensive operations, hoping to catch the enemy and destroy him. However, success often remained elusive as the goal of destruction proved unattainable. The British forces in Malaya also used these standard tactics until 1951. Thereafter, the focus started to shift toward small-unit patrols and the size of the forces available grew.

Whether successful or not, these larger-scale actions, focused on specific terrain and aimed at the destruction of the enemy, greatly increased the chances of noncombatants being killed. The vulnerability of noncombatants increased for a number of reasons, perhaps first of all because of a psychological factor affecting the soldiers who took part in such operations. Action often occurred at unexpected moments and places. An infantry unit on routine patrol might encounter enemy troops, but often it would just meet apparently peaceful civilians going about their business in towns, villages, on the road, or in farmland. Not so with large-scale operations intended to find and destroy enemy forces. These actions took place when there was credible intelligence of the whereabouts of enemy units and commanders considered there was a chance of success. As a result, troops went into action expecting to meet the enemy, which for the soldier entailed danger, excitement, and opportunity, and could make him even more trigger-happy than he might have been on patrol. This dynamic was prevalent everywhere, but perhaps was strongest in Indochina, where the Vietminh time and again was extremely successful in laying both small and large-scale ambushes.[72]

Second, the requirement for secrecy during such actions meant that civilians were often not warned and would suddenly find themselves in the middle of a battlefield. Soldiers, expecting to find the enemy, would be inclined to fire on anything suspicious. Unfortunately, it is not hard to imagine frightened civilians fleeing their homes from the advancing soldiers, only to be mistaken for guerrillas and shot down by troops searching the area or by those manning the cordon.[73]

Third, the topography of intensely cultivated land in both Indonesia and Indochina made this danger especially real, as villages are surrounded by rice paddies. Before those fleeing could reach the (temporary) safety of the next village or woodland, they had to cross the open fields, which any commander with the opportunity would have covered with machine guns and mortars. This situation was worse during the wet seasons, as the high-water levels in the field resulted not only in fewer avenues of movement (creating narrow potential killing grounds) but also forced the enemy to concentrate its forces on dry ground—which usually were the villages.[74]

This was made worse by the inability or unwillingness to even make the distinction between combatants and noncombatants. The previously mentioned Dutch infantry battalion's review of the tactical situation from March 1949 stated that self-preservation "forced" its soldiers to fire on civilians as "the guerrillas do not distinguish themselves in any way from civilians, unless by coincidence they are found carrying arms."[75] Even in Malaya, supposedly the poster child of "minimum force," the situation, especially during the initial years, was not that different. The massive discrepancy in casualty numbers in Kenya and Madagascar should also be seen in this light.[76]

Fourth, large-scale operations were often conducted with insufficient manpower. The lack of manpower in Indochina had a major limiting effect on French operations, while the Dutch in Indonesia, and to a lesser extent the French in Algeria, also suffered from this.[77] As noted, the British were less hampered by a lack of manpower, because of the relatively limited nature of the insurgencies they faced. To solve the problem of not having enough soldiers, the French and Dutch increasingly began to use heavy weapons in lieu of manpower. First in line were the heavy infantry weapons. One or more well-placed machine guns (preferably mounted on a vehicle) could replace many actual infantrymen, freeing up manpower to either search the area or enable the local commander to increase the size of the designated area. Tactical innovation did not end here. Heavy weapons were also used to force an enemy out of hiding and into an area that was covered by machine guns and riflemen.[78]

Heavy support weapons were also deemed suitable to compensate for the lack of manpower. This happened on the largest scale in Indochina. Infantry units were often too depleted of manpower to take all the mortars, recoilless rifles, and machine guns with them on mobile actions. Artillery and close air support therefore became the vital ingredients in ensuing the infantrymen's safety and the destruction of the enemy.[79] For large-scale operations the goal usually was to encircle the enemy and ensure his destruction by artillery and close air support, especially if he was cornered in a village. Artillery was also deemed essential in the protection of French columns venturing out to try to encircle and destroy enemy forces. This also applied to the low-intensity guerrilla war in the Mekong Delta.[80] In Madagascar, the French frequently used naval bombardment and close air support against the insurgents.[81]

Although not as hard-pressed as in Indochina, the French in Algeria also frequently resorted to artillery strikes and air attacks when other means available were not found sufficient.[82] Artillery fire support also formed an integral part of General Maurice Challe's plan for antiguerrilla units (*commandos de chasse*).[83]

FIGURE 7.3 As part of the Commonwealth war effort during the Malayan Emergency, Australian gunners fire their twenty-five-pounder field gun during a nightly shoot against communist insurgent camps or trails in the jungle. (Australian War Memorial, HOB/56/0658/MC)

In Indonesia, the final Dutch tactical publication of the war likewise explicitly stressed the need for heavy weapons to free up manpower (but warned against ammunition wastage because of logistical problems—note that the issue of "collateral damage" did not feature in this warning).[84] In Indochina, Indonesia, Algeria, and to a lesser extent in Malaya, artillery support to the infantry was frequently given and even more often requested. This was also true of air support.[85]

In the final days of the wars in both Indochina and Indonesia, with counterinsurgent morale plunging, the reliance on heavy weapons further increased, reaching the lowest echelons, including routine patrols. Several Dutch memoirs and unit histories recount patrols firing (with small arms and mortars) on villages suspected of harboring enemy troops. And the soldiers' suspicion was easily aroused. As a member of an armored car unit remarked, "We put mortar fire on the village beyond the road before [passing it], as we found it was too quiet."[86] A lack of infantry capacity to follow up the attack tended to limit its tactical effect. As a French officer put it in the wake of the defeat in Indochina, "We were firing more [artillery] without obtaining proportional increase in the results attained."[87] A lack of tactical success notwithstanding, the number of casualties inflicted continued to rise—although certainly not only due to an increased use of heavy weapons. It is telling that almost half of the nearly one hundred thousand Indonesians killed, according to Dutch sources, fell during the last eight months of the four-year conflict.

The use of heavy weapons in the context of counterinsurgency was not limited to the replacement of infantrymen. Heavy weapons were also well suited to carry out actions of collective punishment, which was not uncommon in the wars under consideration in this chapter. Take the following two British examples from Southeast Asia in 1945. Major General Douglas Gracey in southern Vietnam in 1945 threatened local nationalist leaders he would use all heavy weapons available to him if resistance continued.[88] After Brigadier A. W. S. Mallaby was killed in clashes with Indonesian nationalist in the eastern Java port of Surabaya, land forces commander Lieutenant General Philip Christison vowed to "bring the whole weight of my sea, land and air force and all the weapons of modern warfare against them until they are crushed" (see also chapter 4). When Major General Robert Mansbergh arrived with the 5th Indian Division, he let it be known that "crimes against civilization cannot go unpunished." Surabaya was conquered by all means available, with over four hundred British and ten to fifteen thousand deadly Indonesian casualties.[89] As Bayly and Harper note, "The British fought for the city as if it were a full campaign of the Burma war [of 1942–1945]."[90] With the exception of Indochina, no colonial counterinsurgency between 1945 and 1962 witnessed scenes like Surabaya in October and November 1945. But on a smaller scale, the dynamics on display there could be seen everywhere. Whether they were sold to the public as "emergencies," "rebellions," or "police actions," operations were mostly conducted in warlike fashion, with all the resulting casualties that could be expected.

This chapter has sought to explain the discrepancies in casualty numbers and makeup in counterinsurgencies between 1945 and 1962 by highlighting three elements of colonial counterinsurgency warfare during this period in various cases: the continuation of prewar discourses on (colonial) public order and counterinsurgency warfare, the use of modern weaponry, and the (often conventional) types of tactics that were used. All these three elements, combined with population patterns and certain geographical conditions, greatly increased the chances of noncombatants getting killed on or near the battlefield. At least in Indonesia, Indochina, Madagascar, and Algeria, noncombatant casualties as a result of counterinsurgent military conduct probably made up a substantial part of the total numbers of fatal casualties, accounting in a significant way for the discrepancy between insurgent and counterinsurgent losses.

Perhaps the most crucial factor causing high levels of noncombatant deaths was the lack of interest most counterinsurgents showed in sparing noncombatants. The increased risks for noncombatants were accepted, apparently mostly without much reflection. Although the distinction between regular and irregular warfare is not sharply defined at the lowest tactical level, counterinsurgents in this period do not seem to have made an effort to make such a distinction—for example by reflecting on the possible negative effects on the civilian population of employing regular military tactics against guerrillas in densely populated areas. Reflecting on the tactics of clearing villages or terrain, one Dutch officer in 1949 concluded that these operations were "[a] definite act of war, and therefore should be executed like regular combat. A capable officer would even raze the village with machine gun and mortar fire before going in (Okinawa)."[91] Note the explicit reference to the Second World War in the Pacific, and the lack of consideration for possible noncombatants in or near the village. Such an approach made counterinsurgency in the first two decades after 1945 likely to result in many noncombatant causalities—"bloodshed on a rather large scale" indeed.[92]

8

COMPARING THE AFTERLIVES, POLITICAL USES, AND MEMORIES OF EXTREME VIOLENCE DURING THE WARS OF DECOLONIZATION IN FRANCE, THE NETHERLANDS, AND BRITAIN

Raphaëlle Branche

In September 2018, President Emmanuel Macron of France visited an elderly lady near Paris and handed her a text. Knowing that she was very ill, the president's office had rushed to arrange this visit. She had to be there, very much alive, to receive the president's visit and to hold up the mirror he was seeking. What did Macron want to see in the mirror held up by Josette Audin, the widow of a member of the Algerian Communist Party, a man who had been tortured and executed by the French army in Algiers in 1957? Why could the words Macron said to her, in her small apartment, over a cup of coffee, not be said anywhere else? How did this staged scene fully play a part in the political uses of history, and more specifically, the history of France's last decolonization war, the Algerian war? And was this official and public act of penance and the active political use of history uniquely French, or can it be seen as part of a larger and comparable confrontation with the violent colonial past among the former imperial powers central to this volume? If so, how do these processes in the Netherlands and the United Kingdom differ, and to what extent are they similar?

Josette Audin has passed away since then. Over the previous decades her name and that of her husband, Maurice Audin, have become a symbol of the fight for recognition of the crimes committed by the French army during the Algerian War of Independence. She carried this name proudly while working to make sure that it would never be forgotten by France's policy makers. In this fight, she was not alone. She was supported by the French Communist Party and by well-known intellectuals and activists, notably historian Pierre Vidal-Naquet. Maurice Audin was a member of the Algerian Communist Party (at that time, Algeria was considered a part of France). The party was in favor of Algeria's independence and was banned as soon as the war of decolonization began. In 1957, in Algiers, Audin was arrested by French parachutists, along with other party members. Less than a month later, his wife was notified that he had escaped. He would never return. One of his comrades testified that he had seen Audin seriously injured

FIGURE 8.1 Maurice and Josette Audin in Algiers in January 1953. The abduction, torture, and disappearance of the young communist mathematician Audin by the French army in Algiers in 1957 became an iconic example of the systematic torture campaign in Algeria. (Pierre Audin, private collection)

after being tortured.¹ Josette would never accept the official story. Immediately, she alerted the press and attempted to find out what had actually happened to her husband. At the time, Algiers was the site of stiff repression by the French army. This repression was directed against anyone suspected of supporting the struggle for independence: nationalists, as well as communists or progressives. Torture was used systematically, and the army also practiced "enforced disappearances" to an extent never before seen: people were arrested, tortured, and killed, and their corpses were never recovered. An estimated three thousand people or more disappeared from Algiers in 1957.²

Very quickly, Josette Audin was able to present the information she had gathered to a young historian. Pierre Vidal-Naquet became the mainstay of an association—the Maurice Audin Committee—formed to gather evidence that Maurice Audin had been tortured and murdered. The historian gathered documents and wrote a historical critique of great value, denouncing a crime of state masked as an escape. The book was published in May 1958, less than a year after Audin's disappearance, as *L'affaire Audin*.³ The title drew an intentional parallel with the Dreyfus Affair, which at the end of the nineteenth century had stirred passions in France with the case of Alfred Dreyfus, a captain in the French army who was Jewish and had been wrongly accused of treason. Captain Dreyfus's public defense went well beyond military circles. It gave rise in France to the figure of the intellectual who uses his or her public stature to aid a just cause. In the Dreyfus Affair, novelist Émile Zola became an ardent partisan of Dreyfus. Sixty years later, Pierre Vidal-Naquet did not have Zola's reputation nor his eloquence. He would, however, reach the summit in his field of research. Vidal-Naquet was not a novelist. He contributed to Audin's cause as an historian, using the historical method to build the case. *L'affaire Audin* is both a partisan work (the book contradicted the only official truth) and a history book in which he proves his thesis through a careful analysis of sources.

Since then, Vidal-Naquet's thesis has not been proven wrong.⁴ To the contrary, Maurice Audin's disappearance has been situated in a broader context enabling it to be even better understood. The torture and disappearance of Maurice Audin has been shown to be emblematic of an repressive method used with extreme frequency by the French army at that stage of the war.⁵ Unlike other individuals who disappeared after being tortured, Maurice Audin was of European origin, and his wife had resources at hand to publicize his case. She could count on a support network, initially composed of communists and later expanding and giving an echo to her case so that Maurice Audin would not be forgotten. After leaving Algeria, Josette Audin and her three children lived in France, where she continued to pursue her cause. She relied on the engagement of several generations of militants who successively fought for the truth to be recognized and for responsibility to be taken by the French state. Outside France, she was also supported by mathematicians around the world, as her husband had been a mathematician.

What was Josette Audin asking for? What did she continue to request ever since 1957 from the various presidents of France? She asked for the truth about her husband's disappearance. This meant the identity of his murderers, the identity of the ones who ordered his killing, the conditions of his death, and the location of his corpse. Putting his killers on trial was impossible, because the Algerian war ended with an amnesty for all war-related crimes. Thus, the legal avenue was closed, and political recognition was the only avenue that remained open. In 2000, Josette Audin signed, along with Pierre Vidal-Naquet, an appeal calling for general recognition that the French state had practiced torture. She received no answer until François Hollande's election as president in 2012. Hollande allowed her to have access to records about her husband's disappearance held in the army's archives. She went to the archives with a historian. Everything in the records was already known. Vidal-Naquet's work, in particular, had already established most of the facts.

Hollande's response was made on an individual basis, and Josette Audin was granted favorable treatment in many respects. The aim was to give a widow information about the circumstances surrounding her husband's death. The action by Macron, Hollande's successor, was different. The new president decided to address the political dimension of her appeal. By accepting Audin's request, he agreed to make her case an example whereby he could speak more broadly about the violence committed by the French army in Algeria. The declaration had been carefully prepared with historians to avoid any historical errors. The now politically accepted truth was perfectly in tune with the facts as they had been established by researchers. Their investigations had concluded that there were two scenarios for Maurice Audin's death, and both were mentioned in the declaration. The political words were expressly based on the truth-seeking work of historians and journalists.[6]

Yet the objective was two-fold. First, to acknowledge the truth about what happened to Audin, and second, to recognize the truth about the system that led to his death. Macron's statement ended a long process. The French state admitted that Maurice Audin had died at the hands of the army, and it recognized the systematic use of torture during the Algerian war: "In the name of the French Republic [... the president] acknowledges that Maurice Audin had been tortured and executed, or tortured to death, by soldiers who had arrested him at his home. He also recognizes that while Audin's death was, ultimately, a deed committed by certain individuals, it had nevertheless been enabled by a legally instituted system."[7] Macron called for archival records about other disappeared individuals to be opened,[8] and for the people with information that could lead to establishing the truth to be able to speak freely. As the commander in chief of the French armed forces and president of France, Macron, by speaking as he did, established a strong incentive for those still keeping secrets to speak out. At the end of his declaration, Macron came out in favor of taking responsibility for past injustices in order to ease tensions: "By taking this work for truth to a deeper level, the path should be opened up for a better understanding of our past, greater lucidity for the injuries caused in our history, and a new determination to reconcile the memories of the French and Algerian peoples."

The very last words of the declaration referred to what was absent from the rest of the text: the Algerian people. The political act was therefore at least equally important for what it did not say as for what it said. It highlighted, in counterpoint, the absence of any references to the colonial dimension of the Algerian war. It ignored the fact that torture and other forms of abuse and repression were chiefly directed at Algerians, the colonized people, alongside other individuals who rejected France's colonial project. The Algerians and France's colonial past are the forgotten parties in this declaration that focused on the case of Maurice Audin.

By going to Audin's home, Macron wanted to show that he was close to this woman and her fight. He sought also to be a French president who was open to listening, while signaling that his words had an almost magical effect. This was the stage set for this private encounter. The mother, surrounded by her children, in her home, with very few people present. The only camera authorized was that of a journalist and family friend. However, this was indeed a political act, and the fact that it took place in private was an integral part of it. Perhaps the whole scene overwhelmed the young president. He said the word "forgiveness," which was not in the speech as written and would not be included in the Élysée Palace's official communiqué thereafter.[9] Indeed, the word "forgiveness" belongs to another register and has a very hefty meaning following the debates that have shaken French society over the past fifteen years regarding the colonial past. Some have called for repentance or forgiveness, whereas others have considered this word to be a red line that must not be crossed. In January 2021, when receiving the report he had commissioned on "memories of the Algerian War and colonization," Macron (in fact, his special remembrance adviser) reiterated the president's unwillingness to address any official apology for France's colonial past in Algeria.

Building a Comparison, Elaborating a Lexicon

France's situation with regard to the Algerian war is, in many respects, an extreme case. Compared to the Netherlands with regard to the war in Indonesia, the British and their response to the Mau Mau uprising, or even France with regard to the Indochina War, Algeria stands out. First and foremost, this is a result of Algeria's ties to the former metropole. Unlike the other territories of the French colonial empire, Algeria has been considered a part of mainland France and administratively divided into *départements*. Its inhabitants were French citizens (albeit with different rights), and even in late colonial times, the journey across the Mediterranean by boat took only a day. It was more than a territory inhabited by indigenous peoples where a more or less privileged colonial society had settled to exploit its resources. Algeria was the homeland of hundreds of thousands of people who had come from Europe over several generations. When the war broke out, these Europeans numbered one million out of a total population of nine million. Nearly 1.7 million French conscripts were sent off to fight in the war.

Yet, the French-Algerian case works like a magnifying mirror. Taking it as the central case in this comparative study reveals some of the major stakes of the political uses of the history of extreme violence during decolonization wars.[10] By comparing three countries, the specific features of each situation, as well as their common points, are emphasized. Focusing on public uses of history means starting by being aware that there *is* a public use that has meaning in and of itself. Many decolonization conflicts have simply been erased from collective memory. There is no public discourse about them, or at least not in the former colonial metropoles. To understand why certain events are remembered, discussed, and taught while others are not, we need to look behind the events themselves. Scrutinizing which events occurred that are the subject of discourse leads obviously to the present. Why do the societies of former colonial metropoles remember this history, and how?

Two caveats have to be taken into consideration before making the comparison. First of all, this analysis focuses on the political uses of this past *in* the former metropoles: the Netherlands, Great Britain, and France. Research including the former colonies would be very different. Second, it will focus only on legacies of extreme violence in the context of counterinsurgency—that is, wars waged by troops sent by a political entity that considered itself to be an empire. These forces could be both members of the indigenous populations and people from the metropole fighting against armed groups supported by the majority of the population seeking independence. These groups claimed political sovereignty for a nation other than the colonizer. The Algerian nationalists wanted an independent Algeria, the Indonesians an Indonesia that was not the Dutch East Indies, and the Mau Mau a Kenya that was rid of the British and their allies. These wars all led to, or contributed to, independence for these countries and, ultimately, the end of the Dutch, British, and French colonial empires.

The three countries also share a basic characteristic. They were all democracies—at least in their respective metropoles—during the wars in which they used extreme violence, and have remained democracies since. This characteristic sets them apart from Salazar's Portugal, in particular.[11] These democracies did not always acknowledge that they were at war. Their basic principles such as freedom of expression, free association, and human rights were harshly put to trial by the nature of these wars.[12] Memories of this violence are thus a constant reminder of these trials, whether viewed as deviations or successes of democracy. These three characteristics explain the nature of the actors. The political uses of the past are chiefly made by the state. Within the state, various actors are involved, and they must be clearly distinguished. For the purposes of this chapter, the three basic and separate branches will be solely mentioned: the executive, the legislative, and the judiciary. Civil society may also be involved. Actors may vary from political activists for whom the memory of decolonization wars is part of a broader struggle, to militants fighting over a specific memorial event regarding the victims of colonial violence.

The political uses of the past, of any past, must always be understood not in light of the past but in light of the present situation in societies. This is why, despite factual differences in the histories of the decolonization wars we are looking at, there may be common points that refer to specific facts regarding the way Western European societies have dealt with their collective identities more broadly since the Second World War. Borrowing from Lenz and Welzer, it is possible to elaborate the "lexicon" that forms the basic parts of narratives that recount this past of extreme violence and counterinsurgency during decolonization conflicts.[13] These two scholars work on the narratives of the Holocaust across various European countries, and they have identified what can be regarded as a shared lexicon when looking at the contents and meanings of institutionalized memory. Unlike the Holocaust, the wars of decolonization are not all the same and did not all occur at the same time. However, they belonged to the same historical sequence of the Cold War and emergence of what was then called the Third World. The various countries and societies affected by the Holocaust also showed a diversity of situations, but this does not prevent us from thinking about the existence of a shared lexicon that, precisely so, refers perhaps less to a shared experience than to a shared memory manufactured after the event. This chapter seeks out this lexicon chronologically from the end of the decolonization wars to the present day, while simultaneously distinguishing two broad periods in the historical cycle of memory and confrontation with a violent past.

Toward the First Cracks in the Official Narratives

The first item in the lexicon is *model*. This idea emerged directly in the wake of the wars of decolonization. The colonial empires had yielded, but in counterinsurgency terms the methods they used were often presented as victorious models—either as part of a one-off, clear-cut victory, as the repression in Algiers in 1957, or a more far-reaching victory in the case of the Mau Mau rebellion or the Malayan Emergency (1948–1960). The Dutch military obviously had a harder time claiming counterinsurgency victory, but they present their two conventional military offensives in July 1947 and December 1948 (the "police actions") as military accomplishments. The blame for the failing counterinsurgency campaigns in their wake was imputed to national and international political pressure for negotiations and a quick transfer of sovereignty. A back-stabbing myth was born, and, as in France, the question of military defeat never arose.

In the French and British cases, the counterinsurgency methods were theorized and presented as models during and after the wars. They were later advocated within NATO and during bilateral cooperation, also with non-Western states. In fact, the two counterinsurgency schools were built as part of an old rivalry, going back to at least the nineteenth century and the wars of imperial conquest. This rivalry was further fueled during the interwar period, notably in the League of Nations. After having been model colonizers, the French and British developed the idea that they had invented efficient models of repression: colonial policing for the British, and the doctrine of revolutionary war for the French. With regard to the methods per se, the military were ready to admit to the extreme violence that they advocated. It all depended on the audience. And they chose their words carefully. However, the reality of internment camps, torture, or psychological warfare have long been clearly described for this kind of war.[14]

On a more public basis, this modeling coincided with a political discourse that presented the end of colonial sovereignty as an opportunity or a success. The second item in the lexicon is *success*: these wars were presented as having positive outcomes for the former metropoles. In France, Charles de Gaulle insisted on the economic investments that could be redirected to France's productive assets, and he resolutely committed the army to a new direction: the country's engagement to nuclear deterrence and to building France as a nuclear power. The colonial empire was presented as a part of the past that modern France had no reason to regret. Meanwhile, the British were proud of having maintained special ties with Kenya and having helped bring to power a team that was very indebted to the former colonial power.[15] Like the Netherlands, the two countries committed to building the European Community to various degrees. They belonged to the Western bloc and had been founding members of NATO; their supranational context had simply shifted.

The voices that might propagate another narrative were not easily heard in public. The consensus dominated until at least the 1970s. On the issue of extreme violence, the silence was deafening in the years, or even decades, after the war. The end of empires drove a refocusing on national territory; the indigenous populations remained in their native lands and could not be heard in the former metropole, where they had become foreign.[16] Their presence on European soil was seen as a temporary situation for migrant labor. In addition, the wars ended with amnesties that allowed for two things: imprisoned independence fighters were released, and the potential for prosecution of the colonial armed forces became less likely.[17] Not all amnesty decrees had exactly the same scope or covered exactly the same crimes, but the reality was nevertheless that the individuals who had committed crimes during actions to win the war would not be prosecuted. There was an "accountability gap" from the start. This situation pushed away anything that might cast a shadow over the dominant narrative.

In the late 1960s and early 1970s, cracks began to appear in the image of success that these societies projected. There were several reasons for this: the 1968 revolts, echoes of the Vietnam War and protests against the United States as a superpower, as well as domestic political balances whose foundations were shaken and a global economic and monetary crisis. In a few years, the world changed very fast. For a short period, the issue of violence during decolonization wars moved to center stage. However, it still proved difficult to go beyond accepting abuse as "military excesses," mere aberrations from the norm, which was considered to be proper military conduct. The third item in our lexicon is therefore *denial*: repressed memories as well as the denial of the state's responsibility for more structural forms of misconduct.

In the Netherlands, the *Excessennota* (memorandum on excesses) appeared in June 1969 as a direct result of revelations in the media of colonial war atrocities. Several months earlier, veteran Joop Hueting had given, on national television, a detailed eyewitness account of such atrocities, triggering many strong denials, but also supporting statements from other veterans. The hastily drafted *Excessennota* was based on documented cases in the Dutch archives (see also the chapters by Brocades Zaalberg and Luttikhuis, and Bennett and Romijn).[18] During the war, the Dutch authorities had never considered these violent acts to be anything other than "alleged crimes," "alleged excesses," or "misdeeds" at the worst.[19] After the report, their occurrence was recognized, but the official term "excesses" was used by Prime Minister Piet de Jong—a former naval officer—to accentuate their exceptionality. It also allowed the issue of legal accountability to be evaded, as excesses are not necessarily crimes. The term later gained sway to refer to this kind of violence, fueling the idea of misdeeds circumscribed to one region or one kind of service (special forces in South Sulawesi and members of the intelligence services). In the Dutch case, public attention for Dutch atrocities clearly coincided with mounting critique of US military conduct in the Vietnam War. Only several months later, US army lieutenant William Calley would be court-martialed for his leading role in the 1968 My Lai massacre in Vietnam.

Hueting's televised revelations had triggered the notion that the Dutch had their own Vietnam, but the situation had been politically defused, and soon the whole affair seemed to sink into collective oblivion.[20]

In France, the debate was focused on what would be the only topic for debate regarding extreme violence during the Algerian war: torture. No other war crime had affected French public opinion as intensely as this issue at the time of the war, and it remained the focal point of the debate in the early 1970s. The protagonists were Pierre Vidal-Naquet and Generals Massu and Bollardière. In 1972, Vidal-Naquet published a book that detailed the practice of torture during the war.[21] He showed that this violence was long-standing and had already been used by the colonial police. It had been used on a wide basis during the war, and he insisted on the fact that the political authorities had intentionally ignored it, and it had indeed been tolerated without being punished. However, his book reached a much smaller audience than the public debate between the two generals the previous year. General Massu defended his military record during the repression that he had ordered in Algiers in 1957, minimizing the violence of torture. General Bollardière argued against him by asserting the importance of respecting human rights and denouncing the moral deviation of the French army during the war.

However, both men were speaking of a single period of the war that was made notorious by the 1966 film *The Battle of Algiers*. The award-winning film, directed by Gillo Pontecorvo and censored in France, was released for the first time in France in 1971 for a very brief period. This was no coincidence. The term "battle," with its positive connotations (because a "battle" is not a police operation, interrogations involving torture, or murders disguised as escapes), refers to a very short period of the Algerian war: nine months of repression in Algiers, during a war that lasted seven and a half years over a territory four times larger than France.

Both generals were heroes of the Second World War. Their debate raged at a very specific moment in the history of the memory of the Second World War, more specifically, the memory of the French state's behavior during that period. Historian Henry Rousso has called this period "the return of the repressed."[22] The catalyst was a Franco-Swiss documentary filmed in 1969, *The Sorrow and the Pity*, made up of archival images and filmed testimonials. For four hours, former resistance fighters, ordinary citizens, and former collaborators retold their stories of the period. *The Sorrow and the Pity* was disturbing because it did not fit into the dominant memorial theme of the era, which viewed the resistance in heroic terms while being silent about the attitude of the vast majority of the French. This film is considered to be a break in the memory of the Nazi occupation, as it showed the reality of collaboration. In other words, it held up a cracked mirror to the French, whereas the political authorities had held up a smooth, but dishonest, mirror. The film emphasized the Vichy regime's role and, more broadly, the complicity or indecisiveness of most French people. The question of whether torture had been justifiable during the Algerian war resurged in this context. The two historical sequences were not unrelated for the French at the time, since torture had strong connections with the Gestapo in French collective memory.

Similarly, in the Netherlands, the Second World War provided a memorial framework with a strong influence over postwar society. This was also a narrative framework to describe current events. In their diaries, the Dutch soldiers arriving in Indonesia quite often made the comparison with the Nazi occupation.[23] French soldiers had similarly been troubled to see their army behaving much the same way they had seen the Germans operate in France during their childhood.

In the Netherlands, resurging memories connecting the decolonization war to the Second World War had no practical effects on the public memory of the war in Indonesia. In 1971, a bill was passed to lift the statute of limitations on war crimes. It would apply only to crimes committed during the Second World War; war crimes committed by the Dutch in Indonesia would be excluded from it. The De Jong government's stance on this period of history was quite clear: crimes that had come under the statute of limitations could not be prosecuted, "based on the argument that the arbitrary availability of historical files and not the severity of the war crimes would have determined who would be charged and who would not."[24] The comparison served in fact to distinguish between the situation of the Second World War and that of the Dutch East Indies. The violent acts committed during the decolonization war were described as "excesses"—acts that were the responsibility of individuals and not attributable to a system.

Still, the fact that these memories returned to center stage in all three countries at approximately the same time was no accident. It was related to the experience of those who participated in the wars of decolonization, and also to a broader context of looking at the Second World War from a new perspective. In France, the Vichy regime and the role of the French state were being questioned, while in the Netherlands the very high rate of extermination of the Jewish community was questioned. The Netherlands was the only Western European country to rival Eastern European countries on this tragic point. Historian Pieter Lagrou, by comparing France, Belgium, and the Netherlands, has shown how the rediscovery in the 1970s of the scale of the genocide and the number of Jewish victims of the Second World War renewed the focus on these questions and looked at denial as revelatory of postwar societies.[25] Issues of social or political responsibilities during the Second World War overshadowed the same issues regarding the wars of decolonization. For these conflicts, the convergence of the two collective memories strengthened the underestimation of the colonial crimes.

In the Netherlands and France, questions about the wars of decolonization were raised in the public sphere. These questions dealt with the legality of violence and could prompt soul-searching about the legitimacy of power, notably by pointing out the absence of safeguards that could have prevented democratic abuses. These questions were asked in terms that demonstrated new sensibilities and emerging public awareness of human rights issues. The fourth term in the lexicon is *human rights violations*.

The debates about the past that haunted the Netherlands and France in this period were also heated and timely issues in Great Britain.[26] However, the British did not face the same ambiguities regarding their own past, as they had not endured German occupation. Nevertheless, the country also experienced a period of questioning its values, as the "Troubles" in Northern Ireland started in this very same period. From 1969, the public debate became especially agitated, with mixed references both to the Second World War and decolonization. In Northern Ireland, the Royal Ulster Constabulary (RUC) was often taunted by civil rights protesters in the late 1960s and early 1970s for being "RUC-SS," and at the same time, Irish nationalists depicted the British Army's actions in Northern Ireland as a colonial war.[27]

More broadly speaking, the human rights movement affected all three countries, but Great Britain in particular. Two formal complaints were made against Britain by Greece under the European Convention on Human Rights (ECHR) during the Cyprus conflict of 1955–1959, which helped contribute to the founding in 1961 of Amnesty International.[28] One of that NGO's founding members, the Irish lawyer and politician Seán MacBride, had been interned for ties with the IRA in the early 1920s. Amnesty's public campaign for the abolition of torture began in 1972, but there had been previous actions. The 1970s was a major period of international visibility for the fight against the torture of political and military prisoners.[29] An International Conference for the Abolition of Torture was held in Paris in 1973, and the chairman of Amnesty International was awarded the Nobel Peace Prize in 1974. Then, in 1975, the United Nations published a declaration against torture. Two years later, Amnesty International in turn received the Nobel Peace Prize, while the Geneva Convention was amended to take better account of irregular warfare. It was in the spirit of the times to view the extreme violence during the wars of decolonization as a reality that Western societies were no longer willing to accept, a counter-model. However, as it did in the Netherlands, the public discourse on colonial violence faded in France and the United Kingdom after the early 1970s.

Veterans and Victims Speak Out

Not until the 1990s and especially in the two subsequent decades did the issue return to the political forefront. The 1990s were characterized by greater awareness of the individual participants in war: the ordinary soldiers and civilians. The fifth term in the lexicon is *ordinary men* waging a real war. In the Netherlands, the well-known 1947 novella *Oeroeg* was adapted to the cinema in 1993, bringing into sharp focus the violence committed on both sides, but notably by the Dutch. There were several TV documentaries, notably a 1995 film titled *The Excesses of Rawagedeh*.[30] The testimony by survivors and archival documents were devastating, prompting an investigation by the Ministry of Justice following questions in Parliament. Also, the 1969 *Excessennota* report was republished. There were no judicial repercussions, however. Ordinary soldiers were a topic for discussion, but they were not viewed simply as perpetrators. They were increasingly seen as victims of a war that had been fought "on the wrong side of history," as Dutch foreign minister Ben Bot would publicly state in Indonesia in 2005. This view had not been accepted as widely several decades before. The image that soldiers had been forced to fight in a "dirty war" that was waged for the wrong reasons changed the debate on their accountability. They had been sent on impossible missions and obeyed orders for which the political authorities often did not assume responsibility, even though in the end it was the policy makers who should clearly have been held accountable.

In the early 1990s in the Netherlands, a pressing topic in the news was the UN intervention in the former Yugoslavia, and especially the accusations against the Dutch peacekeepers operating under the UN flag in Srebrenica.[31] The lengthy investigation carried out by the Netherlands Institute for War Documentation (1996 to 2002), followed by a parliamentary inquiry (June 2002 to January 2003), insisted on the responsibility of political and military decision makers. This strengthened the view that veterans were more victims than perpetrators. One opinion poll conducted in 2005 defined certain nuances depending on the war in question: veterans of the Second World War were almost unanimously seen as heroes in a just war. For other military operations, from the decolonization war to the present day, the survey respondents clearly distinguished the government's role from the actions of soldiers. The divergence between these two assessments was strongest for the war in Indonesia.[32] This supports the image of ordinary soldiers as victims of war, rather than as perpetrators of possible war crimes. This view was enhanced by the surge of attention worldwide for traumas suffered by veterans, as well as by nonmilitary victims of war.

Also in France in the 1990s and 2000s, fresh emphasis was put on the ordinary experiences of war and notably the experiences of ordinary soldiers, as evidenced

FIGURE 8.2 An Indonesian monument in Balongsari includes a sculpture depicting the December 9, 1947, massacre by Dutch army forces in the town formerly known as Rawagede. Estimates of the number of men executed or killed under other circumstances on that day are still heavily contested but mostly vary from 150 in official Dutch reports to 431 according to Indonesian sources. On September 15, 2011, a civil court in the Netherlands ruled that the Dutch state had to pay indemnities to nine widows of the victims.
(K. W. Brocades Zaalberg, private collection)

by several TV documentaries of the time. *Les années algériennes* by Bernard Favre and *La guerre sans nom* by Bertrand Tavernier recorded the words of civilians and soldiers, who recounted the war on the ground. Violence was not excluded from their narratives, but it was not the central theme, nor was violence limited to acts committed by the French. This was also the period when France officially recognized the war as such. In 1987, all the veterans associations gathered in what they called a "united front" to lobby for a better recognition of their injuries and traumas and an official changing of label from "the maintenance of order operations" to "the war." In 1999 Parliament voted unanimously to change the name, and in 2002 a national monument dedicated to the soldiers and fighters who lost their lives in Algeria was unveiled in Paris for the fortieth anniversary of the end of the war.

What could have been the end of a cycle proved to be the widening of its scope instead. The focus was on violence once more, but now in a broader societal context. From the 2000s onward, the sixth item in the lexicon is *public recognition* of the crime, and material or symbolic reparations. In 2005, the French Parliament passed a law that triggered outrage among historians, and especially in a portion of French society that was unaccustomed to organizing as a political force. This law stipulated, among other things, that schools were to teach the "positive role" of colonization, "notably in North Africa"—the expression traditionally used to speak of Algeria. This law relayed an ideological position. In France, historians and citizens protested publicly and also called for repeal. The president of Algeria protested and called for the controversial article to be revoked. Nearly a year later, the president of France signed an act to withdraw the article. On this subject, the president had lost control over his parliamentary majority. In 2006, tensions needed to be calmed, especially as French cities had endured several weeks of serious urban rioting, with the authorities declaring a "state of emergency" under laws dating back to the beginning of the Algerian war.[33]

What was really new in the public debate on colonial violence after the turn of the twenty-first century was the visibility of the formerly colonized populations or their descendants. Reacting to the February 2005 law, people of color, descendants of formerly colonized migrants, publicly spoke out to proclaim themselves "indigenous people of the Republic." They eventually founded a political party. Their analysis was straightforward: they were "indigenous people of the Republic" because the French Republic discriminated against them, following a pattern of postcolonial discrimination. Their message about the colonial past was very clear: they denounced a fundamentally unequal and violent system. Going well beyond wars, they attacked colonialism and slavery in general and advocated specific political agency for those populations whose history was connected to colonialism. Whereas the previous generations were described as being too passive and complacent toward a Republic viewed as still influenced by a colonial spirit, this generation advocated political action.

Thus, in France, the historical visibility of colonized people occurred through political messages from those who identified as descendants of the colonized. Those who had experienced the Algerian war of liberation were not the most vocal. Nevertheless, an elderly Algerian woman called Louisette Ighilahriz rekindled the process in 2000 by showing the courage to testify in the media about the torture and sexual violence she had endured at the hands of French troops in 1957.[34] She filed a defamation lawsuit against General Maurice Schmitt, the former chief of staff of the French armed forces, who had been a lieutenant in Algeria in 1957 and who had accused her of lying. The general was found guilty and given a symbolic penalty. He appealed and was acquitted on grounds of good faith. Ighilahriz appealed to the supreme court, but her appeal was rejected two years later, and Schmitt's good faith was confirmed. The French judicial system had been unable to deal with the substance of the case because the amnesty law made any criminal prosecution of military personnel impossible. Under French law, the issue of the extreme violence committed during the Algerian war could only be presented before courts in charge of cases dealing with the freedom of expression. The efforts of an Algerian woman, a former militant for the National Liberation Front, would have no judicial impact. Nevertheless, the political effects of the ruling were not trivial for the status of the truth. Lacking a suitable judicial venue, Ighilahriz had made her experience or rape and torture become widely known as a result of free expression.

In Great Britain and the Netherlands, formerly colonized people have also filed cases with the judicial systems. Unlike in France, some of these cases have been successful. In the Netherlands, the question involved crimes committed in Rawagede and South Sulawesi. To begin with, the Prosecuting Office confirmed that the crimes were time barred and that perpetrators could not be prosecuted. The amnesty law still holds sway and protects veterans. However, the Dutch state was sued in civil court by victims. The judicial system accepted the lawsuit filed by nine widows whose husbands had been killed in wartime massacres. The court rejected the state's invocation of the statute of limitations and ordered it to pay the widows compensation for material damage (immaterial damage was rejected). For the other cases in South Sulawesi, the Dutch state initiated a settlement to compensate widows in similar execution cases, outside court. Apart from this financial aspect, there were political stakes: via the justice system, the Dutch state was forced to acknowledge its responsibility for the situation of these women. Thus, in addition to this recognition through the courts, there was recognition by the executive branch of this violence. On 9 December 2011, the sixty-fourth anniversary of the Rawagede massacre, the Dutch ambassador to Indonesia traveled to the town that is now called Balongsari and officially apologized for what had happened there.[35]

In Great Britain, the question of the crimes committed during the repression of the Mau Mau uprising was also raised by formerly colonized people, and also went before the courts. In the early 2010s, four Kenyans filed suit against the British state for torture and violence that they had endured.[36] The lawsuit was ruled to be admissible by the judge, who turned down the Foreign Office's argument that anything that had occurred before 1963 should be handled by the new independent Kenyan government. The Foreign Office also argued that the witnesses who could have shed light on the issue of responsibility at the highest level had all died. However, the judge considered that the archives would be a substitute. Indeed, new archives had been identified, and research by David Anderson, Caroline Elkins, and Huw Bennett had revealed the magnitude of the repressive system.[37] Hence court cases quickly shifted public interest to questions about the archives and the British state's handling of secrecy. Had records been destroyed?

Were they still in Kenya, or had they been shipped to Great Britain, and if so, were they accessible and under what conditions?

In 2013, a court ruled in favor of the Kenyan plaintiffs. As in the Netherlands, the British government made an out-of-court settlement, in this case with more than five thousand Kenyans who had been tortured while in British detention during the Mau Mau uprising of the 1950s.[38] The question of hidden archives became a public affair, widely relayed in the media by David Anderson. The historian had written the first book to analyze the way in which the repression was based on widespread legalization and legitimization of extreme violence. He also clearly established that it was a direct continuation of the ordinary violence of the colonial system, involving land seizures, political violence, and police brutality. Contrary to some of his colleagues, Anderson considered that violence was a topic for historical scholarship that absolutely had to be explained in terms of the context of its appearance and execution. Working in the archives, Anderson became a de facto militant for access to documents. He strongly advocated the need to do historical research on these topics that were inconvenient for a portion of British public opinion and its political class. In this fight against state secrets, the alliance among historians, the media, political personalities, and lawyers proved decisive.

Another alliance formed in the Netherlands also appears to have paid off. In 2012, three major research institutions—the Royal Netherlands Institute of Southeast Asian and Caribbean Studies, the Netherlands Institute of Military History, and the NIOD Institute for War, Holocaust and Genocide Studies—together with some left-wing parties and a portion of the media, advocated a broad scholarly inquiry into the violence of the decolonization war. From the outset the institutes stated that they were distancing themselves from the legal vocabulary, on the one hand, and official euphemisms, on the other. They asked "to conduct research to understand how and why people were motivated to commit cruelties, which so far have been labeled as 'excesses.'" Ultimately, in 2016, the Dutch government decided to provide funding for precisely such a historical research program.[39]

Nothing similar has happened in France. In the early 2000s, the executive branch could still state that torture and summary executions were acts by rogue individuals and "minority actions," but the archives have generally been open, and researchers have been able to demonstrate the systemic nature of torture during the Algerian war and the magnitude of war crimes, summary executions in particular. More recently, in the 2010s, the military court archives were opened up, and they show unequivocally how impunity was built during the war, well before the amnesty. The French president admitted in 2018 to what had long since been historically documented. The declaration, in which he stated that "this system was the unfortunate ground for sometimes terrible acts," was carefully written to avoid offending the armed forces. Macron used predominantly moral terms, but nevertheless clearly admitted that torture had gone "unpunished because it was regarded as a weapon ... considered to be legitimate during that war, despite being illegal." By stating that successive governments had failed to "safeguard human rights, and first and foremost, the physical integrity of the women and men held in custody under their sovereignty," he asserted that political accountability was key. In so doing, he delivered a general message on the actions of the armed forces, stating that his speech was not aimed at casting blanket disgrace on all the individuals who had served in Algeria, and calling on France to look at this page of its history "with courage and lucidity."

On 10 March 2020, some of the courage called for by Macron was also shown when King Willem-Alexander, during a state visit to Indonesia, apologized for "excessive violence on the part of the Dutch" in the late 1940s. As with the 2005 declaration by Foreign Minister Bot, which had subtly denounced the war and its aims, the king's words were weighed carefully. They could still be interpreted as admitting only to "excesses" ("derailments of violence" in Dutch) rather than recognizing the structural nature of the extreme violence used. According to some, particularly in veterans' circles and among the predominantly Eurasian postcolonial migrant community, the king had gone too far. On the other end of the spectrum, some called for collective penance for centuries of Dutch colonial suppression and exploitation. However, the statement, which also emphasized regret for "the pain and the sorrow of the families affected," came as a positive surprise to journalists and scholars alike and was welcomed by many.[40]

In gradually and grudgingly confronting its violent path of decolonization, France has certainly not been unique. Algeria may have been an extreme case, but overall, the shared lexicon emerging in this chapter demonstrates that the broad parallels eclipse the national differences. So, have France, the Netherlands, and the Great Britain reached the end of a cycle, and are they about to start a new one? In each of these countries, that cycle began with victims being unable to speak and with soldiers unable to break their shameful or discreet silence. The state's official positive message was the only one that could be heard. At the end of this cycle—or the beginning of the next—not only could the victims speak, but they were also heard. Soldiers admitted to the ambiguous situation in which they had been placed, and states recognized at least a portion of their responsibility for torture, executions, and other forms of extreme violence during the wars of decolonization.

The conditions for historians to carry out their research into abuse have changed over the decades. While access to archives has overall increased, and witnesses are more willing to testify, society's demands have also increased, and the pressure exerted on those who speak about the past has become stronger. For historians, this does not necessarily mean that their working conditions have unequivocally improved. As new questions have gained public attention, people from different backgrounds, with many different motivations, have appealed to historians to investigate and report "the truth."

These new questions have certain specific features for scholars examining extreme violence during the wars of decolonization. Significantly, this search for historical truth now involves the formerly colonized societies. How is it possible to pursue examinations of this violence in those countries? How do historical narratives of this past resonate with the issues that these countries currently face? What can be done so that the narratives of decolonization and violence developed in the former metropoles do not contribute to a reactivation of colonial domination through prioritizing—be it in financial support, research time, or archival disclosures—the scholarly questions that interest those in the former metropole over questions of importance to the former colony?

The field of historical scholarship is not separate from other fields, judicial or political. Historians are placed at the heart of the way in which formerly imperial states and societies think of and depict themselves. The various national cases and societal contexts that have been compared in this book must also be positioned within a broader framework. The issue of extreme violence against colonized people is one of the key historical themes of our period, which links up to wider engagement with our colonial pasts and postcolonial present, and our current place in the world. Studying this key historical theme may help European societies finally face up to the complex legacies of their colonial identities, past and present.

Contributors

Pierre Asselin is professor of history and Dwight E. Stanford Chair in American Foreign Relations at San Diego State University. He holds a PhD from the University of Hawai'i at Manoa, Honolulu.

Huw Bennett is a reader in international relations at Cardiff University. He holds a PhD from the University of Wales, Aberystwyth.

Raphaëlle Branche is a professor of contemporary history at Paris Nanterre University. She received her PhD from the Paris Institute of Political Studies (Sciences Po).

Thijs Brocades Zaalberg holds positions as associate professor at the Netherlands Defence Academy and assistant professor in contemporary military history at Leiden University. He holds a PhD from the University of Amsterdam.

Roel Frakking is a lecturer in political history in the History and Art History Department at Utrecht University. He received his PhD from the European University Institute, Florence.

Christiaan Harinck holds a PhD from Leiden University and currently teaches at the University of Utrecht.

Azarja Harmanny is a researcher with the Netherlands Institute of Military History (NIMH). As a PhD candidate at the University of Utrecht he is completing his dissertation on the use of heavy weapons in the Indonesian War of Independence.

Brian McAllister Linn is professor of military history at Texas A&M University. He holds a PhD from Ohio State University.

Bart Luttikhuis holds a PhD from the European University Institute, Florence. He was a fellow at the Netherlands Institute of Southeast Asian and Caribbean Studies (KITLV), taught at Leiden University, and now teaches at Alberdingk Thijm School in Utrecht.

Peter Romijn is senior researcher / head of research at the NIOD Institute for War, Holocaust, and Genocide Studies in Amsterdam and professor of twentieth-entury history at the University of Amsterdam. He received his PhD from the University of Groningen.

Stef Scagliola is a postdoctoral researcher at the Centre for Contemporary and Digital History at Luxembourg University and a fellow at the Netherlands Institute of Southeast Asian and Caribbean Studies (KITLV) in Leiden. She holds a PhD from Erasmus University Rotterdam.

Henk Schulte Nordholt is professor emeritus of Indonesian history at Leiden University and former head of research at the Netherlands Institute of Southeast Asian and Caribbean Studies (KITLV). He holds a PhD from Vrije Universiteit Amsterdam.

Martin Thomas is professor of imperial history at Exeter University. He holds a PhD from Oxford University.

Natalya Vince is a reader in North African and French studies at the University of Portsmouth, UK. She holds a PhD from the University of London.

Notes

1. INTRODUCTION

1. A small selection from this wide-ranging debate: Huw Bennett, "'A Very Salutary Effect': The Counter-terror Strategy in the Early Malayan Emergency, June 1948 to December 1949," *Journal of Strategic Studies* 32, no. 3 (2009): 415–444; Brian Drohan, *Brutality in the Age of Human Rights: Activism and Counterinsurgency at the End of the British Empire* (Ithaca, NY: Cornell University Press, 2017). Karl Hack has even called for post-revisionism as a counterweight to what he perceives as tendency to overcorrect the narrative on (British) counterinsurgency: Karl Hack, "Everyone Lived in Fear: Malaya and the British Way of Counter-insurgency," *Small Wars & Insurgencies* 23, no. 4–5 (2012): 671–699, and Karl Hack, "'Devils That Suck the Blood of the Malayan People': The Case for Post-revisionist Analysis of Counter-insurgency Violence," *War in History* 25, no. 2 (2018).

2. Newspapers and other media in the UK, US, and France hardly covered the Dutch king's apologies. Only the *Guardian* treated it in a broader European context. John Henley, Phillip Oltermann, and Daniel Boffey, "European Powers Still Loth to Admit Historical Evils," *Guardian*, 11 March 2020. On Macron's apologies see the final chapter to this volume by Raphaëlle Branche.

3. For some examples see Daniel Marston and Carter Malkasian, eds., *Counterinsurgency in Modern Warfare* (Oxford: Osprey, 2008); Gregory Fremont-Barnes, ed., *A History of Counterinsurgency: From South Africa to Algeria, 1900–1954*, 2 vols. (Santa Barbara, CA: Praeger, 2015); Isabelle Duyvesteyn and Paul Rich, eds., *The Routledge Handbook of Insurgency and Counterinsurgency* (London: Routledge, 2012).

4. The Committee of Dutch Debts of Honour (led by chairman Jeffry Pondaag) filed its first lawsuit against the Dutch state on behalf of Indonesian victims in the West Javanese town Rawagede (now Bolongsari) in 2008. For more on these cases see Bart Luttikhuis, "Juridisch afgedwongen excuses. Rawagedeh, Zuid-Celebes en de Nederlandse terughoudendheid," *BMGN—Low Countries Historical Review* 129, no. 4 (2014): 92–105; Nicole L. Immler, "Hoe koloniaal onrecht te erkennen? De Rawagede-zaak laat kansen en grenzen van rechtsherstel zien," *BMGN—Low Countries Historical Review*, 133, no. 4 (2018): 57–87.

5. Rémy Limpach, *De brandende kampongs van Generaal Spoor* (Amsterdam: Boom, 2016). For "trail of burning kampongs" see p. 737. For a discussion in English on Limpach's analysis see Rémy Limpach, with Bart Luttikhuis, Abdul Wahid, Robert Cribb, and Harry Poeze, "Debate on *De brandende kampongs van Generaal Spoor*," *Bijdragen tot de Taal-, Land- en Volkenkunde* 173, no. 4 (2017): 557–579.

6. The three institutes involved are KITLV, NIMH, and NIOD. For more information on the program "Independence, Decolonization, Violence and War in Indonesia, 1945–1950" and its eight subprojects see www.ind45-50.org/en.

7. Frances Gouda and Thijs Brocades Zaalberg, *American Visions of the Netherlands East Indies / Indonesia: U.S. Foreign Policy and Indonesian Nationalism, 1920–1949* (Amsterdam: Amsterdam University Press, 2002); Robert J. McMahon, *Colonialism and Cold War: The US and the Struggle for Indonesian Independence, 1945–1949* (Ithaca, NY: Cornell University Press, 1981).

8. Examples of the most comprehensive such efforts are David B. Abernethy, *The Dynamics of Global Dominance: European Overseas Empires, 1415–1980* (New Haven, CT: Yale University Press, 2000), and Jane Burbank and Frederick Cooper, *Empires in World History: Power and the Politics of Difference* (Princeton, NJ: Princeton University Press, 2010).

9. Martin Thomas, *Fight or Flight: Britain, France and Their Roads from Empire* (Oxford: Oxford University Press, 2014); Martin Shipway, *Decolonization and Its Impact: A Comparative Approach to the End of Empires* (Malden, MA: Blackwell, 2010).

10. For a critique on the simplistic comparison between Indochina and Malaya see Thomas, *Fight or Flight*, 161–163. A recent volume that conceptualizes national "styles" of counterinsurgency is Beatrice Heuser and Eitan Shamir, eds., *Insurgencies and Counterinsurgencies: National Styles and Strategic Cultures* (Cambridge: Cambridge University Press, 2016).

11. Limpach, *De brandende kampongs*, 25 (emphasis in original letter).

12. Gert Oostindie, *Soldaat in Indonesië 1945–1950. Getuigenissen van een oorlog aan de verkeerde kant van de geschiedenis* (Amsterdam: Boom, 2015) 82, 138, 156–157, 206, 233, 236, 237, 242. For a comparison to the German razzia on Putten see also Limpach, *De brandende kampongs*, 435, 753. It should be noted that all these comparisons by contemporaries of Dutch behavior with extreme violence during the German occupation leave the Shoah out of the equation, focusing instead on German reprisal measures against non-Jewish Dutch civilians.

13. Ian Cobain and Jessica Hatcher, "Kenyan Mau Mau Victims in Talks with UK Government over Legal Settlement," *Guardian*, 5 May 2013.

14. Quote in Raphaëlle Branche, *"Papa, qu'as-tu fait en Algérie?" Enquête sur un silence familial* (Paris: La Découverte, 2020), 184, 199. The trial of the perpetrators of Oradour had fueled a huge debate in France in 1953 since some of the perpetrators were Alsatian men, forcibly engaged to fight in Nazi uniform.

15. J. A. A. van Doorn and W. J. Hendrix, *Ontsporing van geweld: Het Nederlands-Indonesisch conflict* (Amsterdam: Bataafse Leeuw, 1985), 47. This conclusion was underwritten in Loe de Jong, *Het Koninkrijk der Nederlanden in de Tweede Wereldoorlog 12II* (The Hague: Sdu, 1988), 1015.

16. For example, Martien Hoogland, "Nederland moet het optreden in Nederlands-Indië in historisch perspectief plaatsen," *HP de Tijd*, 3 May 2017; J. J. P. de Jong, "Het kantelende beeld van dekolonisatie," *Clingendael Spectator*, 6 February 2018. Limpach has also commented on this tendency: Rémy Limpach, "Zwarte Bladzijden in Nederland, Duitsland, Frankrijk en Groot-Brittannië," *Geschiedenis Magazine*, June 2017, 52–57.

17. For "league table" see David Anderson, *Histories of the Hanged: The Dirty War in Kenya and the End of Empire* (New York: W. W. Norton, 2005), 6.

18. Thomas, *Fight or Flight*, 7.

19. For a classic example of this debate see Huw Bennett, "The Other Side of the COIN: Minimum Force and Exemplary Force in British Army Counterinsurgency in Kenya," *Small Wars & Insurgencies* 18, no. 4 (2007): 638–664; Rod Thornton, "'Minimum Force': A Reply to Huw Bennett," *Small Wars and Insurgencies* 20, no. 1 (2009): 215–226.

20. See for instance Simon Innes-Robbins, *Dirty Wars: A Century of Counter-insurgency* (Stroud, Gloucestershire: History Press, 2016); Benjamin Grob-Fitzgibbon, *Imperial Endgame: Britain's Dirty Wars and the End of Empire* (London: Palgrave, 2011).

21. Jan Bank, ed., *De excessennota* (The Hague: Sdu, 1995).

22. Gert Oostindie et al., "'Alles is natuurlijk te begrijpen als je erover nadenkt,' Interview met Prof. dr. Cees Fasseur," *Leidschrift* 31, no. 3 (2016): 95–107.

23. Oostindie, *Soldaat in Indonesië*; Peter Romijn, "Learning on 'the Job': Dutch War Volunteers Entering the Indonesian War of Independence, 1945–46," *Journal of Genocide*

Studies 14 (2012): 317–336; Stef Scagliola, *Last van de oorlog: De Nederlandse oorlogsmisdaden in Indonesië en hun verwerking* (Amsterdam: Balans, 2002).

24. Limpach, *De brandende kampongs*, 45. Limpach himself uses both "extreme violence" and "mass violence," largely interchangeably. Cf. on terminology Limpach et al., "Debate."

25. Stathis N. Kalyvas, *The Logic of Violence in Civil War* (Cambridge: Cambridge University Press, 2006), 20. Along somewhat similar lines, Tarak Barkawi argues that violence is a broader concept than "war," because especially in colonial situations the use of force should be conceived as "an ordinary dimension of politics." Tarak Barkawi, "Decolonising War," *European Journal of International Security* 1 (2016): 199–214.

26. Benjamin Valentino, Paul Huth, and Dylan Balch-Lindsay, "'Draining the Sea': Mass Killing and Guerrilla Warfare," *International Organization* 58 (2004): 375–407; Alexander B. Downes, "Draining the Sea by Filling the Graves: Investigating the Effectiveness of Indiscriminate Violence as a Counterinsurgency Strategy," *Civil Wars* 9, no. 4 (2007): 420–444; David H. Ucko, "'The People Are Revolting': An Anatomy of Authoritarian Counterinsurgency," *Journal of Strategic Studies* 39, no. 1 (2016): 29–61.

27. The original Third Geneva Convention was signed as early as 1929.

28. See, for example, Boyd van Dijk, "The Making of the Geneva Conventions: Decolonization, the Cold War, and the Birth of Humanitarian Law" (diss., European University Institute, 2017); A. Dirk Moses, Marco Duranti, and Roland Burke, *Decolonization, Self-Determination, and the Rise of Global Human Rights Politics* (Cambridge: Cambridge University Press, 2020). For the influence of ideas and declarations on human rights on decolonization wars and on counterinsurgency methods see Fabian Klose, *Human Rights in the Shadow of Colonial Violence: The Wars of Independence in Kenya and Algeria* (Philadelphia: University of Pennsylvania Press, 2013); Drohan, *Brutality in the Age of Human Rights*.

29. Cf. also Limpach, *De brandende kampongs*, 45; Sibylle Scheipers, *Unlawful Combatants: A Genealogy of the Irregular Fighter* (Oxford: Oxford University Press, 2015). See also the chapters by Harinck and by Frakking and Thomas in this volume, who deal with the complications of defining combatant status in colonial counterinsurgencies.

30. For a comparative analysis of forced resettlement see Moritz Feichtinger, "Strategic Villages: Forces Relocation, Counterinsurgency and Social Engineering in Kenya and Algeria, 1952–1962," in *Decolonization and Conflict: Colonial Comparisons and Legacies*, ed. Martin Thomas and Gareth Curless (London: Bloomsbury Academic, 2017), 137–158; Moritz Feichtinger, "'A Great Reformatory': Social Planning and Strategic Resettlement in Late Colonial Kenya and Algeria, 1952–63," *Journal of Contemporary History* 52, no 1 (2017): 45–72.

31. If this is indeed the case, then this "classic" colonial method of burning and razing villages was eventually counterproductive. After all, the lack of Dutch population-control measures seems to have driven the population into the arms of the guerrillas. We thank Petra Groen for the latter contrasting insight adding to our comparison between mass burning and organized population and resources control.

32. On "icons of memory" see Paul Bijl, *Emerging Memory: Photographs of Colonial Atrocity in Dutch Cultural Memory* (Amsterdam: Amsterdam University Press, 2009).

33. Rémy Limpach (NIMH, The Hague) is currently working on a study of the Dutch intelligence services in Indonesia, which will focus extensively on the issue of torture.

34. Thomas and Curless, *Decolonisation and Conflict*, 100.

35. Figures on Kenya and Algeria as assembled by Feichtinger, "'Great Reformatory,'" 49. For some of these general notions see also Limpach, "Zwarte Bladzijden," 52–53.

36. Christopher Goscha, "A 'Total War' of Decolonization? Social Mobilization and State-Building in Communist Vietnam, 1949–54," *War & Society*, 31 no. 2 (2012): 136–162.

37. See Frances Gouda and Thijs Brocades Zaalberg, *American Visions of the Netherlands East-Indies / Indonesia: US Foreign Policy and Indonesian Nationalism, 1920–1949* (Amsterdam: Amsterdam University Press, 2002), 305. See also Petra Groen, *Marsroutes and Dwaalsporen* (The Hague: Sdu, 1991), 289–290.

38. For this rough comparison see Thijs Brocades Zaalberg, "The Civil and Military Dimensions of Dutch Counterinsurgency on Java, 1947–49," *British Journal for Military History* 1, no. 2 (2015): 67–83. For the figure 150,000 Dutch forces in 1949 as well as 120,000 in 1947 see Petra Groen, Anita van Dissel, Mark Loderichs, Rémy Limpach, and Thijs Brocades Zaalberg, *Krijgsmacht en kolonie: Opkomst en ondergang van Nederland als koloniale macht 1816–2010* (Amsterdam: Boom, 2021), 364.

39. For Dutch casualties see Van Doorn and Hendrix, *Ontsporing van geweld*, 165. Figures for the Indochina War are from Christopher Goscha, *Historical Dictionary of the Indochina War, 1945–1954* (Copenhagen: NiAS, 2011), 17, 88–89. These numbers exclude significant casualties among locally recruited paramilitary and police forces. Including these would significantly raise the casualty figures in especially Kenya and Algeria. For more detailed figures see Harinck's contribution to this volume.

40. Goscha, *Historical Dictionary*, 88–89; Christiaan Harinck, Nico van Horn, and Bart Luttikhuis, "Wie telt de Indonesische Doden?," *De Groene Amsterdammer*, no. 30 (2017); Anderson, *Histories of the Hanged*, 4–5. For discussion on other casualty figures see Harinck's contribution in this volume.

41. Goscha, *Historical Dictionary*, 165.

42. Limpach, *De brandende kampongs*, 308.

43. Bart Luttikhuis, "Generating Distrust through Intelligence Work: Psychological Terror and the Dutch Security Services in Indonesia, 1945–1949," *War in History* 25, no. 2 (2018): 154–158.

44. For example, in chapter 10 of *De brandende kampongs van Generaal Spoor*, Limpach discusses seventeen (partially interrelated) causes, not counting additional intrinsic motivations such as sadism.

45. On causal hierarchy cf. E. H. Carr's classic *What Is History?* (London: Penguin, 1961). On the "brutalizing" effect of war we take inspiration from George Mosse's *Brutalization Theory*: George Mosse, *Fallen Soldiers: Reshaping the Memory of the World Wars* (Oxford: Oxford University Press, 1990).

46. Limpach, *De brandende kampongs*, 740–745.

47. Apart from Limpach, for instance cf. Jacques Frémeaux, "The French Experience in Algeria: Doctrine, Violence and Lessons Learned," *Civil Wars* 14, no. 1 (2012): 49–62; Shipway, *Decolonization*, 161–166.

48. Dierk Walter, *Colonial Warfare: European Empires and the Use of Force* (London: Hurst, 2017), 6, 265–267. See also Thoralf Klein and Frank Schumacher, eds., *Kolonialkriege: Militärische Gewalt im Zeichen des Imperialismus* (Hamburg: Hamburger Edition, HIS Verlag, 2006).

49. Kim A. Wagner, "Calculated to Strike Terror: The Amritsar Massacre and the Spectacle of Colonial Violence," *Past & Present* 233, no. 1 (2016): 189, 204, 205, 209, 219–221; Kim A. Wagner, "Savage Warfare: Violence and the Rule of Colonial Difference in Early British Counterinsurgency," *History Workshop Journal* 85 (Spring 2018): 218, 231; Kim A. Wagner, *Amritsar 1919: An Empire of Fear and the Making of a Massacre* (New Haven, CT: Yale University Press, 2019). See also Nancy Rose Hunt, *A Nervous State: Violence, Remedies, and Reverie in Colonial Congo* (Durham, NC: Duke University Press, 2016); Henk Schulte Nordholt, "A Genealogy of Violence," in *Roots of Violence in Indonesia: Contemporary Violence in Historical Perspective*, ed. Freek Colombijn and J. Thomas Lindblad (Leiden: KITLV, 2002), 33–60.

50. Limpach, *De brandende kampongs*, 708–717; Stef Scagliola, *Last van de oorlog*, 81–83, 89; Oostindie, *Soldaat in Indondesië*, 17–20, 242–243.

51. Carl von Clausewitz, *On War*, ed. and trans. Michael Howard and Peter Paret (1832; Princeton, NJ: Princeton University Press, 1984), 75–90.

52. Wayne Lee, *Barbarians and Brothers: Anglo-American Warfare, 1500–1865* (Oxford: Oxford University Press, 2011); Wayne Lee, ed., *Warfare and Culture in World History*, 2nd ed. (New York: NYU Press, 2020); Patrick Porter, *Military Orientalism: Eastern War through Western Eyes* (London: Hurst, 2009).

53. Sönke Neitzel and Harald Welzer, *Soldaten: On Fighting, Killing and Dying* (London: Simon & Schuster, 2013).

54. This builds on a similar notion in relation to ethnic violence and ethnic war in Kalyvas, *Logic of Violence*, 390.

2. NOT AN AFTERTHOUGHT

1. Eerste Kamer der Staten-Generaal, Verslag der Handelingen, Rijksbegroting voor het Dienstjaar 1949, politieke beschouwingen, 25 Januari 1949, J. Haken.

2. House of Commons Hansard, 9 December 1953, accessed online 14 June 2019, https://hansard.parliament.uk/Commons/1953-12-09/debates/3a8fe752-a8e7-4c28-a673-2668676d2d25/Mau-MauCasualties.

3. Fabian Klose, *Human Rights in the Shadow of Colonial Violence* (Philadelphia: University of Pennsylvania Press, 2013), 5.

4. David Anderson, *Histories of the Hanged: Britain's Dirty War in Kenya and the End of Empire* (London: Orion, 2005); Richard Stubbs, *Hearts and Minds in Guerrilla Warfare: The Malayan Emergency 1948–1960* (Oxford: Oxford University Press, 1993).

5. John MacKenzie, *Propaganda and Empire: The Manipulation of British Public Opinion 1880–1960* (Manchester: Manchester University Press, 1984), 2; Bernard Porter, *The Absent-Minded Imperialists* (Oxford: Oxford University Press, 2004), 307.

6. Wim van den Doel, *Zo ver de wereld strekt: De geschiedenis van Nederland overzee vanaf 1800* (Amsterdam: Bert Bakker, 2011), 303.

7. Petra Groen, Anita van Dissel, Mark Loderichs, Rémy Limpach, and Thijs Brocades Zaalberg, *Krijgsgeweld en kolonie: Opkomst ondergang van Nederland als koloniale mogendheid 1816–2010* (Amsterdam: Boom, 2021), 351 and 368.

8. Eerste Kamer der Staten-Generaal, Verslag der Handelingen, Rijksbegroting voor het Dienstjaar 1949, politieke beschouwingen, 25 Januari 1949, A. B. Roosjen.

9. Elizabeth Buettner, *Europe after Empire: Decolonization, Society, and Culture* (Cambridge: Cambridge University Press, 2016), 40.

10. Alexander L. George and Andrew Bennett, *Case Studies and Theory Development in the Social Sciences* (Cambridge, MA: MIT Press, 2005), 18, 79.

11. James Mahoney and Dietrich Rueschemeyer, eds., *Comparative Historical Analysis in the Social Sciences* (Cambridge: Cambridge University Press, 2003), 8.

12. Tom Mackie and David Marsh, "The Comparative Method," in *Theory and Methods in Political Science*, ed. David Marsh and Gerry Stoker (Basingstoke, UK: Macmillan, 1995), 175.

13. George and Bennett, *Case Studies and Theory Development*, 67.

14. James Mahoney and Kathleen Thelen, "Comparative-Historical Analysis in Contemporary Political Science," in *Advances in Comparative-Historical Analysis*, ed. James Mahoney and Kathleen Thelen (Cambridge: Cambridge University Press, 2015), 20.

15. Floribert Baudet, *Het vierde wapen: Voorlichting, propaganda en volksweerbaarheid 1944–1953* (Amsterdam: Boom, 2013).

16. Louis Zweers, *De gecensureerde oorlog: Militairen versus media in Nederlands-Indië 1945–1949* (Zutphen, Netherlands: Walburg Pers, 2013).

17. Andrew Defty, *Britain, America and Anti-Communist Propaganda 1945–53: The Information Research Department* (London: Routledge, 2004), 29.

18. W. Scott Lucas and C. J. Morris, "A Very British Crusade: The Information Research Department and the Beginning of the Cold War," in *British Intelligence, Strategy and the Cold War, 1945–51*, ed. Richard Aldrich (London: Routledge, 1992), 87.

19. For instance, files containing confidential reports of Army Public Relations Office to Indies Government Information Service (RVD-Batavia), in National Archives, The Hague, Ministerie van Koloniën, collection no. 2.10.29, inventory no. 89 (hereafter NL-HaNA, followed by entry number and inventory number).

20. Zweers, *De gecensureerde oorlog*; Gerda Janssen Hendriks, "Een voorbeeldige kolonie: Nederlands-Indië in 50 jaar overheidsfilms 1912–1962" (PhD diss., University of Amsterdam, 2014).

21. Demonstrated in detail in Arend Lijphart, *The Politics of Accommodation: Pluralism and Democracy in the Netherlands* (Berkeley: University of California Press, 1968).

22. Reports produced by Van Goudoever in NL-HaNA, Collectie W. A. van Goudoever 2.21.205.20/10.

23. Phillip Deery, "The Terminology of Terrorism: Malaya, 1948–52," *Journal of Southeast Asian Studies* 34, no. 2 (2003): 236, 237, 241, 245.

24. Myles Osborne, "'The Rooting Out of Mau Mau from the Minds of the Kikuyu Is a Formidable Task': Propaganda and the Mau Mau War," *Journal of African History* 56, no. 1 (2015): 78, 80, 93.

25. Erik Linstrum, "Facts about Atrocity: Knowing Violence in the Postwar British Empire," *History Workshop Journal* 84 (Autumn 2017): 109, 115–116.

26. Osborne, "Rooting Out of Mau Mau," 80, 82.

27. Susan L. Carruthers, *Winning Hearts and Minds: British Governments, the Media and Colonial Counter-insurgency 1944–1960* (London: Leicester University Press, 1995), 72, 97–98, 167.

28. Bruce Rocheleau, "Politics, Accountability, and Information Management," in *Selected Readings on Information Technology Management: Contemporary Issues*, ed. George Kelley (Hershey, PA: Information Science Reference, 2009), 323–357.

29. Neil Mitchell, *Democracy's Blameless Leaders: From Dresden to Abu Ghraib, How Leaders Evade Accountability for Abuse, Atrocity, and Killing* (New York: NYU Press, 2012), 2–4.

30. Ryan Grauer, "Uncertain Victory: Information Management and Military Power," *Journal of Global Security Studies* 2, no. 1 (2017): 18–38.

31. Richard K. Betts, "Analysis, War, and Decision: Why Intelligence Failures Are Inevitable," *World Politics* 31, no. 1 (1978): 61–89.

32. David M. Anderson and Daniel Branch, "Allies at the End of Empire—Loyalists, Nationalists and the Cold War, 1945–76," *International History Review* 39, no. 1 (2017): 1–13.

33. David Edgerton, *The Rise and Fall of the British Nation: A Twentieth-Century History* (London: Allen Lane, 2018), 342.

34. NL-HaNA, Ministerie van Buitenlandse Zaken, Bureau DIRVO, 2.05.52/551, 557. Connections between Bureau DIRVO (Directie Verre Oosten / Directorate for the Far East) and RVD-Batavia.

35. NL-HaNA, Collectie P. J. Koets, 2.21.100/436 and 439. Memoranda by P. J. Koets, Chief of Cabinet High Commissioner of the Crown in Jakarta, 16 January 1949 and 12 March 1949.

36. Rémy Limpach, *De brandende kampongs van Generaal Spoor* (Amsterdam: Boom, 2016), 439–442.

37. Examples of such reporting in NL-HaNA, Ministerie van Koloniën, 2.10.29/91–96 and 193–205.
38. NL-HaNA, Ministerie van Koloniën 2.10.29/96.
39. NL-HaNA, Ministerie van Koloniën 2.10.29/98.
40. NL-HaNA, Ministerie van Koloniën 2.10.29/89, and further, reporting by "Dienst Legercontacten" (Army Public Relations Service) to Lt. Governor-General in Batavia; Reporting by Lt. Governor-General to Minister of Colonies / Overseas Territories, in the same, inventory no. 91 (and further); reporting by RVD-Batavia to Minister of Colonies / Overseas Territories), in the same, inventory no. 42.
41. Reporting in NL-HaNA, Ministerie van Buitenlandse Zaken, Bureau DIRVO, 2.05.52/551.
42. Reporting in NL-HaNA, Ministerie van Buitenlandse Zaken, Bureau DIRVO, 2.05.52/557.
43. NL-HaNA, Ministerraad, 2.02.05.02/388, Minutes of Cabinet Meetings, 23 April 1946; NL-HaNA, Ministerraad, 2.02.05.02/389, Minutes of Cabinet Meetings, 8 April 1947.
44. NL-HaNA, Collectie J. J. A. Logemann, 2.21.111/33, Letters MP Logemann to Minister Van Maarseveen, 14 November 1949, and Van Maarseveen to Logemann, 17 November 1949.
45. David Goldsworthy, *Colonial Issues in British Politics, 1945–1961: From "Colonial Development" to "Wind of Change"* (Oxford: Oxford University Press, 1971), 64–68.
46. Michael S. Goodman, "Creating the Machinery for Joint Intelligence: The Formative Years of the Joint Intelligence Committee, 1936–1956," *International Journal of Intelligence and CounterIntelligence* 30, no. 1 (2017): 66–84.
47. Rory Cormac, *Confronting the Colonies: British Intelligence and Counterinsurgency* (London: Hurst, 2013), 27–30.
48. Calder Walton, *Empire of Secrets: British Intelligence, the Cold War and the Twilight of Empire* (London: Harper, 2013), 125.
49. S. R. Ashton and S. E. Stockwell, *British Documents on the End of Empire*, series A, vol. 1, *Imperial Policy and Colonial Practice 1925–1945* (London: HMSO, 1996), xxvi.
50. Anne Thurston, *Records of the Colonial Office, Dominions Office, Commonwealth Relations Office and Commonwealth Office* (London: HMSO, 1995), 18–21.
51. Huw Bennett, "Soldiers in the Court Room: The British Army's Part in the Kenya Emergency under the Legal Spotlight," *Journal of Imperial and Commonwealth History* 39, no. 5 (2011): 719.
52. British National Archives, Kew [TNA], FCO 141/5750: Nanyuki District Intelligence Committee Summary for the week ending 20 August 1953.
53. TNA FCO 141/5824: Rift Valley Provincial Intelligence Summary for the fortnight ending 11 May 1954.
54. TNA FCO 141/6555: Twentieth Meeting of the Colony Emergency Committee, 11 May 1953.
55. Jennifer L. Foray, *Visions of Empire in the Nazi-Occupied Netherlands* (Cambridge: Cambridge University Press, 2012).
56. Limpach, *De brandende kampongs*, 590, 686–688.
57. Peter Romijn, "Learning on 'the Job': Dutch War Volunteers Entering the Indonesian War of Independence, 1945–1946," in *Colonial Counterinsurgency and Mass Violence: The Dutch Empire in Indonesia*, ed. Bart Luttikhuis and A. Dirk Moses (Abingdon, UK: Routledge, 2014), 103.
58. Romijn, "Learning on 'the Job,'" 104.
59. Jan T. M. Bank, ed., *De Excessennota: Nota betreffende het archiefonderzoek naar de gegevens omtrent excessen in Indonesië begaan door Nederlandse militairen in de periode 1945–1950* (The Hague: Sdu, 1995), *Annex*, 12, 4.

60. Luttikhuis and Moses, *Colonial Counterinsurgency*, 1–4
61. Bank, *Excessennota Annex*, 12, 3–4.
62. Bank, 8–9
63. Chris van der Heijden, "Nederlandse excessen en publieke opinie tussen 1945 en 1955," *De Groene Amsterdammer*, February 27, 2013.
64. Bank, *Excessennota Annex*, 10.
65. NL-HaNA, Ministerie van Koloniën: Indisch Archief, serie v, 2.10.36.15/76, Letter Minister Van Maarseveen to Frans J. Goedhart, 23 September 1949.
66. Dane Kennedy, *The Imperial History Wars: Debating the British Empire* (London: Bloomsbury, 2018), 95.
67. John Newsinger, "The Military Memoir in British Imperial Culture: The Case of Malaya," *Race and Class* 35, no. 3 (1994): 55.
68. Wendy Webster, *Englishness and Empire 1939–1965* (Oxford: Oxford University Press, 2005), 119–129.
69. David Anderson, "Mau Mau at the Movies: Contemporary Representations of an Anti-colonial War," *South African Historical Journal* 48, no. 1 (2003): 71–89.
70. Miles Kahler, *Decolonization in Britain and France: The Domestic Consequences of International Relations* (Princeton, NJ: Princeton University Press, 1984), 246.
71. Stephen Howe, *Anticolonialism in British Politics: The Left and the End of Empire, 1918–1964* (Oxford: Clarendon, 1993), 1, 147, 152, 157, 237–238.
72. Richard Whiting, "The Empire and British Politics," in *Britain's Experience of Empire in the Twentieth Century*, ed. Andrew Thompson (Oxford: Oxford University Press, 2012), 161.
73. Martin Thomas, *Fight or Flight: Britain, France, and Their Roads from Empire* (Oxford: Oxford University Press, 2014), 118.
74. Goldsworthy, *Colonial Issues in British Politics*, 210–213.
75. Howe, *Anticolonialism in British Politics*, 201–207.
76. Spencer Mawby, "The Limits of Anticolonialism: The British Labour Movement and the End of Empire in Guiana," *History* 101, no. 344 (2016): 85–87.
77. Kahler, *Decolonization in Britain and France*, 151.
78. Katherine Bruce-Lockhart, "The 'Truth' about Kenya: Connection and Contestation in the 1956 Kamiti Controversy," *Journal of World History* 26, no. 4 (2016): 815–838.
79. Yolana Pringle, "Humanitarianism, Race and Denial: The International Committee of the Red Cross and Kenya's Mau Mau Rebellion, 1952–60," *History Workshop Journal* 84 (Autumn 2017): 89–107.
80. Richard Toye, "Arguing about Hola Camp: The Rhetorical Consequences of a Colonial Massacre," in *Rhetorics of Empire: Languages of Colonial Conflict after 1900*, ed. Martin Thomas and Richard Toye (Manchester: Manchester University Press, 2017), 187–207.
81. Mitchell, *Democracy's Blameless Leaders*, 23–26.
82. Mitchell, 26–31.
83. NL-HaNA, toegangsnummer 2.20.36.15/76 (Ministerie van Koloniën), High Commissioner Lovink to Minister Van Maarseveen, 19 July 1949.
84. NL-HaNA, 2.20.36.15/76, Correspondence of Chief Intelligence, Army Commander, High Commissioner and Minister of Overseas Territories, 15 February–15 March 1949.
85. NL-HaNA, 2.20.36.15/76, Letter Major J. H. Somer to Lieutenant-General Spoor, 15 February 1949, and Spoor to High Commissioner Beel, 18 February 1949.
86. NL-HaNA, 2.20.36.15/76, Letter Beel to Van Maarseveen, 28 February 1949, Van Maarseveen to Beel, 19 March 1949.
87. NL-HaNA, toegangsnummer 2.21.11/33 (Collectie J. H. A. Logemann), Minister of Reconstruction L. H. Neher to M. P. Logemann, 23 April 1948.

88. NL-HaNA, 2.20.36.15/76, Letter M. van der Goes van Naters, MP, to aan Van Maarseveen.

89. NL-HaNA, Algemeen Secretarie, 2.10.14/4724, Letter General Secretary with the High Commissioner to the Head of the Colonial Department of Justice, 1 August 1949.

90. Limpach, *De brandende kampongs*, 643; Romijn, "Learning on 'the Job,'" 105; Maurice Swirc, "Vijftig jaar Excessennota. De sneeuwbal rolt dan verder," *De Groene Amsterdammer*, November 7, 2019, 26–31.

91. Nicholas Owen, "Critics of Empire in Britain," in *The Oxford History of the British Empire*, vol. 4, *The Twentieth Century*, ed. Judith M. Brown and William Roger Louis (Oxford: Oxford University Press, 1999), 206.

92. Anderson, *Histories of the Hanged*, 90–91.

93. General Sir George Erskine, "Message to be distributed to all officers of the army, police and security forces, 23 June 1953," reproduced in Huw Bennett and David French, eds., *The Kenya Papers of General Sir George Erskine 1953–1955* (Stroud, UK: History Press for the Army Records Society, 2013), 36.

94. Huw Bennett, *Fighting the Mau Mau: The British Army and Counter-insurgency in the Kenya Emergency* (Cambridge: Cambridge University Press, 2012), 112–118.

95. Bennett, *Fighting the Mau Mau*, 118–125, 203–211.

96. C. J. M. Schuyt, "Politiek, staat en samenleving: Is een vernieuwing van hun onderlinge verhouding mogelijk?," *Socialisme en Democratie* 55, no. 5 (1998): 213–218.

97. Matthew Connelly, *A Diplomatic Revolution: Algeria's Fight for Independence and the Origins of the Post–Cold War Era* (Oxford: Oxford University Press, 2002).

98. Brian Drohan, *Brutality in an Age of Human Rights: Activism and Counterinsurgency at the End of the British Empire* (Ithaca, NY: Cornell University Press, 2017).

99. On the diplomatic, military, and propaganda dimensions see, respectively, Robert Holland, *Britain and the Revolt in Cyprus* (Oxford: Oxford University Press, 1998); David French, *Fighting EOKA: The British Counter-insurgency Campaign on Cyprus, 1955–1959* (Oxford: Oxford University Press, 2015); and Maria Hadjiathanasiou, *Propaganda and the Cyprus Revolt: Rebellion, Counter-insurgency and the Media, 1955–59* (London: I. B. Tauris, 2020).

100. A. W. Brian Simpson, *Human Rights and the End of Empire: Britain and the Genesis of the European Convention* (Oxford: Oxford University Press, 2001).

3. WINDOWS ONTO THE MICRODYNAMICS OF INSURGENT AND COUNTERINSURGENT VIOLENCE

1. Pioneered by comparative politics scholars, essential works on the microdynamics of violence include Stathis Kalyvas, *The Logic of Violence in Civil War* (Cambridge: Cambridge University Press, 2006); Kalyvas, "The Ontology of 'Political Violence': Action and Identity in Civil Wars," *Perspectives on Politics* 3, no. 3 (2003): 475–484; Elizabeth Jean Wood, *Insurgent Collective Action and Civil War in El Salvador* (Cambridge: Cambridge University Press, 2003); Jeremy Weinstein, *Inside Rebellion: The Politics of Insurgent Violence* (Cambridge: Cambridge University Press, 2006); Christopher Cramer, *Civil War Is Not a Stupid Thing: Accounting for Violence in Developing Countries* (London: Hurst, 2006); Stathis Kalyvas, Ian Shapiro, and Tarek Masoud, eds., *Order, Conflict, and Violence* (Cambridge: Cambridge University Press, 2008); Erica Chenoweth and Adria Lawrence, eds., *Rethinking Violence: States and Non-state Actors in Conflict* (Cambridge, MA: MIT Press, 2010); Paul Staniland, *Networks of Rebellion: Explaining Insurgent Cohesion and Collapse* (Ithaca, NY: Cornell University Press, 2014); Jessica Stanton, *Violence and Restraint in Civil War: Civilian Targeting in the Shadow of International Law* (Cambridge: Cambridge

University Press, 2016); James D. Fearon and David D. Laitin, "Ethnicity, Insurgency, and Civil War," *American Political Science Review* 97, no. 1 (2001): 75–90.

2. Gil Merom, *How Democracies Lose Small Wars* (Cambridge: Cambridge University Press, 2003); Ivan Arreguín-Toft, *How the Weak Win Wars: A Theory of Asymmetric Conflict* (Cambridge: Cambridge University Press, 2005), 23–47; Ana Arjona, Nelson Kasfir, and Zahariah Mampilly, eds., *Rebel Governance in Civil War* (Cambridge: Cambridge University Press, 2015).

3. The point is illustrated by the Algerian security services' inability to monitor the large numbers of Algerian detainees interned following the 1945 Sétif uprising, many of whom absconded over the winter of 1945–1946: Archives nationales d'outre-mer (ANOM), sous-série: Gouvernement-général d'Algérie (GGA), 40g: Centre d'Informations et d'Études (CIE) / Services des liaisons nord-africains, carton 40G/32, sous-dossier: Haute Police, no. 5,547/POL/NA, Direction de la Sécurité Générale, to Prefects of Algiers, Constantine, and Oran, 12 February 1946.

4. On the importance of ALN sanctuary bases in Morocco and, especially, Tunisia as strategic redoubts and political forcing grounds see Saphia Arezki, *De l'ALN à l'ANP: La construction de l'Armée Algérienne 1954–1991* (Algiers: Éditions Barzakh, 2018), 133–137, 145–154.

5. For evidence of these violence workers operating in different colonial and postcolonial contexts see Eileen Ryan, "Violence and the Politics of Prestige: The Fascist Turn in Colonial Libya," *Modern Italy* 20, no. 2 (2015): 123–135; David M. Anderson and Øystein H. Rolandsen, "Violence as Politics in Eastern Africa, 1940–1990: Legacy, Agency, Contingency," *Journal of Eastern African Studies* 8, no. 4 (2014): 539–557.

6. For analysis of the "loyalism" phenomenon and its limitations see David M. Anderson and Daniel Branch, eds., *Allies at the End of Empire: Loyalists, Nationalists, and the Cold War, 1945–76* (Abingdon, UK: Routledge, 2016), 1–13.

7. For a clear example of this criminalization of civilian activity see Matthew Hughes, *Britain's Pacification of Palestine: The British Army, the Colonial State, and the Arab Revolt, 1936–1939* (Cambridge: Cambridge University Press, 2019), 51–65, 135–168.

8. ANOM, Aix-en-Provence, Cabinet Jacques Soustelle, carton 11cab/41t, no. 114, "Instruction interministérielle du 30 Avril 1955 créant un Commandement dans la zone d'application de la loi sur l'état d'urgence: Département de Constantine." On "lawfare": David French, *The British Way in Counter-insurgency, 1945–1967* (Oxford: Oxford University Press, 2011), esp. chaps. 4 and 5; and French, "Nasty Not Nice: British Counterinsurgency Doctrine and Practice, 1945–1967," *Small Wars & Insurgencies* 23, no. 4–5 (2012): 744–761.

9. See note 1.

10. ANOM, 11cab/41, no. 58/CA1, Département d'Alger, Arrondissement d'Aumale, Commune mixte de Bou Saada, Administrateur des services civils à M. Le Préfet du département, "Situation générale—sécurité," 28 June 1955.

11. ANOM, 11cab/41, no. 1263/F/Dv-3, GGA, Direction Générale des Finances, 2ème Division, "Note à M. le Directeur des Cabinet Civil et Militaire," 15 July 1955. On neutralism or, in French parlance, *attentisme*, see Neil MacMaster, "The 'Silent Native': *Attentisme*, Being Compromised, and Banal Terror during the Algerian War of Independence, 1954–62," in *The French Colonial Mind: Violence, Military Encounters, and Colonialism*, ed. Martin Thomas (Lincoln: University of Nebraska Press, 2012), 283–303.

12. ANOM, 11cab/89, no. 1485/F-Dv-2, GGA Direction Générale des Finances, "Note: recouvrement de l'impôt—tournées de perception/Sécurité," 21 October 1955.

13. Stathis Kalyvas, "Warfare in Civil Wars," in *Rethinking the Nature of War*, ed. Isabelle Duyvesteyn and Jan Angstrom (Abingdon, UK: Routledge, 2005), 88–108; Kalyvas, *Logic*

of Violence. See also Ryan, "Violence and the Politics of Prestige," 124–131, which also discerns the same dynamics and continuities to violence in Italian colonial Libya.

14. The most revealing treatment of Armée de Libération Nationale activity in the Aurès, and the infighting behind it, is Saphia Arezki, *De l'ALN à l'ANP*, 114–116, 141–144.

15. ANOM, 11cab/51, H. P. Eydoux note, "Opinion de Germaine Tillion sur le 'palabre' de l'Aurès," 31 March 1955. The fullest account of village structures on the Algerian front line is Neil MacMaster, *War in the Mountains: Peasant Society and Counterinsurgency in Algeria, 1918–1958* (Oxford: Oxford University Press, 2020), 56–78, pt. 3.

16. ANOM, 11cab/41, Dr Cadi, Assemblée Nationale, letter to Governor-General Soustelle, 27 June 1955. The letter highlighted the insecurity of notables and *djemâa* loyalists in the Aurès settlement of Ichemoul.

17. ANOM, 11cab/51, H. P. Eydoux, Note pour M Juillet, 2 June 1955.

18. Insurgent violence against "loyalist" Muslims was also most intense in these interior borderlands; see ANOM, 11cab/38, Direction de la Sécurité Générale Service Centrale des RG, "Nombre d'attentats commis contre les musulmans francophiles," 109e synthèse sur la situation en Algérie," 24 April 1955; for other Algerian examples see MacMaster, *War in the Mountains*, 298–303.

19. For two forms of violence that are specifically hard to trace see the chapters in this volume by Azarja Harmanny and Brian Linn and by Stef Scagliola and Natalya Vince.

20. ANOM, Madagascar, 6(2)D123: Notes de renseignements des services de police adressées au cabinet civil du GGM, 1947–Jan. 1948, sous-dossier Renseignements Sûreté Mars 1947, no. 2772/DISCF, R. Baron, Chef de la Sûreté Générale Tananarive "Renseignements," "Réunion des membres du MDRM de la section de Faravohitra du 24 Mars 1947."

21. ANOM, Madagascar, 3D32/Mission Demaille, Chef de Mission report, "Service de la Trésorerie Générale de Madagascar et Dépendances," Tananarive, 11 June 1948. The provincial tax burden in areas of intense rebel activity further increased as local populations were required to meet the costs of military and police reinforcements.

22. These administrative problems were highlighted during the Ministry of Overseas France inspection mission of former rebel-held areas after the uprising ended: ANOM, 3D34, Mission Mérat, Inspection des Colonies, Mission 1948, "Rapport concernant l'organisation de la gendarmerie et de la garde indigène à Madagascar," Tananarive, 1 May 1949. The statement by Inspector M. Y. Blin is revealing: "Je n'ai pas besoin d'insister sur ce qu'il y avait d'anormal dans l'absence quasi-complète, depuis de longues années, de toute politique indigène. Dans les circonstances actuelles, une telle carence de la part de l'administration d'une colonie comme Madagascar équivaut à une démission virtuelle de la France à l'égard des populations auxquelles nous avons jadis montré le chemin de la civilisation et du mieux-être."

23. The National Archives (TNA), London, FO 371/67721, Z6417/3290/69/G, Maj.-Gen. Salisbury-Jones, WO Director of Military Intelligence, "Situation in Madagascar and Indo-China," 2 July 1947.

24. Philippe Le Billon, "The Geopolitical Economy of 'Resource Wars,'" in *The Geopolitics of Resource Wars: Resource Dependence, Governance and Violence*, ed. Philippe Le Billon (London: Frank Cass, 2005), 7.

25. ANOM, Madagascar, 3D32/Mission Demaille, "Rapport concernant le rétablissement de la confiance franco-malgache," Tananarive, 4 June 1948.

26. Eric T. Jennings, *Perspectives on French Colonial Madagascar* (New York: Palgrave Macmillan, 2017), 131–136.

27. Historians Christopher Bayly and Tim Harper, for instance, make a similar point about what they call "the Great Asian War" in their *Forgotten Wars: Freedom and Revolution in Southeast Asia* (Cambridge, MA: Belknap Press of Harvard University Press, 2007), 7.

28. Adria Lawrence, "Driven to Arms? The Escalation to Violence in Nationalist Conflicts," in Chenoweth and Lawrence, *Rethinking Violence*, 144–146.

29. Roel Frakking, "'Collaboration Is a Delicate Concept': Alliance-Formation and the Colonial Defense of Indonesia and Malaysia, 1945–1957" (PhD diss., European University Institute, Florence, 2017), 17–18, 111; Cheah Boon Kheng, *Red Star over Malaya: Resistance and Social Conflict during and after the Japanese Occupation of Malaya, 1941–46*, 4th ed. (Singapore: National University of Singapore Press, 2012), 150, 155; Staniland, *Networks of Rebellion*, 186–188; James P. Ongkili, *Nation-Building in Malaysia, 1946–1974* (Singapore: Oxford University Press, 1985), 21–29.

30. TNA, CAB 129/28, Colonial Secretary memo, "The Situation in Malaya," July 1, 1948; "600 Suspects Held," *Straits Times*, June 22, 1948.

31. Institute of Southeast Asia Studies (ISEAS), Singapore, Tan Cheng Lock Papers (TCL) 24.4h, Yap Mau Tatt, "Emergency and Chinese Co-operation"; ISEAS, TCL 37.170.02, "Memorandum on the Future of the Chinese in Malaya," December 1946.

32. TNA, CO 825/35/10, H. A. L. Luckham, Some Causes of the Loss of Malaya, 30 March 1942; Ongkili, *Nation-Building in Malaysia*, 41, 57–58; ISEAS, TCL 6.1., "Report on a Visit to Malaya from 20 August to 20 September 1952 at the Invitation of the Malayan Chinese Association," by Victor Purcell and Francis Carnell. For the broader background see Wen-Qing Ngoei, *Arc of Containment: Britain, the United States, and Anticommunism in Southeast Asia* (Ithaca, NY: Cornell University Press, 2019), chaps. 2–3.

33. Some sources estimate that the MRLA had five hundred thousand active supporters, collectively known as the Min Yuen: R. W. Kromer, *The Malayan Emergency in Retrospect: Organization of a Successful Counterinsurgency Effort* (Santa Monica, CA: RAND Corp., 1972), 7; Huw Bennett, "'A Very Salutary Effect': The Counter-terror Strategy in the Early Malayan Emergency, June 1948 to December 1949," *Journal of Strategic Studies* 32, no. 3 (2009): 416–418.

34. "Worried 200 Have Nowhere to Go," *Malay Mail*, January 14, 1953; Tan Teng-Phee, "Like a Concentration Camp, *lah*: Chinese Grassroots Experience of the Emergency and New Villages in British Colonial Malaya," *Chinese Southern Diaspora Studies* 3 (2009): 219–221; Arkib Negara Malaysia, Kuala Lumpur (ANM), TPD 311/1952 New Villages Federation of Malaya; State Agricultural Officer to Director of Agriculture, 21 August 1951, no. 17 in SAO.PK.Conf.5/50; A. L. Barcroft, Settlement Agricultural Officer, Malacca, to Director of Agriculture, 14 July 1951, (4) in AOM.84/51, both in ANM, D.A.Gen/47 Emergency Authorities, Liaison With; ANM, Selangor Secretariat 980/1953 Brief notes by State War Exec Officer on this visit to New Villages, (2)SEL/WEC/Sec.28/52, 20 April 1953; (4) Sel/WEC/Sec.28/52, 6 May 1953; L. C. Cerell to All British Advisers and Resident Commissioners, 5 June 1953, Def: 9182/51/25, ANM, TPD 311/1952 New Villages FOM.

35. ANM, Extract from a talk on New Villages given by the New Villages Liaison Officer to "D.W.E.C. Courses," TPD 311/1952 New Villages Federation of Malaya; ANM, Wong Yin Fah, Labour Officer, Klang, Report on Survey of Unemployed in Division "D" of the Pandaharan New Village, Port Swettenham, 8 June 1953, Sel.Sec. 1937 PT/1952 6A, ANM, Selangor Secretariat 1937 Pt./1952 Unemployment at Pandamaran New Village.

36. We borrow the phrase from Laleh Khalili, "Counterterrorism and Counterinsurgency in the Neo-liberal Age," in *The Oxford Handbook of Contemporary Middle Eastern and North African History*, ed. Amal Ghazal and Jens Hanssen (Oxford: Oxford University Press, 2020), 4.

37. R. dhu Renick Jr., "The Emergency Regulations of Malaya: Causes and Effect," *Journal of Southeast Asian Studies* 6, no. 2 (1965): 11–12.

38. Karl Hack, "Everyone Lived in Fear: Malaya and the British Way of Counterinsurgency," *Small Wars & Insurgencies* 23, no. 4–5 (2012): 674.

39. ISEAS, H. S. Lee Papers 21.81a. Director of Operations, Malaya, Administration of Chinese Settlements, Directive No. 13, 26 February 1951, FSY 18/A/50; TNA,

CO 1022/449, Monthly Administrative Report for December 1952, 12 January 1953, no. 51/33.

40. ANM, (SR) 15/15 Bandits/Communists Terrorist -Propaganda. H. Holder, Circle Special Branch Officer to Captain Howard, Operations Branch, 22 February 1955, SB/2525KT/SF10/1, ANM, (SR) 15/15 Bandits/Communists Terrorist -Propaganda.

41. TNA, CO 1022/14, Monthly Review January, Security Forces Weekly Intelligence Summary no. 92 for the Week Ending 7 February 1952.

42. *Freedom News* 26, 15 June 1952; *Freedom News* 45, January 1954.

43. TNA, AIR 22/507, Weekly Intelligence Summary no. 193 for week ending 14 January 1954.

44. ANM, L.D., M.No.(CIC)6/53 (1) Phuah Chak (m) H.G. High Commander, (2) Lim Seh Hoon (f) Husband & Wife Killed by Terrorists in Kebon Bahru New Village. TRY/COMP/578 28 April, 1953 Compensation Officer, Emergency (Civil Injuries Compensation) Regulations 1949, P. E. G. Bates to District Officer, Segamat, Johore; Ref. (3) in L.D.M. (CIC) 6/53 Deputy Commissioner for Labour, North Johore, Muar, J. D. H. Neill to District Officer, Segamat, 19 March 1953. Death of Home Guard Commander Phuah Chack & His Wife, Lim Seh Hoon near Kebon Bahru New Village.

45. On the prevalence of sexual humiliation as a counterinsurgent strategy see the chapter by Scagliola and Vince in this volume.

46. "Labour Condemns 'Semenyih Outrage': Strong Protest to London," *Straits Echo & Times of Malaya*, 18 January 1956; "Semenyih: Call for Evidence," *Straits Times*, 3 February 1956; "Semenyih: More Arrests," *Straits Times*, 13 June 1956. For more evidence of how internal bordering proved conducive to sexual violence see in this volume the chapter by Scagliola and Vince, 6–8.

47. The relative impunity with which Algeria's FLN initially operated in the Aurès massif and Grande Kabylia, the two regional centers of rural rebellion in 1954–1955, lends weight to this conclusion; see ANOM, 11cab/89, no. 17/CAB/AAE, Governor Soustelle to Algiers Prefect, "Implantation des renforts administratifs en Kabylie," 7 October 1955.

48. "Chineesch-Indonesische Conferentie," *Het Dagblad*, 24 August 1946; *Portrait of a Patriot: Selected Writings by Mohammad Hatta*, ed. Noer (The Hague: Mouton, 1972), 447–448; *Constitution of the Indonesian Republic*, chap. 14, art. 33, in Charles Wolf Jr., *The Indonesian Story: The Birth, Growth and Structure of the Indonesian Republic* (New York: John Day, 1948), 170–171.

49. Roel Frakking, "Collaboration," 264–267; Politiek Verslag over Sumatra van Gouverneur, Chief Commanding Officer, Amacab Sumatra (Spits) over de Maand April 1946, in *Officiële bescheiden betreffende de Nederlands-Indonesische betrekkingen 1945–1950* (*NIB*), ed. S. L. van der Wal, P. J. Drooglever, and M. J. B. Schouten (The Hague: Instituut voor Nederlandse Geschiedenis, 1971), 4, 211; Nationaal Archief, The Hague (NL-HaNA), Ministerie van Defensie: Strijdkrachten in Nederlands-Indië, 2.13.132/392, Kort Verslag van de Bespreking, Gehouden op 2 April 1948, Ten Kantore van de IVPA Betreffende Politieaangelegenheden; NL-HaNA, Nefis en CMI, 2.10.62/1685, Vechtpartij Chin. Veiligheidscorps en NICA-Amboneesen, 23 September 1946, no. ER8/39635.

50. NL-HaNA, Defensie/Strijdkrachten Ned. Indië 2.12.132/1340, Chinees Veiligheids [illegible] (Pao An Tui), 3 December 1947.

51. Frakking, "Collaboration," 197–198.

52. NL-HaNA, Defensie/Strijdkrachten Ned. Indië, 2.13.132/ 3937, Richtlijnen en aanbevelingen i.v.m. Ondernemingswachten, het contact met Militair en Burgerlijk Gezag en de beveiliging van de ondernemingen in het algemeen, RV ALS Buitenzorg, H. J. van Holst Pellekaan aan de Commandant Ie Infanteriebrigade Buitenzorg, de HTB Buitenzorg, de Commandant MP, de ALS Prae-rehabilitatie in Batavia, 19 December 1947.

53. See, for example, NL-HaNA, Alg. Secretarie Ned.-Ind. Regering, 2.10.14/2676, "Memorandum: Outlining Acts of Violence and Inhumanity Perpetrated by Indonesian

Bands on Innocent Chinese before and after the Dutch Police Action Was Enforced on July 21, 1947," Compiled by Chung Hua Tsung Hui, Federation of Chinese Associations in Batavia, 3. The Institute for Southeast Asian Studies in Singapore holds a copy of the memorandum in the Tan Cheng Lock Papers.

54. NL-HaNA, Defensie/Strijdkrachten Ned. Indië, 2.13.132/1340, Chinees Veiligheids [illegible] (Pao An Tui), 3 December 1947.

55. Frakking, "Collaboration"; Politiek Verslag over Sumatra van Gouverneur, Chief Commanding Officer, Amacab Sumatra (Spits) over de Maand April 1946, *NIB* 4, 211; NL-HaNA, Defensie/Strijdkrachten Ned. Indië, 2.13.132/392, Kort Verslag van de Bespreking, 2 April 1948, Ten Kantore van de IVPA Betreffende Politieaangelegenheden; NL-HaNA, Nefis en CMI, 2.10.62/1685, Vechtpartij Chin. Veiligheidscorps en NICA-Amboneesen, 23 September 1946, no. ER8/39635.

56. Roel Frakking, "Het Middel Erger dan de Kwaal? De Opkomst en het Failliet van het Instituut der Ondernemingwacht in Nederlands-Indië, 1946–50" (MA diss., University of Utrecht, 2011), 259.

57. "Ondernemingswacht Verdwenen," *Het Nieuwsblad voor Sumatra*, 11 December 1948, 1.

58. NL-HaNA, Federabo, 2.20.50/67, Résumé Nr. 21 dd 8 June 1948, ALS en ZWSS; Notulen van de op 27-2-1948 te 09.000 uur te Soerabaja gehouden bespreking over de Ondernemingswachten, Collection H. J. de Vries, Colonel Inf., KNIL, Nederlands Instituut voor Militaire Historie, The Hague; Résumé Nr. 14, 13 April 1948; NL-HaNA, Defensie/Strijdkrachten Ned. Indië, 2.13.132/1396, Verslag over de reis naar Oost Java van Majoor A. Roskam en 1ᵉ Luitenant Tan Gwan Djiang; Hoge Vertegenwoordiger van de Kroon (Lovink) aan Minister van Overzeese Gebiedsdelen (Van Maarseveen), 27 October 1949, *NIB* 20, 437.

59. J. A. B. Plomp, *De theeonderneming: Schets van werk en leven van een theeplanter in Indië/Indonesië voor en na de oorlog* (Breda, Netherlands: Warung Bambu T.Z., 1992).

60. NL-HaNA, Nederlandsche Handel-Maatschappij (NHM), 2.20.10/8911, Afschrift van enkele passages uit Résumé Nr. 4 van de vergadering van de Dagelijkse Besturen van A.L.S, Z.W.S.S. en C.P.V. met de Ondervoorzitters der Bonden, gehouden op 7 maart 1950, bijlage bij Nr. F. 601., de Algemeen Secretaris Federabo (onleesbaar), namens de Voorzitter, aan Dr. Ir. Ph. Levert, Ir. H. van der Meyden, A. G. Ostermann, K. Raadsheer, J. C. F. Schor, K. F. Zeeman, C. C. Zeverijn; NL-HaNA, Federabo 2.20.50/67, Uit Federatie Mail Nr. 5 dd. 11 maart 1950 Nr. F. 526/L 12; Uit Résumé Nr. 4 dd. 7 maar t 1950, Bespreking DB Syndicaten A.L.S. enz. en Onder-Voorzitters Bonden, archief.

61. Frakking, "Collaboration," 207.

62. ANOM, carton 11cab/41, PR/GJ. Constantine Prefect Dupuch to Governor-General, "Objet: Retrait des parachutistes de l'Aurès," February 22, 1955.

63. ANOM, 11cab/89, GGA, "Note sur le déclenchement de l'opération *Sauterelle*," 6 May 1955.

64. ANOM, GGA, 40G/32, sous-dossier: Haute Police, no. 5,547/POL/NA, sous-dossier: Groupes Mobiles de Police Rurale (GMPR), "Règlement relatif au fonctionnement et à l'emploi des GMPR," 12 May 1955. To complement these rural security measures, in March 1955 five hundred additional riot police of the Compagnies Républicains de Sécurité (CRS) were recruited for service in Algerian cities. Six additional urban police stations opened a month later, in April; see ANOM, 11cab/55, H. P. Eydoux note pour M. Vaujour, 26 March 1955, and ANOM, 11cab/36, no. 17676/POL-S, GGA, Note pour M. le Directeur des Cabinets Civil et Militaire, "Réorganisation de la Direction de la Sécurité générale," 15 April 1955.

65. For mounting government concern that the GMPR–*police judiciare* liaison was not working see ANOM, GGA, 40G/32, sous-dossier: Divers, AR/JS, "S/C de M. le Secrétaire

Général du Gouvernement: Coordination entre la police et les autorités locales," 12 January 1957.

66. ANOM, GGA, 40G/32, sous-dossier: Haute Police, no. 5,547/POL/NA, sous-dossier: GMPR, "Règlement relatif au fonctionnement et à l'emploi des GMPR," 12 May 1955. Individual GMPR units were administered by a regional delegate who reported to the inspector of police at *département* level.

67. ANOM, 11cab/51, Note pour M. le Directeur de la Sécurité Générale, 24 August 1955.

68. ANOM, Cabinet Soustelle, 11cab/51, H. P. Eydoux, "Note sur la situation dans la zone d'urgence du Constantinois," 16 May 1955.

69. ANOM, 11cab/89, sous-dossier: action administrative et économique, H. P. Eydoux, Note pour le Colonel Constans and M. Vrolyk, 19 October 1955: "État d'esprit dans les campagnes." The original French reads: Il se confirme de différentes sources que les populations des douars sont fatigues des exactions des fellaghas et demandent à être protégées. Les collectes forcées, le ravitaillement obligatoire, les exécutions sommaires, les énasements, etc. ruinent les fellahs et les font vivre dans une atmosphère de frayeur.

70. ANOM, 11cab/51, H. P. Eydoux, "Situation dans la zone d'urgence du Constantinois," 16 May 1955.

71. ANOM, Archives Département de Constantine, carton 93/139, no. 2129/EMM/SEC. GGA, État-Major Mixte, Sommaire de la réunion du 1 Août 1956: organisation et emploi des GMPR.

72. For example, see ANOM, GGA, 40G/32, "Renseignement, Source: très bonne, 'Attaque du 36e GMPR à El Fahoul (commune mixte de Remchi) du 23 septembre 1956.'"

73. ANOM, 11cab/89, GGA Cabinet, "Note pour Colonel Schoen," 16 December 1955.

74. ANOM, carton 11cab/41, tel. 562, Constantine Prefect to Resident Minister, April 21, 1956; on the events of August 1955 see Mahfoud Kaddache, "Les tournants de la guerre de libération au niveau des masses populaires," in *La guerre d'Algérie et les Algériens*, ed. Charles-Robert Ageron (Paris: Armand Colin, 1997), 52–54; Claire Mauss-Copeaux, *Algérie, 20 août 1955—Insurrection, répression, massacres* (Paris: Payot, 2011).

75. For good summaries: Natalya Vince, *The Algerian War, the Algerian Revolution* (London: Bloomsbury Academic, 2020), 106–108; Arezki, *De l'ALN à l'ANP*, 114–131; more broadly: Gilbert Meyner, *Histoire intérieur du FLN* (Paris: Fayard, 2002).

76. Philippe Gaillard, *L'Alliance: La guerre d'Algérie du Général Bellounis (1957–1958)* (Paris: L'Harmattan, 2009); Charles-Robert Ageron, "Une troisième force combattante pendant la guerre d'Algérie. L'armée nationale du peuple algérien et son chef le 'général' Bellounis. Mai 1957–juillet 1958," *Outre-Mers* 321 (1998): 65–76.

77. ANOM, GGA, 40G/32, sous-dossier: Haute Police, no. 21,699/SNA/RG3, Direction de la Sûreté Nationale en Algérie, Sous-direction des services actifs de police, RG, A. Benoit, Sûreté Directeur, "État d'esprit parmi les éléments musulmans des GMPR," 31 December 1957; Jacques Valette, "Un contre-maquis durable de la guerre d'Algérie: L'affaire Si Cherif (1957–1962)," *Guerres Mondiales et Conflits Contemporains* 208, no. 4 (2002): 7–34.

78. ANOM, GGA, 40G/32, sous-dossier: Haute Police, Ministre résident en Algérie to Directeur du Service des Affaires Algériennes, GGA, no date, but probably late 1958.

79. During 1958 a replacement rural police militia, the Groupes Mobiles de Sécurité, under tighter police control, supplanted the GMPR: ANOM, GGA, 40G/32, sous-dossier GMS.

80. For more on the challenges of remaining neutral see also the chapter in this volume by Harmanny and Linn.

81. NL-HaNA, Alg. Secretarie Ned.-Ind. Regering, 2.10.14/2417, Rapport betreffende de Partei Ra'jat Pasoendan, 27 December 1946; idem, A. K. Widjojoatmodjo to the Director of the Cabinet of the Lt. Gouverneur-Generaal, undated; idem, Kort Verslag betreffende de Bestuursvoering in de Preanger over de Maand Maart 1947, undated;

Lt. Gouverneur-Generaal (Van Mook) to Minister van Overzeese Gebiedsdelen (Sassen), 11 October 1948, *NIB* 15, 401; J. Bank, *Katholieken en de Indonesische Revolutie* (Baarn, Netherlands: Ambo, 1983), 216–231. Verslag van de Openingsconference van de Malino-Conferentie op 16 July 1946, *NIB* 5, 1–2; Articles 1 and 4.1 of the Ontwerp-Overeenkomst van Linggadjati, *NIB* 5, 753–754; Regeerings Voorlichtings Dienst, *Malino Maakt Historie* (Batavia: De Regeerings Voorlichtings Dienst, 1946), 8; Nederlands Interdisciplinair Demografisch Instituut, *De Demografische Geschiedenis van Indische Nederlanders* (The Hague: NIDI, 2002), 25.

82. Lt. Gouverneur-Generaal (Van Mook) aan Minister van Overzeese Gebiedsdelen (Jonkman), 15 December 1946, *NIB* 6, 577; Frakking, "Collaboration," 223–227.

83. P. M. H. Groen, *Marsroutes en Dwaalsporen: Het Nederlands militair-strategisch beleid in Indonesië 1945–1950* (The Hague: Sdu, 1991), 78; Heru Sukadri K, Soewarno, Ny, Umiati RA, *Sejarah Revolusi Kemerdekaan (1945–1949) Daerah Jawa Timur* (Jakarta: Proyek Inventarisasi dan Dokumentasi Sejarah Nasional, 1991 [1984]), 246.

84. Frakking, "Collaboration," 224.

85. NL-HaNA, Proc.-Gen. Hooggerechtshof Ned.-Ind., 2.10.17/108, Conferentie Coördinatie Berichtgeving 24/5/1947; NL-HaNA, Alg. Secretarie Ned.-Ind. Regering, 2.10.14/2417, Kort Verslag betreffende de Bestuursvoering in de Preanger over de Maand Maart 1947.

86. Frakking, "Collaboration," 229–230.

87. Frakking, 102.

88. Service Historique de la Défense (SHD), Vincennes, Indochina files, 10H2897, no. 697/3, Forces Terrestres du Nord Vietnam, Lieutenant-Colonel Huot, Commandant le secteur de Phúc Yên, to M. le Chef de Province de Vinh Phúc, 18 May 1954.

89. For details of background and aftermath see, on the Vietnamese side, Pierre Asselin, "Choosing Peace: Hanoi and the Geneva Agreement on Vietnam, 1954–55," *Cold War History* 9, no. 2 (2007): 95–126; Asselin, "The Democratic Republic of Vietnam and the 1954 Geneva Conference: A Revisionist Critique," *Cold War History* 11, no. 2 (2011): 163–178; Lien-Hang T. Nguyen, *Hanoi's War: An International History of the War for Peace in Vietnam* (Chapel Hill: University of North Carolina Press, 2012), 29–30. And on the French side, Ministère des Archives Étrangères (MAE), La Courneuve, 120QO/319, Pourparlers de paix en Indochine, "Fiche concernant un 'cessez le feu' en Indochine," 16 April 1954; MAE, 120QO/319, tel. 32171, COMIGAL Saigon, to États Associés, Paris, 17 August 1954.

90. SHD, 10H2897, sous-dossier: Chrono—*départ*, June–July 1954.

91. SHD, 10H160, sous-dossier: *Pacific*, no. 108/CAB-CE/DC/TS, Commandant en Chef en Indochine, "Note: Comité de Guerre," Saigon, 11 October 1953.

92. SHD, 10H160, sous-dossier: *Pacific*, Haut Comité de Guerre, Direction de la Guerre, Conduite des Opérations, Colonel Guillard, 5 August 1953.

93. Sophie Quinn-Judge, "Giving Peace a Chance: National Reconciliation and a Neutral South Vietnam, 1954–1964," *Peace and Change* 38, no. 4 (2013): 385–397; Jessica Elkind, "'The Virgin Mary Is Going South': Refugee Resettlement in South Vietnam, 1954–1956," *Diplomatic History* 38, no. 5 (2014): 987–1016; Philip E. Catton, "'It Would Be a Terrible Thing If We Handed These People over to the Communists': The Eisenhower Administration, Article 14(d), and the Origins of the Refugee Exodus from North Vietnam," *Diplomatic History* 39, no. 2 (2015): 331–358.

94. SHD, 10H2897, no. 697/3, Forces Terrestres du Nord Vietnam, Lieutenant-Colonel Huot, Commandant le Secteur de Phúc Yên, to M. le Chef de Province de Vinh Phúc, 18 May 1954.

95. ANOM, 11cab/80, no. 688/EMM/D, Governor-General Soustelle circular to army divisional commanders, prefects, subprefects, and *officiers d'affaires algériennes*, "Attitude à observer à l'égard des populations musulmanes dans la lutte contre le terrorisme," 22 November 1955.

96. SHD, 1H1463: Synthèses hebdomadaires de renseignements sur les activités subversives, no. 6283/EMA/2/EG, Colonel Dalstein, Chef du 2ᵉ Bureau/EMA, Paris, Synthèse de renseignements sur les activités subversives en Afrique du Nord, semaine du 23 au 30 mars 1956, 1–3.

97. For Mollet's complicity in the war's expansion see Denis Lefebvre, *Guy Mollet face à la torture en Algérie, 1956–1957* (Paris: Bruno Leprince, 2001).

98. SHD, 1H1379/D1, EMA-1, "Plan d'urgence 1ᵉ partie," 18 March 1956; Martin Evans, *Algeria: France's Undeclared War* (Oxford: Oxford University Press, 2013); Martin Thomas, *The French North African Crisis: Colonial Breakdown and Anglo-French Relations, 1945–1962* (Basingstoke, UK: Macmillan, 2000), 109–120.

99. Martin Thomas, "Order before Reform: The Spread of French Military Operations in Algeria, 1954–1958," in *Guardians of Empire: The Armed Forces of the Colonial Powers, c. 1700–1964*, ed. David Killingray and David Omissi (Manchester: Manchester University Press, 1999), 198–220.

100. SHD, 1H1463: Synthèses hebdomadaires de renseignements sur les activités subversives, no. 6283/EMA/2/EG, Colonel Dalstein, Chef du 2ᵉ Bureau/EMA, Synthèse de renseignements sur les activités subversives en Afrique du Nord, semaine du 23 au 30 mars 1956, p. 2.

101. SHD, 1H1463, no. 9787/EMA/2/EG, Dalstein, Synthèse de renseignements sur les activités subversives, semaine du 11 au 18 mai 1956.

102. Mohamed Harbi, *Les archives de la révolution algérienne* (Paris: Éditions du Jaguar, 1992); Matthew Connelly, *A Diplomatic Revolution: Algeria's Fight for Independence and the Origins of the Post–Cold War Era* (Oxford: Oxford University Press, 2002); Arezki, *De l'ALN à l'ANP*, 109–114.

103. David Kilcullen, "Globalisation and the Development of Indonesian Counterinsurgency Tactics," *Small Wars & Insurgencies* 17, no. 1 (2006): 51–52.

104. Patricia Owens has written most thoughtfully about these social policy dimensions to counterinsurgency, in *Economy of Force: Counterinsurgency and the Historical Rise of the Social* (Cambridge: Cambridge University Press, 2015), esp. chaps. 4 and 5.

105. SHD, 1H2403: "Création, organisation et dissolution des bureau et organismes et actions psychologique, moyens et effectifs d'action psychologique."

106. SHD, 1H1374/D3, EMA summary, "Situation des trois armées en Algérie, 1956."

107. TNA, WO 291/1773, "A Study of the Reasons for Entering the Jungle among Chinese Communist Terrorists in Malaya"; Uit de "Nieuwsgier" van Woensdag 15 September 1948; NL-HaNA, NHM, 2.20.01/8910, Mr. J. G. van 't Oever, Waarnemend Voorzitter ALS/ZWSS aan Jhr. Mr. W. J. de Jonge, Voorzitter Federabo, 16 September 1948, annex to V.V./no. 76; NL-HaNA, Defensie/Strijdkrachten Ned.-Indië, 2.13.132/1300, Systeem van Beveiliging in Onrustige Gebieden op Java en Sumatra, No.: Kab./237, 31 January 1949.

108. Roel Frakking, "The Plantation as Counterinsurgency Tool," in *Decolonization and Conflict: Colonial Comparisons and Legacies*, ed. Martin Thomas and Gareth Curless (London: Bloomsbury Academic, 2017), 65–67.

109. Ronald Robinson, "Non-European Foundations of European Imperialism: Sketch for a Theory of Collaboration," in *Studies in the Theory of Imperialism*, ed. Roger Owen and Bob Sutcliffe (Harlow, UK: Longman, 1972), 118–120; Colin Newbury, "Patrons, Clients, and Empire: The Subordination of Indigenous Hierarchies in Asia and Africa," *Journal of World History* 11, no. 2 (2000): 227–263.

110. Henri Eckert, "Double-Edged Swords of Conquest in Indo-China: *Tirailleurs Tonkinois, Chasseurs Annamites* and Militias, 1883–1895," in *Colonial Armies in Southeast Asia*, ed. Karl Hack and Tobias Rettig (London: Routledge, 2009), 126.

111. For introductions see Daniel Branch, *Defeating Mau Mau, Creating Kenya: Counterinsurgency, Civil War, and Decolonization* (Cambridge: Cambridge University Press, 2009); Kalyvas, *Logic of Violence*. On the contentious politics of naming civil wars, or so

designating them in international law, see Jacob Mundy, *Imaginative Geographies of Algerian Violence: Conflict Science, Conflict Management, Antipolitics* (Stanford, CA: Stanford University Press, 2015), 31–46.

112. Khalili, "Counterterrorism and Counterinsurgency," 6, 8.

113. Tramor Quémeneur, "La détention ou l'illégalité: Trois parcours de refus d'obéissance dans la guerre d'Algérie," in *Des hommes et des femmes en guerre d'Algérie*, ed. Jean-Charles Jauffret (Paris: Éditions Autrement, 2003), 431–442; "Testimony of Georges Mattéi," in *The Algerian War and the French Army: Experiences, Images, Testimonies*, ed. Martin S. Alexander, Martin Evans, and J. V. F. Keiger (Basingstoke, UK: Palgrave Macmillan, 2002), 249–253.

4. CRACKING DOWN ON REVOLUTIONARY ZEAL AND VIOLENCE

1. One of the most comprehensive studies is by political scientist Tuong Vu, but he analyzes the experiences of Indonesia and Vietnam separately, not comparatively. See Tuong Vu, *Paths to Development in Asia: South Korea, Vietnam, China, and Indonesia* (New York: Cambridge University Press, 2010).

2. Stein TØnnesson, "Filling the Power Vacuum: 1945 in French IndoChina, the Netherlands East Indies and British Malaya," in *Imperial Policy and Southeast Asian Nationalism, 1930–1957*, ed. Hans Antlöv and Stein TØnnesson (London: Routledge, 1995), 110–143.

3. Ethan Mark, *Japan's Occupation of Java in the Second World War: A Transnational History* (London: Bloomsbury, 2018).

4. George Kanahele, "The Japanese Occupation of Indonesia: Prelude to Independence" (PhD diss., Cornell University, 1967); Aiko Kurasawa, "Mobilization and Control: A Study of Social Change in Rural Java, 1942–1945" (PhD diss., Cornell University, 1988); Shigeru Sato, *War, Nationalism and Peasants: Java under the Japanese Occupation, 1942–1945* (New York: M. E. Sharpe, 1994).

5. Pierre van der Eng, "Food Supply in Java during War and Decolonization, 1940–1950," *Munich Personal RePEc Archive*, May 2008, consulted online on 4 March 2021 at https://mpra.ub.uni-muenchen.de/8852/1/Food_supply_Java_1940-50.pdf.

6. On the famine see Ngo Vinh Long, *Before the Revolution: The Vietnamese Peasants under the French* (New York: Columbia University Press, 1991), 122–133; Stein TØnnesson, *Vietnamese Revolution of 1945: Roosevelt, Ho Chi Minh and de Gaulle in a World at War* (London: Sage, 1991), 281–298; David G. Marr, *Vietnam 1945: The Quest for Power* (Berkeley: University of California Press), 96–107.

7. Benedict Anderson, *Java in a Time of Revolution: Occupation and Resistance, 1944–1946* (Ithaca, NY: Cornell University Press, 1972), 125–166; Robert Cribb, *Gangsters and Revolutionaries: The Jakarta People's Militia and the Indonesian Revolution 1945–1949* (Honolulu: University of Hawai'i Press, 1991), 57–67; William Frederick, *Visions and Heat: The Making of the Indonesian Revolution* (Athens: Ohio University Press, 1989); William Frederick, "The Appearance of Revolution," in *Outward Appearances: Dressing State and Society in Indonesia*, ed. Henk Schulte Nordholt (Leiden: KITLV Press, 1997), 199–248.

8. Moloccan, Menadonese, and some other smaller ethnic communities had traditionally been recruited into the colonial army as "martial races."

9. Cribb, *Gangsters and Revolutionaries*, 66–67; William Frederick, "The Killing of Dutch and Eurasians in Indonesia's National Revolution (1945–49): A 'Brief Genocide' Reconsidered," *Journal of Genocide Studies* 14 (2012): 359–401. Assimilated Chinese—so-called *peranakan*—were also attacked by *pemuda*. Members of the *peranakan* elite had played a key role in the domestic economy. During the Japanese occupation they were deeply involved in the forced rice deliveries.

10. George Kahin, *Nationalism and Revolution in Indonesia* (Ithaca, NY: Cornell University Press, 1952), 143; Rémy Limpach, *De brandende kampongs van Generaal Spoor* (Amsterdam: Boom, 2016), 183–184.

11. Hoang Van Dao, *Viet Nam Quoc Dan Dang: A Contemporary History of a National Struggle, 1927–1954* (Pittsburgh: Rosedog Books, 2008).

12. Quoted in François Guillemot, *Dai Viet, indépendance et révolution au Viêt-Nam: L'échec de la troisième voie (1938–1955)* (Paris: Les Indes savantes, 2012), 191. The collapse of wartime European and Asian national resistance (i.e., antifascist) movements owing to communist intransigence is a central theme in Ian Buruma, *Year Zero: A History of 1945* (New York: Penguin, 2013).

13. François Guillemot, "Autopsy of a Massacre on a Political Purge in the Early Days of the Indochina War (Nam Bo 1947)," *European Journal of East Asian Studies* 9, no. 2 (2010): 229.

14. Quoted in Daniel Guérin, *Au service des colonisés: 1930–1953* (Paris: Éditions de Minuit, 1956), 22. According to François Guillemot, Thau's death "symbolically marked the onset of revolutionary violence in southern provinces" (Guillemot, *Dai Viet*, 255).

15. Marr, *Vietnam 1945*, 519.

16. Alex Holcombe, "The Role of the Communist Party in the Vietnamese Revolution: A Review of David Marr's *Vietnam: State, War, and Revolution (1945–1946)*," *Journal of Vietnamese Studies* 11, nos. 3–4 (2016): 317.

17. Christopher E. Goscha, "Intelligence in a Time of Decolonization: The Case of the Democratic Republic of Vietnam at War (1945–50)," *Intelligence and National Security* 22, no. 1 (February 2007): 129.

18. S. L. van der Wal, *Officiële bescheiden betreffende de Nederland-Indonesische betrekkingen 1945–1950*, vol. 1 (The Hague: Martinus Nijhoff, 1971), 288.

19. Mary van Delden, *De republikeinse kampen in Nederlands-Indië, oktober 1945—mei 1947: Orde in chaos?* (Proefschrift Radboud Universiteit Nijmegen, 2007), 178. Herman Bussemaker, *Bersiap: Opstand in het paradijs. De Bersiap-periode op Java en Sumatra 1945–1946* (Zutphen, Netherlands: Walburg Pers, 2005), 309, mentions a number of seventy-five thousand Eurasian internees.

20. Quoted in T. O. Smith, *Britain and the Origins of the Vietnam War: UK Policy in Indo-China, 1943–50* (Houndmills, UK: Palgrave, 2007), 41–42.

21. Geraint Hughes, "A 'Post-war' War: The British Occupation of French-Indochina, September 1945–March 1946," *Small Wars and Insurgencies* 17, no. 3 (September 2006): 269; John Springhall, "'Disaster in Surabaya': The Death of Brigadier Mallaby during the British Occupation of Java, 1945–46," *Journal of Imperial and Commonwealth History* 24, no. 3 (September 1996): 422–443.

22. John Springhall, "'Kicking out the Vietminh': How Britain Allowed France to Reoccupy South Indochina, 1945–46," *Journal of Contemporary History* 40, no. 1 (January 2005): 116, 129.

23. "Déclaration du gouvernement en date du 24 mars 1945 relative à l'Indochine," in *La guerre d'Indochine, 1945–1954: Textes et documents*, vol. 1, *Le retour de la France en Indochine*, ed. Gilbert Bodinier (Paris: Service Historique de L'Armée de Terre, 1987), 141–143; M. Kathryn Edwards, *Contesting Indochina: French Remembrance between Decolonization and Cold War* (Berkeley: University of California Press, 2016), 16.

24. Quoted in Thierry d'Argenlieu, *Chronique d'Indochine, 1945–1947* (Paris: Albin Michel, 1985), 30.

25. Springhall, "'Kicking out the Vietminh,'" 118.

26. "Note," September 20, 1945; GR 10H (Indochine) 949, Service Historique de la Défense, Paris, 1, 2.

27. "Instructions politiques de l'Amiral d'Argenlieu, Haut-commissaire de France pour l'Indochine, du 15 septembre 1945," in Bodinier, *La guerre d'Indochine*, 171–173.

28. Quoted in Jacques Dalloz, "Indochine, 1945–1947: Leclerc face à d'Argenlieu," *Guerres mondiales et conflits contemporains*, no. 192 (1998): 152.

29. Hughes, "'Post-war' War," 269.

30. Amiral d'Argenlieu to EMGDE Paris, 27 September 1945, GR 10H (Indochine) 161, Service Historique de la Défense, Paris, 1.

31. Paul Isoart, *Le phénomène national vietnamien: De l'indépendance unitaire à l'indépendance fractionnée* (Paris: Librairie générale de droit et de jurisprudence, 1961), 337.

32. David G. Marr, *Vietnam: State, War, and Revolution (1945–1946)* (Berkeley: University of California Press, 2013), 114.

33. Christopher Bayly and Tim Harper, *Forgotten Wars: Freedom and Revolution in Southeast Asia* (Cambridge, MA: Harvard University Press, 2007), 148.

34. Hughes, "'Post-war' War," 269.

35. "Rapport verbal du Lt Mathiot, retour de Saigon," 1 October 1945, GR 10H (Indochine) 161, Service Historique de la Défense, Paris, 1. "Troupes sur place ne valent rien— pourrie par long séjour colonie et propagande," Mathiot added. "Officiers sans autorité sur leurs hommes—tenue de la Marine nettement plus correcte" (2).

36. Charles Gottarel letter to Thierry d'Argenlieu, 9 September 1946, #14, SLOTFOM XIV Archives nationales d'outre-mer, Aix-en-Provence, 1.

37. "Association des familles des victimes des massacres des 24–25–26 septembre 1945 à Saigon letter to Monsieur Marius Moutet, Ministre de la France d'Outre-mer," undated, #14, SLOTFOM XIV Archives nationales d'outre-mer, Aix-en-Provence, 6; "Les massacres de Septembre à Saigon (Extrait des 'Écrits de Paris' de Décembre 1949)," undated, #14, SLOTFOM XIV Archives nationales d'outre-mer, Aix-en-Provence, 7.

38. "Témoignage," undated, #14, SLOTFOM XIV Archives nationales d'outre-mer, Aix-en-Provence, 6.

39. "Association des familles des victimes des massacres des 24–25–26 septembre 1945 à Saigon letter to Monsieur Marius Moutet, Ministre de la France d'Outre-mer," undated, #14, SLOTFOM XIV Archives nationales d'outre-mer, Aix-en-Provence, 6.

40. "La situation en Indochine (exposé du 10 Octobre 1945)," undated, GR 10H (Indochine) 165, Service Historique de la Défense, Paris, 4–5.

41. "Section de liaison française en Extrême-Orient, Bulletin de renseignement No 2418 du 27 Septembre 1945: Situation en Indochine au 27–9–1945," GR 10H (Indochine) 165, Service Historique de la Défense, Paris, 1.

42. See "Document No. 10: Terrorisme et atrocités au Nam Bo (quelques exemples après 6 mars et 30 Octobre)," undated, 174QO/73, États Associés, Archives du Ministère des états associés, 1945–1957 (Section II), Archives diplomatiques de France, La Courneuve [hereafter ADF], 5.

43. "La situation en Indochine (exposé du 10 Octobre 1945)," undated, GR 10H (Indochine) 165, Service Historique de la Défense, Paris, 1, 11.

44. "Bulletin de renseignement No 2664 du 27 Octobre 1945: État d'esprit des populations," 17 October 1945, GR 10H (Indochine) 161, Service Historique de la Défense, Paris, 1.

45. Quoted in Thomas Vaisset, *L'Amiral d'Argenlieu: Le moine soldat du Gaullisme* (Paris: Belin, 2017), 376.

46. "La situation en Extrême-Orient (exposé du 26.9.1945)," 27 September 1945, GR 10H (Indochine) 161, Service Historique de la Défense, Paris, 13.

47. Vaisset, *L'Amiral d'Argenlieu*, 376.

48. Jean-Marc Lepage, *Les services secrets en Indochine* (Paris: Nouveau Monde éditions, 2014), 36.

49. "Note," September 20, 1945, GR 10H (Indochine) 949, Service Historique de la Défense, Paris, 3.

50. "Note," September 20, 1945, GR 10H (Indochine) 949, Service Historique de la Défense, Paris, 1, 2.

51. Quoted in Vaisset, *L'Amiral d'Argenlieu*, 377.

52. "The Secretary of State to the Assistant Chief of the Division of Southeast Asian Affairs (Landon), then at Saigon," 28 January 1946 in United States Department of State, *Foreign Relations of the United States, 1946: The Far East, Volume VIII* (Washington, DC: Government Printing Office, 1971), 15/Document 16.

53. "La dernière absurdité serait de considérer aujourd'hui l'Indochine comme un pays mûr pour l'indépendance, possédant une élite avec laquelle on peut traiter." Quoted in Dalloz, "Indochine, 1945–1947," 154–155.

54. According to a confession by d'Argenlieu's chef Étienne Schlumberger. See Vaisset, *L'Amiral d'Argenlieu*, 483, 572n3.

55. On the reconquest of southern Vietnam see William Waddell, *In the Year of the Tiger: The War for Cochinchina, 1945–1951* (Norman: University of Oklahoma Press, 2018).

56. "Directive No I concernant la conduite à tenir au Tonkin jusqu'à nouvel ordre," 6 April 1946, 174QO/73, ÉA II, ADF, 1.

57. "Dossier Annexe No IX—Document No 41: Protestations du délégué vietnamien en date du 23.7.1946 a.s. incident de HONGAY du 8.7.1946," 23 July 1946, 174QO/73, ÉA II, ADF, 2.

58. Valluy's directive is reproduced in "Rapport du Général de Division Morlière, Commandant les Troupes Françaises en Indochine du Nord, et Commissaire de la République par intérim en Indochine du Nord, d'Août à Décembre 1946," 10 January 1947, 174QO/73, ÉA II, ADF, 12.

59. "Étude préliminaire concernant l'exécution d'un coup de force au Tonkin: Solution No 2—Hypothèse: Abandon de Hanoi," undated, GR 10H (Indochine) 949, Service Historique de la Défense, Paris, 1, 3, 4.

60. "Étude préliminaire concernant l'exécution d'un coup de force au Tonkin: Solution No 2," 13.

61. "Incidents de HAIPHONG 20–21 Novembre 1946—Compte rendu No 1," 22 novembre 1946, GR 10H (Indochine) 2444, Service Historique de la Défense, Paris, 2.

62. Stein Tønnesson, *Vietnam 1946: How the War Began* (Berkeley: University of California Press, 2010), 135.

63. Reproduced in "Rapport du Général de Division Morlière, Commandant les Troupes Françaises en Indochine du Nord et Commissaire de la République par intérim au sujet de la situation en Indochine du Nord," 28. Emphasis in original. "Incidents de HAIPHONG 20–21 Novembre 1946—Compte rendu No 1," 28.

64. Anderson, *Java in a Time of Revolution*, 146–151; Cribb, *Gangsters and Revolutionaries*, 72–83.

65. John Smail, *Bandung in the Early Revolution, 1945–1946: A Study in the Social History of the Indonesian Revolution* (Ithaca, NY: Modern Indonesia Project Cornell University, 1964), 147–157.

66. Frederick, *Visions and Heat*, 278–279.

67. Tom van den Berge, "Indonesisch geweld tegen de burgerbevolking in West-Java, 1945–1949. Een verkenning," *Leidschrift* 31, no. 3 (2016): 57–78.

68. Michael Williams, "Banten: Rice Debts Will Be Repaid with Rice, Blood with Blood," in *Regional Dynamics of the Indonesian Revolution*, ed. Audrey Kahin (Honolulu: University of Hawai'i Press, 1985), 55–82; Anton Lucas, *One Soul One Struggle: Region and Revolution in Indonesia* (Sydney: Allen & Unwin, 1991).

69. Anthony Reid, *The Blood of the People: Revolution and the End of Traditional Rule in Northern Sumatra* (Kuala Lumpur: Oxford University Press, 1979), 194–227.

70. Jaap de Moor, *Westerling's oorlog: Indonesië 1945–1950* (Amsterdam: Balans, 1999), 104–112.

71. Reid, *Blood of the People*, 228–263; Mary Steedly, *Rifle Reports: A Story of Indonesian Independence* (Berkeley: University of California Press, 2013).

72. Bussemaker, *Bersiap*, 342; Robert Cribb, "The Brief Genocide of Eurasians in Indonesia, 1945/46," in *Empire, Colony, Genocide: Conquest, Occupation, and Subaltern Resistance in World History*, ed. A. Dirk Moses (New York: Berghahn Books, 2008), 424–436; Frederick, "Killing of Dutch and Eurasians," 359–380; Bart Immerzeel, "Bersiap: De werkelijke cijfers," *Javapost*, consulted on 4 March 2021 at https://javapost.nl/2014/02/07/bersiap-de-werkelijke-cijfers/; Mary Somers-Heidhues, "Anti-Chinese Violence in Java during the Indonesian Revolution 1945–49," *Journal of Genocide Research* 14, no. 3–4 (2012): 381–401.

73. Bussemaker, *Bersiap*, 331.

74. Tom van den Berge, *H. J. van Mook 1894–1965: Een vrij en gelukkig Indonesië* (Bussum, Netherlands: Uitgeverij Toth, 2014).

75. Nyoman S. Pendit, *Bali Berjuang* (Jakarta: Gunung Agung, 1979), 191–238; Geoffrey Robinson, *The Dark Side of Paradise: Political Violence in Bali* (Ithaca, NY: Cornell University Press, 1996), 129–150.

76. Barbara Harvey, "Tradition, Islam, and Rebellion: South Sulawesi 1950–1965" (PhD diss., Cornell University, 1974), 128–153.

77. Limpach, *De brandende kampongs*, 247–323; De Moor, *Westerling's oorlog*, 135–153.

78. Limpach, *De brandende kampongs*, 279, 293–294, 319, 762; Heather Sutherland, "History of Makassar," unpublished ms., chap. 9.

79. Limpach, *De brandende kampongs*, 269, 308.

80. Christiaan Harinck, "Zoeken, aangrijpen en vernietigen: De theorie, praktijk en prijs van het Nederlandse militaire optreden in Indonesië, 1945–1949" (PhD diss., Leiden University, 2021).

81. Frances Gouda and Thijs Brocades Zaalberg, *American Visions of the Netherlands–East Indies / Indonesia, 1920–1949* (Amsterdam: Amsterdam University Press, 2002), 282–302.

5. THE PLACES, TRACES, AND POLITICS OF RAPE IN THE INDONESIAN AND THE ALGERIAN WARS OF INDEPENDENCE

Khedidja Adel, from the Université Constantine 2 Abdelhamid Mehri in Algeria, and Galuh Ambar, from Gadjah Mada University of Yogyakarta in Indonesia, conducted inquiries for us in local languages, shared as-yet-unpublished research, and provided feedback on our approach. We thank Jonathan Verweij (PhD candidate and curator at Museum Bronbeek) and Dr. Marius Loris-Rodionoff (Centre d'Histoire Sociale, Université Paris I Panthéon-Sorbonne) for sharing their sources with us. We are grateful to Liesbeth Zegveld (law firm Prakken d'Oliveira) for allowing us access to the court files of Mrs. Tremini's 2016 case against the Dutch state.

1. Elizabeth Jean Wood, "Variation in Sexual Violence during War," *Politics and Society* 34, no. 3 (2006): 307–341; Elizabeth Jean Wood, *Insurgent Collective Action and Civil War in El Salvador* (Cambridge: Cambridge University Press, 2010).

2. Raphaëlle Branche and Fabrice Virgili, eds., *Viols en temps de guerre* (Paris: Payot, 2011).

3. We focus in this article on rape committed by members of the Dutch and French armed forces. This does not imply that we deny the existence of acts of rape committed by their adversaries. While some references to rape committed by members of the Algerian National Liberation Army (ALN) against Algerian women exist in military archives and

memoirs, the evidence does not indicate that this was a widespread practice. See Ryme Seferdjeli, "Rethinking the History of the Mujahidat during the Algerian War: Competing Voices, Reconstructed Memories and Contrasting Historiographies," *Interventions* 14, no. 2 (2012): 238–255. A different impression is given by documents seized from Indonesian troops in December 1947, found in the archive of the NEFIS (the Dutch military intelligence service) by military historian Rémy Limpach, containing the explicit order to intensify "pillage and rape" in the area of Central Java. We thank him for sharing this important document with us. National Archives, The Hague, Archive NEFIS/CMI, collection number 2.10.37.02/5552, documents with orders seized on 6 January 1948 from an Indonesian TNI Bataljon II Resimen 15 Brigade VI Divisi II.

4. In addition, analysis of eighty-nine private contemporary diaries of Dutch military personnel reveals nine references to sexual violence. Nederlands Instituut voor Militaire Historie (NIMH), Den Haag, Dagboekenproject Nederlandse militairen in Indonesië 1945–1949 [Database of unpublished diaries, Netherlands Institute for Military History]. A similar perusal of a database of 659 full-text published memoirs, edited diaries, or correspondence provides only two references to rape. Database "Soldiers in Indonesia," Royal Netherlands Institute of Southeast Asian and Caribbean Studies (KITLV), 2016. An equivalent database does not exist in the French context.

5. Marius Loris-Rodionoff, "Crises et reconfigurations de la relation d'autorité dans l'armée française au défi de la guerre d'Algérie, 1954–1966" (PhD, Université Paris I, 2018), 336.

6. Khedidja Adel, "La prison des femmes de Tifelfel: Enfermement et corps en souffrance," *L'Année du Maghreb*, no. 20 (2019): 123–138.

7. Simone de Beauvoir and Gisèle Halimi, *Djamila Boupacha* (Paris: Gallimard, 1962).

8. Abdul Haris Nasution, *Sekitar Perang Kemerdekaan* (Historische Dienst Indonesische Landmacht, 1991).

9. Raphaëlle Branche, "Des viols pendant la guerre d'Algérie," *Vingtième siècle. Revue d'histoire*, no. 75 (2002/3): 123–132; Marnia Lazreg, *Torture and the Twilight of Empire: from Algiers to Baghdad* (Princeton, NJ: Princeton University Press, 2008); Judith Surkis, "Ethics and Violence: Simone de Beauvoir, Djamila Boupacha and the Algerian War," *French Politics, Culture and Society* 28, no. 2 (2010): 38–55.

10. National Archives, The Hague, Archief Procureur Generaal [archive of the general prosecutor], collection no. 2.10.17, inventory no. 1314 (hereafter NL-HaNA, followed by entry number and inventory number).

11. NL-HaNA, Krijgsraad te Velde [court-martial], 2.09.19/58, vonnis 940, 26 August 1948.

12. NL-HaNA, Commissie Gedragingen en Onderscheidingen KNIL [Commission for assessment of conduct and military awards] 2.10.58/53, vonnis 670, 5 August 1948.

13. Mouloud Feraoun, *Journal 1955–1962* (Paris: Seuil, 1962), 184.

14. Raphaëlle Branche, *La torture et l'armée pendant la guerre d'Algérie, 1954–1962* (Paris: Gallimard, 2001), 309.

15. Natalya Vince, "Transgressing Boundaries: Gender, Race, Religion and 'Françaises musulmanes' during the Algerian War of Independence," *French Historical Studies* 33, no. 3 (2010): 445–474.

16. Netherlands Institute for Military History (NIMH), "NIMH Dagboekenproject Nederlandse militairen in Indonesië 1945–1949," citaat uit: Collection 457/3, Diary H. Keegstra, 1949.

17. J. J. A. van Doorn and W. Hendrix, *Onstporing van geweld, over Nederlands Indisch/Indonesisch conflict* (Rotterdam: Rotterdam University Press, 1970), 251.

18. NL-HaNA, Commission on behavior and decorations KNIL, 2.10.58–53/7, Verdict 1948–04–20–672.

19. Loris-Rodionoff, "Crises et reconfigurations," 331–332.

20. Dossier de procedure de RR, TG and CP, no judgment 924/4555 TPFA Alger, Archives de la Justice Militaire Le Blanc. Quoted in Loris-Rodionoff, "Crises et reconfigurations," 332–335.

21. NL-HaNA, Krijgsraad te Velde, 2.09.19/33, verdict 905 in Malang op 12 February 1949.

22. Pieter de Kam, *Het reizende bataljon: Herdenkingsboek 8 RS. stoottroepen en KNIL (Gadja Merah) in de Y-brigade 1944–1948* (Hilversum, Netherlands, 1996). In modern Indonesian spelling "sir" is rendered as "tuan," but in the veteran's memoir the old spelling is used.

23. NIMH, "NIMH Dagboekenproject," Collection 57/4709, Diary of H. van Hoorn, 1948/1949.

24. Annegriet Wietsma and Stef Scagliola, *Liefde in Tijden van Oorlog: Onze jongens en hun verzwegen kinderen in de Oost* (Amsterdam: Boom, 2013), 8.

25. Susan Blackburn, *Women and the State in Modern Indonesia* (Cambridge: Cambridge University Press, 2009). Blackburn cites the following Indonesian works, which discuss the role of these women independence fighters: R. T. Condronagoro, ed., *Riwayat Laskar Putri Indonesia di Surakarta* (Surakarta, Indonesia: Wirjowitono, 1979); N. Nurliana, M. P. B. Manus, G. A. M. Ohorella, et al., *Peranan Wanita Indonesia di Masa Perang Kemerdekaan 1945–1950* (Jakarta: Departemen Pendidikan dan Kebudayaan, 1986).

26. Beauvoir and Halimi, *Djamila Boupacha*, 21–24.

27. Sitti Hasanah Nu'mang, "Saya diancam Westerling," in *A Thousand Faces of Women Fighters in the '45 Revolutionary Field* (Jakarta: Grasindo, 1995), 258–263.

28. Michel Cornaton, *Les camps de regroupement de la guerre d'Algérie* (Paris: L'Harmattan, 1998). Fabien Sacriste, "Surveiller et moderniser. Les camps de 'regroupement' de ruraux pendant la guerre d'indépendance algérienne," *Métropolitiques.eu* (2012), https://www.metropolitiques.eu/Surveiller-et-moderniser-Les-camps.html#nh5. Moritz Feichtinger, "'A Great Reformatory': Social Planning and Strategic Resettlement in Late Colonial Kenya and Algeria, 1952–63," *Journal of Contemporary History* 52, no. 1 (2017): 45–72.

29. Florence Beaugé, *Une guerre sans gloire: Histoire d'une enquête* (Paris: Calmann-Lévy, 2005), 88.

30. Adel, "La prison des femmes de Tifelfel."

31. Joanna Bourke, *Rape: Sex, Violence, History* (Emeryville, CA: Shoemaker and Hoard, 2007), 360.

32. Cynthia Enloe, *Maneuvers: The International Politics of Militarizing Women's Lives* (Berkeley: University of California Press, 2000), 109–110.

33. Paul Kirby, "How Is Rape a Weapon of War? Feminist International Relations, Modes of Critical Explanation and the Study of Wartime Sexual Violence," *European Journal of International Relations* 19, no. 4 (2012): 797–821; Madeline Morris, "By Force of Arms: Rape, War, and Military Culture," *Duke Law Journal* 45, no. 4 (1996): 651–781.

34. Dominique Olivier (4K 19), Oral archives of the Service historique de la Défense (Army archives), quoted in Loris-Rodionoff, "Crises et reconfigurations," 127–128.

35. Hylke Speerstra, *Op klompen door de dessa. Indië-gangers vertellen* (Amsterdam: Atlas, 2015), 182.

36. A well-known counterexample to this logic is the My Lai massacre in 1968, when twenty civilians were raped by soldiers belonging to the US Army Charlie Company, despite the extensive accessibility of prostitutes for US soldiers in Vietnam. Gina Marie Weaver, *Ideologies of Forgetting: Rape in the Vietnam War* (Albany: SUNY Press, 2010).

37. De Jonge 1997: 80–81 -Soldaat in Indonesië database.

38. Louisette Ighilahriz with Anne Nivat, *Algérienne* (Paris: Fayard and Calmann Lévy, 2001).

39. Sitti Hasanah, "Saya diancam," 262.

40. H. G. Esméralda's *Un été en enfer. Barbarie à la française: Témoignage sur la généralisation de la torture, Algérie 1957* (Paris: Exils, 2004) is based on an account written in 1958 by the author, extracts of which were published in the newspaper *Le Monde* at the time. This 2004 publication anonymized the names of the torturers and also did not contain some passages about sexual violence—the full original 1958 version is published in Jacques Duquesne's *Carnets secrets de la guerre d'Algérie* (Paris: Bayard, 2012), 17.

41. Branche, *La torture et l'armée*.

42. Rémy Limpach, *De brandende kampongs van Generaal Spoor* (Amsterdam: Boom, 2016), 466.

43. Branche, "Des viols pendant la guerre d'Algérie"; Lazreg, *Torture and the Twilight of Empire*.

44. Branche, "Des viols pendant la guerre d'Algérie," 128.

45. Wood, "Variation in Sexual Violence during War," 332.

46. Malek Alloula, *The Colonial Harem*, trans. Myrna Godzich and Wlad Godzich (Minneapolis: University of Minnesota Press, 1986); see also Pascal Blanchard, Nicolas Bancel, Gilles Boetsch, et al., eds., *Sexe, race et colonies: La domination des corps du XVe siècle à nos jours* (Paris: La Découverte, 2018).

47. Christelle Taraud, *La prostitution coloniale, Algérie, Tunisie, Maroc (1830–1962)* (2003; Paris: Payot, 2009).

48. Christina Wu, "Le mythe de la femme du Sud-Est Asiatique," in Blanchard, Bancel, et al., *Sexe, race et colonies*, 261. See also Patricia Park, "The Madame Butterfly Effect: Tracing the History of a Fetish," bitchmedia, 30 July 2014, https://www.bitchmedia.org/article/the-madame-butterfly-effect-asian-fetish-history-pop-culture.

49. Jonathan Verweij, "'Hoeveel wreekt de bruidegom de bruid'; seksueel geweld en de Nederlandse krijgsmacht in Indonesië, 1945–1950" [How the bride doth suffer the groom's wrath: Sexual violence and the Dutch armed forces in Indonesia, 1945–1950], *Tijdschrift voor geschiedenis* 129, no. 4 (2016).

50. Ann Laura Stoler, *Carnal Knowledge and Imperial Power: Race and the Intimate in Colonial Rule* (Berkeley: University of California Press, 2002). For the Algerian equivalent see Judith Surkis, *Sex, Law, and Sovereignty in French Algeria, 1830–1930* (Ithaca, NY: Cornell University Press, 2019).

51. Susie Protschky, "Home at the Front: Violence against Indonesian Women and Children in Dutch Military Barracks during the Indonesian National Revolution," in *Gender, Violence and Power in Indonesia: Across Time and Space*, ed. Katharine McGregor, Ana Dragojlovic, and Hannah Loney (London: Routledge, 2020), 65.

52. *Résistance algérienne*, 16 May 1957, a newspaper published in French and Arabic by the FLN between October 1955 and June 1957.

53. Frantz Fanon, *A Dying Colonialism*, trans. Haakon Chevalier (New York: Grove, 1965), 45.

54. An estimated two hundred thousand to four hundred thousand Algerian men served as auxiliaries in the French army between 1954 and 1962, representing approximately 10 to 20 percent of the entire Algerian rural population. François-Xavier Hautreux, "Quelques pistes pour une meilleure compréhension de l'engagement des harkis (1954–1962)," *Les Temps Modernes*, no. 666 (2011): 44–52. When the Dutch colonial army (Koninklijk Nederlands Indisch Leger) was disbanded in 1950, there were fifty thousand local troops, of which twenty-six thousand were incorporated into the Indonesian Armed Forces and twenty thousand were demobilized in Indonesia. Four thousand local troops of Moluccan descent refused to join the Indonesian army and were transported to the Netherlands. Source: Timeline, website Dutch

Institute for Military History, consulted 1 May 2020, https://www.defensie.nl/onderwerpen/tijdlijn-militaire-geschiedenis/1945-1949-van-nederlands-indie-naar-indonesie.

55. Raphaëlle Branche, "'The Best *Fellagha* Hunter Is the French of North African Descent': Harkis in French Algeria," in *Unconventional Warfare from Antiquity to the Present Day*, ed. B. Hughes and F. Robson (Cham, Switzerland: Palgrave Macmillan, 2017), 47–66, 47.

56. Interview with Chérifa Akache, in Natalya Vince, *Our Fighting Sisters: Nation, Memory and Gender in Algeria, 1954–1962* (Manchester: Manchester University Press, 2015), 62.

57. Christiaan Harinck, "'Zoeken, aangrijpen en vernietigen!' De theorie, praktijk en prijs van het Nederlandse militaire optreden in Indonesië 1945–1949" (PhD diss., to be defended at Leiden University in 2022). Also see Harinck's contribution to this volume. For special forces see Limpach, *De brandende kampongs*, 100, 744.

58. Muhammad Yuanda Zara, "Voluntary Participation, State Involvement: Indonesian Propaganda for the Struggle of Maintaining Independence, 1945–1949" (PhD diss., University of Amsterdam, 2016); Matthew Connelly, *A Diplomatic Revolution: Algeria's Fight for Independence and the Origins of the Post–Cold War Era* (Oxford: Oxford University Press, 2002).

59. Antoine Weijzen, *De Waarheid: De Indië-weigeraars: De vergeten slachtoffers van een koloniale oorlog* (Utrecht: Omniboek, 2015); Martin Evans, *The Memory of Resistance: French Opposition to the Algerian War (1954–1962)* (Oxford: Berg, 1997).

60. *Minggu Pagi*, 20 April 1952. *Minggu Pagi* (Sunday morning) was a weekly Sunday magazine. A report about the meeting of women's organizations in 1952 was published by an anonymous author on this date.

61. Kawar Wati, *Wanita Lima Nama* (1982). The protagonist is an Indonesian woman, who is first sexually exploited as a "comfort girl" during the Japanese occupation, then raped by a Dutch soldier, and then again by a member of an Indonesian militia.

62. Branche, "Des viols pendant la guerre d'Algérie"; Lazreg, *Torture and the Twilight of Empire*.

63. Todd Shepard and Catherine Brun, eds., *Guerre d'Algérie: Le sexe outragé* (Paris: CNRS Éditions, 2016).

64. Yuki Tanaka, *Japan's Comfort Women: Sexual Slavery and Prostitution during World War II and the U.S. Occupation* (New York: Routledge, 2002), 78. Tanaka argues in his study of sexual slavery during and after World War II that "as much as the Japanese were unconcerned about the exploitation of non-Europeans, the Dutch were equally indifferent to victims who were not white and Dutch."

65. Zohra Drif, *La mort de mes frères* (Paris: Maspero, 1961), 11–12.

66. Vince, *Our Fighting Sisters*, 86.

67. Saadia-et-Lakhdar (the pseudonyms for Salima and Rabah Bouaziz), *L'aliénation colonialiste et la résistance de la famille algérienne* (Lausanne, Switzerland: La Cité, 1961), first published in the French journal *Temps Modernes* in June 1961 and then published as a book by the supporter of the FLN, Nils Andersson.

68. Surkis, "Ethics and Violence"; Lee Whitfield, "The French Military under Female Fire: The Public Opinion Campaign and Justice in the Case of Djamila Boupacha, 1960–62," *Contemporary French Civilization* 20, no. 1 (1996): 76–90.

69. *Times* (London), 10 November 1961

70. J. Frémeaux, "Les SAS (Sections administratives spécialisées)," *Guerres mondiales et conflits contemporains*, no. 208 (2002): 55–68.

71. Archives nationales d'outre-mer [Center for Overseas Archives, CAOM], France: 5/SAS/5 Aghribs.

72. Blackburn, *Women and the State*, 196.

73. Camille Lacoste-Dujardin, *Opération Oiseau Bleu: Des Kabyles, des ethnologues et la guerre d'Algérie* (Paris: La Découverte, 1997), 158.

74. Sitti Hasanah Nu'mang, in *A Thousand Faces of Women Fighters in the '45 Revolutionary Field* (Jakarta: Grasindo, 1995).

75. Adel, "La prison des femmes de Tifelfel."

76. Poems presented in a paper given by Souhila Benkhellat's PhD supervisor, Professor Khaled Chérif Sabeur, "Les tirailleurs sénégalais à travers quelques extraits inédits de poèmes populaires kabyles," at "The Algerian War of Independence: Global and Local Histories, 1954–62, and Beyond," Oxford Algeria Conference 2017, University of Oxford, 10–12 May 2017.

77. Vince, *Our Fighting Sisters*, 159.

78. Ighilahriz, *Algérienne*; "Les viols pendant la guerre d'Algérie," *Envoyé Spécial* (France 2, 2002).

79. KUKB stands for Komite Utang Kehormatan Belanda (Committee of Dutch Honorary Debts).

80. The case followed on from the successful lawsuit against the Dutch state for a mass execution perpetrated by a Dutch military unit in the same village of Peniwen. After the success of the Tremini case, the Dutch state lodged an appeal (ongoing), out of fear of setting a precedent. Freek Schravesande, "In 1949 verkracht, dus is haar zaak nu verjaard?," *NRC Handelsblad*, 2 May 2016.

81. Mrs. Tremini's testimony in the court case. Archives held at Prakken d'Oliveira law firm.

82. Protschky, "Home at the Front," 80.

83. Nicole L. Immler and Stef Scagliola, "Seeking Justice for the Mass Execution in Rawagede / Probing the Concept of 'Entangled History' in a Post-colonial Setting," *Rethinking History: The Journal of Theory and Practice* 20, no. 1 (2020): 1–28.

84. Protschky, "Home at the Front," 65.

85. Alloula, *Colonial Harem*.

86. Cynthia Enloe, *Bananas, Beaches and Bases: Making Feminist Sense of International Politics* (1990; Berkeley: University of California Press, 2014), 105.

87. Report found in the archive of the city of Yogyakarta, about the losses in the neighborhood of Kapanewon Pedes / Bantul as the consequence of the Dutch military attack on the city in December 1948 (M.Sc. 128). Daftar Dari Adanja Kerugian Ra'jat Akibat Agresi Militer Belanda dalam Daerah Kapanewon Pedes / Bantul.

88. Darto Harnoko Tanggal, interview by Galuh Ambar, 12 January 2017, Waktu: 09.30–13.00. This is an interview with the Indonesian retired historian, Dr. Darto Harnoko, who was part of a focus group, with eighteen other historians, to review the history of the revolution. In the interview, he recounted how he talked to Ventje Sumual, the former leader of the sub-Wehrkreis in West Sleman (a neighborhood in Yogyakarta), at the premises of his research institute (date unknown). Sumual told him about mass rape that took place in this neighborhood by Dutch soldiers.

89. Laâtra, from Rouffi (Aurès, Algeria), interview with Khedidja Adel, June 2019.

6. "THE NORMAL ORDER OF THINGS"

1. David Halberstam, *The Making of a Quagmire: America and Vietnam during the Kennedy Era*, rev. ed. (1964; Lanham, MD: Rowman & Littlefield, 1987), 84.

2. Raymond "Turk" Westerling, *Challenge to Terror* (1952; Kindle edition, 2018), 850–963.

3. Richard B. Johnson, *The Biggest Stick: The Employment of Artillery Units in Counterinsurgency* (Fort Leavenworth, KS: Combat Studies Institute, 2011), 1–20.

4. J. A. A. van Doorn and W. Hendrix, *Ontsporing van geweld: Het Nederlands-Indonesisch conflict*, 4th rev. ed. (Zutphen, Netherlands: Walburg Pers, 2012), 242–250. The authors also used the term *mechanisch geweld* to refer to the same phenomenon. Neither term has an Anglo-American military equivalent, and a literature search reveals "technical violence" refers to cyber bullying and malicious social engineering.

5. Stef Scagliola, *Last van de oorlog: De Nederlandse oorlogsmisdaden in Indonesië en hun verwerking* (Amsterdam: Balans, 2002), 56; Jan Hoffenaar, Joep van Hoof, and Jaap de Moor, *Vuur in beweging: 325 jaar veldartillerie, 1627–2002* (Amsterdam: Boom, 2002), 127; Gert Oostindie, Ireen Hoogeboom and Jonathan Verwey, *Soldaat in Indonesië 1945–1950: Getuigenissen van een oorlog aan de verkeerde kant van de geschiedenis* (Amsterdam: Prometheus, 2015), 146, 163; Rémy Limpach, *De brandende kampongs van generaal Spoor* (Amsterdam: Boom, 2016), 391–92, 395, 768, photo caption no. 48.

6. Bart Luttikhuis, "What Makes Violence Extreme, and Who Is Responsible?," in "Debate on *De brandende kampongs van Generaal Spoor* by Rémy Limpach, with Bart Luttikhuis, Abdul Wahid, Robert Cribb, Harry Poeze," *Bijdragen tot de taal-, land- en volkenkunde / Journal of the Humanities and Social Sciences of Southeast Asia* 173, no. 4 (2017): 560.

7. Limpach, *De brandende kampongs*, 389, 780; "Debate on *De brandende kampongs*," 559–579.

8. On military revolutions see Macgregor Knox and Williamson Murray, *The Dynamics of Military Revolution, 1300–2050* (New York: Cambridge University Press, 2001); Clifford J. Rogers, ed., *The Military Revolution Debate: Readings on the Military Transformation of Europe* (Boulder, CO: Westview, 1995). On the firepower revolution see J. B. A. Bailey, *Field Artillery and Firepower* (Annapolis, MD: Naval Institute Press, 2004); Shelford Bidwell and Dominick Graham, *Fire-Power: British Army Weapons and Theories, 1904–1945* (London: Unwin Hyman, 1985); Michael D. Grice, *On Gunnery: The Art and Science of Field Artillery* (North Charleston, NC: Booksurge, 2009); Bruce I. Gudmundsson, *On Artillery* (Westport, CT: Greenwood, 1993).

9. Erik Dorn Brose, *The Kaiser's Army: The Politics of Military Technology in Germany during the Machine Age, 1870–1918* (New York: Oxford University Press, 2001), 26–42. On allegations of excessive violence against civilians see Bastian Matteo Scianna, "A Predisposition to Brutality? German Practices against Civilians and *Francs-tireurs* during the Franco-Prussian War, 1870–1871, and Their Relevance for the German 'Military *Sonderweg*' Debate," *Small Wars & Insurgencies* 30 (2019): 968–993.

10. Stephen Biddle, *Military Power: Explaining Victory and Defeat in Modern Battle* (Princeton, NJ: Princeton University Press, 2004), 87.

11. Wesley Frank Craven and James Lea Cate, eds., *The Army Air Forces in World War II*, vol. 3, *Europe: Argument to V-E Day, January 1944 to May 1945* (1951; repr., Washington, DC: Office of Air Force History, 1983), 209–219; Tami Davis Biddle, *Rhetoric and Reality in Air Warfare: The Evolution of British and American Ideas about Strategic Bombing, 1914–1945* (Princeton, NJ: Princeton University Press, 2002); Richard Overy, *The Bombers and the Bombed: Allied Air War over Europe, 1940–1945* (New York: Penguin Books, 2013); Kenneth P. Werrell, *Death from the Heavens: A History of Strategic Bombing* (Annapolis, MD: Naval Institute Press, 2009).

12. J. Knowles, "Medium Artillery in Burma," *Field Artillery Journal* 35 (1945): 21–27. On Japan's race war in China a good entry is Richard Frank, *Tower of Skulls: A History of the Asia-Pacific War, June 1937–May 1942* (New York: W. W. Norton, 2020).

13. Biddle, *Military Power*, 1–13; Shelford Bidwell, *Modern Warfare: A Study of Men, Weapons and Theories* (London: Allen Lane, 1973); Jonathan M. House, *Combined Arms Warfare in the Twentieth Century* (Lawrence: University Press of Kansas, 2001); David Jordan, James D. Kiras, David J. Lonsdale, Ian Speller, Christopher Tuck, and C. Dale Walton, *Understanding Modern Warfare* (New York: Cambridge University Press, 2008).

14. Charles E. Callwell, *Small Wars: Their Principles and Practice*, 3rd ed. (London: Harrison and Sons, 1906), 152, see also 153–158, 429–439.

15. Hilaire Belloc and Basil S. Blackwell, *The Modern Traveller* (London: Edward Arnold, 1898), 41; Daniel R. Headrick, *The Tools of Empire: Technology and European Imperialism in the Nineteenth Century* (New York: Oxford University Press, 1981). On imperial policing see David Omissi, *Air Power and Colonial Control* (Manchester: Manchester University Press, 1990); James S. Corum and Wray R. Johnson, *Airpower in Small Wars: Fighting Insurgents and Terrorists* (Lawrence: University Press of Kansas, 2003), 51–86.

16. Abdul Haris Nasution, *Fundamentals of Guerrilla Warfare* (1953, repr., New York: Praeger, 1965); Robert Cribb, "Military Strategy in the Indonesian Revolution: Nasution's Concept of 'Total People's War' in Theory and Practice," *War and Society* 19 (October 2001): 143–154; Christopher Goscha, "Bringing Asia into Focus: Civilians and Combatants in the Line of Fire in China and Indochina," *War and Society* 31 (August 2012): 87–105. For an astute critique of Mao's military thought see Douglas Porch, *Counterinsurgency: Exposing the Myths of the New Way of War* (New York: Cambridge University Press, 2013), 154–161.

17. Mark M. Boatner, "Countering Communist Artillery," *Combat Forces Journal* 4 (September 1953): 24; Kevin M. Boylan, "No 'Technical Knockout': Giap's Artillery at Dien Bien Phu," *Journal of Military History* 78 (October 2014): 1329–1383; D. M. Giangreco, *Artillery in Korea: Massing Fires and Reinventing the Wheel* (Fort Leavenworth, KS: Combat Studies Institute, 2003).

18. C. A. Bayly and T. N. Harper, *Forgotten Wars: Freedom and Revolution in Southeast Asia* (Cambridge, MA: Belknap Press of Harvard University Press, 2007).

19. Andrew J. Birtle, *U.S. Army Counterinsurgency and Contingency Operations Doctrine, 1942–1976* (Washington, DC: Center of Military History, 2006); Anthony Clayton, *The Wars of French Decolonization* (New York: Longman, 1994); David French, *The British Way in Counter-insurgency, 1945–1967* (Oxford: Oxford University Press, 2011).

20. For a translation of a GDA counterinsurgency manual see "Suppression of Irregular (Bandit) Operations," 1949, file 319.1, box 41, entry 32B, RG 337, National Archives II, College Park, MD; Birtle, *U.S. Army Counterinsurgency*, 42–55; Corum and Johnson, *Airpower in Small Wars*, 93–110; Charles R. Schrader, *The Withered Vine: Logistics and Communist Insurgency in Greece, 1945–1949* (Westport, CT: Praeger, 1999); Amikam Nachmani, "Civil War and Foreign Intervention in Greece, 1946–49," *Journal of Contemporary History* 25 (October 1990): 489–522.

21. 8th Army Korea, "Special Problems in the Korean Conflict," 1952, Combined Arms Library, Fort Leavenworth, KS; Birtle, *U.S. Army Counterinsurgency*, 85–122; Allan R. Millett, *The War for Korea, 1945–1950: A House Burning* (Lawrence: University Press of Kansas, 2005); Ronald H. Spector, *In the Ruins of Empire: The Japanese Surrender and the Battle for Postwar Asia* (New York: Random House, 2007), 138–166, 268–272.

22. Thomas C. Hone, "Strategic Bombardment Constrained: Korea and Vietnam," in *Case Studies in Strategic Bombardment*, ed. C. Cargill Hall (Washington, DC: Government Printing Office, 1998), 487; Conrad C. Crane, *American Airpower Strategy in Korea, 1950–1953* (Lawrence: University Press of Kansas, 2000).

23. Bryan R. Gibby, *The Will to Win: American Military Advisors in Korea, 1946–1953* (Tuscaloosa: University of Alabama Press, 2012), 211; G. Kirk Alexander, "Operational Artillery in Korea" (thesis, US Army School of Advanced Military Studies, 2013); Roy E. Appleman, *South to the Natkong, North to the Yalu (June–November 1950)* (Washington, DC: Office of Chief of Military History, 1961), 19–24; William Glenn Robertson, "The Korean War: The United Nations' Response to Heavy Bombardment," in *Tactical Responses to Concentrated Artillery* (Fort Leavenworth, KS: Combat Studies Institute, 1990), 107–118.

24. A. H. Peterson, G. C. Reinhardt, and E. E. Conger, eds., *Symposium on the Role of Airpower . . . Philippine Huk Campaign* (Santa Monica, CA: RAND, 1963), 57.

25. Uldarico S. Baclagon, *Lessons from the Huk Campaign in the Philippines* (Manila: M. Colcol, 1960); Corum and Johnson, *Airpower in Small Wars*, 110–136; Lawrence M. Greenburg, *The Hukbalahap Insurrection: A Case Study of a Successful Anti-insurgency Operation in the Philippines, 1946–1955* (Washington, DC: Center of Military History, 1995); Napoleon D. Valeriano and Charles T. R. Bohannon, *Counterguerrilla Operations: The Philippine Experience* (New York: Frederick A. Praeger, 1962).

26. Corum and Johnson, *Airpower in Small Wars*, 179–199; Johnson, *Biggest Stick*, 26, 39–64; Riley Sutherland, *Army Operations in Malaya, 1947–1960* (Santa Monica, CA: RAND, 1964); Steven Paget, "A Sledgehammer to Crack a Nut? Naval Gunfire Support during the Malayan Emergency," *Small Wars and Insurgencies* 28, no. 2 (2017): 361–384. The British relocation plan, one observer noted rather callously, was to "absquat, unsquat, or desquat the squatter villages," see Paul M. A. Linebarger, "They Call 'em Bandits in Malaya," *Army Combat Forces Journal* 2 (January 1951): 29.

27. Baclagon, *Lessons from the Huk Campaign*, 57.

28. Peterson, Reinhardt, and Conger, *Symposium on the Role of Airpower*, 45–46.

29. Ronald H. Spector, *The U.S. Army in Vietnam: Advice and Support; The Early Years, 1941–1960* (Washington, DC: Center of Military History, 1983), 106.

30. Luis Taruc, *He Who Rides the Tiger: The Story of an Asian Guerrilla Leader* (New York: Frederick A. Praeger, 1967), 38–42; William J. Pomeroy, *The Forest: A Personal Record of the Huk Guerrilla Struggle in the Philippines* (New York: International, 1963).

31. Paget, "Sledgehammer," 369; Larry Yates, *Field Artillery in Military Operations Other Than War: An Overview of the US Experience* (Fort Leavenworth, KS: Combat Studies Institute, 2005).

32. Peterson, Reinhardt, and Conger, *Symposium on the Role of Airpower*.

33. Baclagon, *Lessons from the Huk Campaign*, 160–162; Tomás Tirona, "The Philippine Anti-Communist Campaign," *Air University Quarterly Review* 7, no. 2 (Summer 1954): 42–55; Valeriano and Bohannon, *Counterguerrilla Operations*, esp. 131–133.

34. HQ, Department of the Army, *FM 31–22: U.S. Army Counterinsurgency Forces* (November 1963), 54. In another possible example of lessons learned from other conflicts, the US Army advisers to the Republic of Vietnam's army in the 1950s recommended very small and light artillery organizations. See Spector, *Advice and Support*, 264, 296, 299.

35. The following paragraphs were researched by Azarja Harmanny for his forthcoming dissertation.

36. Petra Groen, *Marsroutes en dwaalsporen. Het Nederlands militair-strategisch beleid in Indonesië, 1945–1950* (The Hague: Sdu, 1991), 212–214, tables in appendices 12–15. See also table on http://www.kitlv.nl/wp-content/uploads/2017/07/Overzicht-doden-versie-14-juli-2017.pdf (accessed 1 May 2020), as appendix to Christiaan Harinck et al., "Wie telt de Indonesische doden?," *De Groene Amsterdammer* 30 (2017).

37. David Wehl, *The Birth of Indonesia* (London: Allen & Unwin, 1948), 62.

38. A. H. Nasution, *Fundamentals of Guerrilla Warfare* (Jakarta: Seruling Masa, 1970), 16.

39. National Archives, The Hague, Archief Procureur Generaal (hereafter NL-HaNA), collection no. 2.13.126, Archief Mariniersbrigade in Nederlands-Indië, inventory no. 993, *Stukken betreffende het uitvoeren van werkzaamheden op het gebied van inlichtingen en veiligheid., 1946–1946*, "Training Instruction No.7."

40. Nugroho Notosusanto, *The Battle of Surabaja* (Jakarta: Department of Defence and Security, Centre for Armed Forces History, 1970), 14; M. R. H. Calmeyer and J. Hoffenaar, *Herinneringen: Memoires van een christen, militair en politicus* (The Hague: Sdu, 1997), 111–114. See also the chapter by Asselin and Schulte Nordholt in this volume.

41. NL-HaNA, Mariniersbrigade, inv. no. 151, *Commandant Nederlandse Mariniersbrigade aan Commandant Korps Mariniers, Soerabaja, 5 april 1946*. Mansergh was

commander in chief of the Allied Forces Netherlands East Indies (AFNEI) from April to November 1946.

42. A. J. F. Doulton, *The Fighting Cock, Being the History of the 23rd Indian Division, 1942–1947* (Aldershot, UK: Gale & Polden, 1951), 256; Bayly and Harper, *Forgotten Wars*, 180.

43. Notosusanto, *Battle of Surabaja*; Roeslan Abdulgani, *Heroes Day and the Indonesian Revolution* (Jakarta: Prapantja, 1964); Wayan Agus Apriana, "Bamboo Spear as Indonesian Traditional Weapon: Study Case on Singaparna Struggle in Tasikmalaya, West Java, Indonesia, 1944," in *ACTA 2012: Technology and Warfare. 38th ICMH Congress Proceedings Sofia, Bulgaria, 25 August—1 September 2012* (Sofia: Sofia University Press, 2013), 533–544.

44. Batara Hutagalung, *10 November '45: Mengapa Inggris membom Surabaya? Analisis latar belakang agresi militer Inggris* (Jakarta: Millennium, 2001).

45. O. G. Ward, *De militaire luchtvaart van het KNIL in de na-oorlogse jaren 1945–1950* (Houten, Netherlands: Van Holkema & Warendorf, 1988), 156–161; W. Geneste and T. Postma, *Squadron 860: 1943–1993: In 50 jaar van "stringbag" tot "fly by wire"* (Leeuwarden, Netherlands: Eisma, 1993), 12–14; Groen, *Marsroutes en dwaalsporen*, 17; Nederlands Instituut voor Militaire Historie (NIMH), 567 Collection Cats, inv. no. 38, *Stukken en documentatie betreffende de regimenten Veldartillerie in Nederlands-Indië, 1946–1950*.

46. Martin S. Alexander and J. F. V. Keiger, *France and the Algerian War, 1954–1962: Strategy, Operations and Diplomacy* (London: Routledge, 2013), 28.

47. NL-HaNA, Mariniersbrigade, inv. no. 1598, "Verslag over Artillerie Afdeeling der Mariniers Brigade van 1/3/46 tot 1/11/46."

48. R. W. Hoksbergen and J. Kroon, *De Nederlandse artillerie vanaf 1945* (Amersfoort, Netherlands: Vereniging Officieren Artillerie, 1998), 21; J. Hoffenaar and B. Schoenmaker, *Met de blik naar het Oosten: De Koninklijke Landmacht, 1945–1990* (The Hague: Sdu, 1994), 13.

49. Limpach, *De brandende kampongs*, 410–411; B. C. Cats, *L.I.B.'s in de tropen: Een overzicht van het verblijf van onze oorlogsvrijwilligers bij de lichte infanteriebataljons in het voormalige Nederlands-Indië, 1945–1949* (Maastricht, Netherlands: Departement van Defensie, 1961), 63; NL-HaNA, 2.13.106, Indisch Instructie Bataljon, inv. no. 6, *Ingekomen en minuten van uitgaande stukken, 1945–1946*; NIMH, 512, Antonietti, inv. no. 88, *Tabel en toelichting 'Voorlopige oorlogsorganisatie van een bataljon parachutisten van het KNIL', maart—oktober 1949*.

50. P. E. van Loo, "Metalen vogels onder de tropenzon: De Indische militaire luchtvaart 1914–1950," *Onze Luchtmacht* 66, no. 4 (2014): 11.

51. Ward, *De militaire luchtvaart van het KNIL in de na-oorlogse jaren 1945–1950*, 291.

52. The incident is briefly mentioned in P. C. Boer, *De jachtvliegtuigen, Army Co-operation- en lesvliegtuigen van de Militaire Luchtvaart KNIL 1945–1950* (Amsterdam: Bataafsche Leeuw, 2009), 66–67, and Ward, *Militaire luchtvaart*, 291–292. Both reproduce the official Dutch version that the plane hit the treetops accidentally, which is highly questionable, considering the circumstances. Louis Zweers, *De crash van de Franeker. Een Amerikaanse persreis naar Nederlands-Indië in 1949* (Amsterdam: Boom, 2001), 17–22, gives a more accurate representation.

53. Yos Bintoro, *Fly to Fight: Biografi Komodor Muda Agustinus Adisutjipto* (Jakarta: Rayyana Komunikasindo, 2014), 295–308; Irna H. N. Hadi Soewito, Nana Nurliana Suyono, and Soedarini Suhartono, *Awal kedirgantaraan di Indonesia: Perjuangan AURI 1945–1950* (Jakarta: Yayasan Obor Indonesia, 2008), 107–108.

54. NIMH, 509, Dekolonisatie Nederlands-Indië, inv. no. 331, "Interview met luitenant-generaal S. H. Spoor."

55. Van Doorn and Hendrix, *Ontsporing van geweld*, 211–212.
56. Hoffenaar, Van Hoof, and De Moor, *Vuur in beweging*, 127.
57. NL-HaNA, Strijdkrachten Ned.-Indië, 2.13.132, inv. no. 2277, *3–6 Regiment Veldartillerie. 1947 juli 21–1949 maart 3, Verslag over het 1e kwartaal 1949*.
58. Many examples are given in Roelf Spreeuwers, *De lange weg* (Stadskanaal, Netherlands: Roorda, 1980).
59. W. A. Schouten and H. B. Evers, "Het gebruik van de artillerie, ingedeeld bij de V-Brigade gedurende en na de politionele actie," *Militaire spectator* 4 (1949): 225–236: 232.
60. J. Lizé, "De lucht boven de sawa's: Over de offensieve bijdrage van de luchtstrijdkrachten tijdens de dekolonisatieoorlog in Nederlands-Indië (1945–1950)" (MA thesis, Universiteit Utrecht, 2015), 212.
61. Groen, *Marsroutes en dwaalsporen*, 246, 259.
62. A. H. Nasution, *Sekitar Perang Kemerdekaan Indonesia / Jil. 10, Perang gerilya semesta II* (Bandung, Indonesia: Angkasa, 1979), 45, 90, 128, 145, 161, 253, appendix 8.
63. T. B. Simatupang, *Report from Banaran: Experiences during the People's War*, trans. B. R. O'G. Anderson and E. E. Graves (Ithaca, NY: Modern Indonesia Project, Cornell University, 1972), 71–72.
64. Seskoad, *Serangan umum 1 Maret 1949 di Yogyakarta: Latar belakang dan pengaruhnya* (Jakarta: Citra Lamtoro Gung Persada, 1993), 254–255.
65. J. de Moor, *Westerling's oorlog: Indonesië 1945–1950: De geschiedenis van de commando's en parachutisten in Nederlands-Indië 1945–1950* (Amsterdam: Balans, 1999), 350–352; NL-HaNA, Strijdkrachten, inv. no. 2260, "Bevel tot vermeestering en bezetting Gading op 10 Maart 1949, Djocja, 5 Maart 1949."
66. NIMH, 545 Collection Sweep, Egodocumenten Nederlands-Indië 1945–1950, inv. no. 101, *Memoires getiteld 'Dienstplichtig tussen macht en onmacht. Notities omtrent eigen- en andermans belevenissen in de jaren 1945–1950' van M. A. P. de Lange . . .*, 65; email mr. De Lange to Harmanny, June 26, 2019. Account based on fellow members from his battalion that took part in the operation.
67. UN Archives, S-0681, Subject Files—Good Offices Committee and United Nations Commission for Indonesia 1940–1951 (GOC/UNCI), inv. no. S-0681–0027–04, "L. N. Palar, Chief of the Indonesian Delegation to the Security Council to the President of the Security Council, Lake Success, 25 March 1949."
68. UN Archives, GOC/UNCI, inv. no. S-0681–0011–07, *Wonosari Incident*.
69. R. P. Budding, *Beheersing van geweld. Het optreden van de Nederlandse landstrijdkrachten in Indonesië, 1945–1950* (Amsterdam: Bataafsche Leeuw, 1996), 53–54; Limpach, *De brandende kampongs*, 408; Piet Hagen, *Koloniale oorlogen in Indonesië: Vijf eeuwen verzet tegen vreemde overheersing* (Amsterdam: Arbeiderspers, 2018), 774.
70. De Moor, *Westerling's oorlog*, 352.
71. NL-HaNA, Strijdkrachten, inv. no. 2260, *2 Regiment Veldartillerie, 1948 december—september 1949 (bundel VII–XII)*, notes in handwritten notebook.
72. Nasution, *Sekitar Perang Kemerdekaan Indonesia / Jil. 10, Perang gerilya semesta II*, appendix 8.
73. Jan Bank, *De excessennota: Nota betreffende het archiefonderzoek naar de gegevens omtrent excessen in Indonesië begaan door Nederlandse militairen in de periode 1945–1950* (The Hague: Sdu, 1995).
74. Limpach, *De brandende kampongs*, 389–419.
75. E. H. M. Vallen and P. Heurter, eds., *Gedenkboek 402 Bataljon Infanterie* (Maastricht, Netherlands: Goffin, 1951), 189; Hagen, *Koloniale oorlogen*, 775.

7. "BLOODSHED ON A RATHER LARGE SCALE"

1. I would like to thank Bart Luttikhuis and Nico van Horn. Together with them, the author laid the groundwork for the numerical analysis of the Indonesian fatal casualties presented in this chapter. Martin Thomas and Gareth Curless, eds., *Decolonization and Conflict: Colonial Comparisons and Legacies* (London: Bloomsbury, 2017); Philip Dwyer and Amanda Nettelbeck, eds., *Violence, Colonialism and Empire in the Modern World* (London: Palgrave Macmillan, 2018).

2. Daniel Marston and Carter Malkasian, *Counterinsurgency in Modern Warfare* (Oxford: Osprey, 2008, rev. paperback ed. 2010); Gregory Fremont-Barnes, ed., *A History of Counterinsurgency*, 2 vols. (Santa Barbara, CA: Praeger, 2015).

3. Martin Bürgin, "From the Classics to Cultural History: Perspectives for Insurgency and Counterinsurgency Research," in *Insurgency and Counterinsurgency: Irregular Warfare from 1800 to the Present*, ed. Thijs Brocades Zaalberg, Jan Hoffenaar, and Alan Lemmers (The Hague: NIMH, 2011), 245–255; Sibylle Scheipers, "Counterinsurgency or Irregular Warfare? Historiography and the Study of 'Small Wars,'" *Small Wars & Insurgencies* 25, no. 5–6 (2014): 879–899.

4. The numbers are often based on estimations and are at the same time possibly both incomplete and over-complete, in the sense that groups of victims might have been excluded from the total tally, while total tallies might also include indirect casualties of war, such as those deprived of food or medical attention by the circumstances.

5. Christopher A. Goscha, *Historical Dictionary of the Indochina War (1945–1954): An International and Interdisciplinary Approach* (Copenhagen: NIAS, 2011), "casualties," 88–89; Christopher A. Goscha, *The Penguin History of Modern Vietnam* (London: Allen Lane, 2016), 244–245.

6. No fewer than thirty thousand and perhaps up to one hundred thousand Madagascans died in the insurrection—most of them as a result of hunger, depravation, and neglect. In typical colonial fashion, the French authorities after the revolt counted and estimated the victims in two categories, "European" and "Madagascan," putting in the latter group the insurgents killed, along with the locally raised pro-French forces, Madagascan public servants, and civilians killed by the insurgents. This system of counting makes the historian's task rather daunting. Antony Clayton, *The Wars of French Decolonization* (London: Longman, 1994), 83, 85–86; Jacques Trochon, *L'insurrection malgache de 1947* (Fianarantsoa, Madagascar: Éditions Ambozontany, 1982), 70–73; Jean Fremigacci, "La vérité sur la grande révolte de Madagascar," *L'Histoire* 318 (2007): 36–43.

7. J. J. A. van Doorn and W. Hendrix, *Ontsporing van geweld: Het Nederlands-Indonesisch conflict*, 4th rev. ed. (1970; Amsterdam: Walburg Pers, 2012), 165. The number of policemen and local irregular allies killed is not known.

8. C. H. C. Harinck, Nico van Horn, and Bart Luttikhuis, "Wie telt de Indonesische doden?," *Groene Amsterdammer*, 26 July 2017, 12–15. For a slightly adapted English translation see https://imperialglobalexeter.com/2017/08/14/do-the-indonesians-count-calculating-the-number-of-indonesian-victims-during-the-dutch-indonesian-decolonization-war-1945-1949/.

9. Richard McMillen, *The British Occupation of Indonesia 1945–1946* (Abingdon, UK: Routledge, 2005), 73.

10. Despatch No. 14 from High Commissioner for the United Kingdom to Secretary of State for Commonwealth Relations, Kuala Lumpur, 5 November 1960, as cited in Henry John Coates, *Suppressing Insurgency: An Operational Analysis of the Emergency in Malaya, 1948–1954* (Boulder, CO: Westview, 1922), 202.

11. David Anderson, *Histories of the Hanged: Britain's Dirty War in Kenya and the End of Empire* (2005; paperback ed., London: Phoenix, 2006), 4; Daniel Branch, "The Enemy

Within: Loyalists and the War against Mau Mau in Kenya," *Journal of African History* 48 (2007): 291–315, 292.

12. Xavier Yacono, "Les pertes algériennes de 1954 à 1962," *Revue des mondes musulmans et de la Méditerranée* 34 (1982): 119–134; Charles-Robert Ageron, "Les pertes humaines de la guerre d'Algérie," in *Genèse de l'Algérie algérienne* (Paris: Éditions Bouchène, 2005): 655–662; Peter McCutcheon, "Breaking the Camel's Back: The Departure from the Philosophy of Cultured Force—the French Counterinsurgency Campaign in Algeria, 1954–1962," in Fremont-Barnes, *History of Counterinsurgency*, vol. 1, *From South Africa to Algeria, 1900–1954*, 205–254, 206; Philippe François, "Waging Counterinsurgency in Algeria—a French Point of View," *Military Review* 9–10 (2008): 56–67, 56.

13. Goscha, *Historical Dictionary*, 88–89.

14. Adrian Vickers, *A History of Modern Indonesia* (Cambridge: Cambridge University Press, 2005), 100–101.

15. McCutcheon, "Breaking the Camel's Back," 206.

16. Jim Storr, *The Hall of Mirrors: War and Warfare in the Twentieth Century* (Warwick, UK: Helion, 2018), 114–119, 234–235.

17. Bruce Cronin, "Reckless Endangerment Warfare: Civilian Casualties and the Collateral Damage Exception in International Humanitarian Law," *Journal of Peace Research* 50, no. 2 (2013): 175–187, 175; Michael Howard, *War in European History*, rev. paperback ed. (1976; Oxford: Oxford University Press, 2009), 138.

18. Martin Thomas, *Violence and Colonial Order: Police, Workers and Protest in the European Colonial Empires, 1918–1940* (Cambridge: Cambridge University Press, 2012), 51–52, 325, 326, 333; Simon Robbins, "The Defeat of a Colonial School of Pacification: The French in Indochina, 1945–54," in Fremont-Barnes, *History of Counterinsurgency*, 1:105–124, 112–114; Jacques Frémeaux, "The French Experience in Algeria: Doctrine, Violence and Lessons Learnt," *Civil Wars* 14, no. 1 (2012): 49–62, 55; P. M. H. Groen, "Colonial Warfare and Military Ethics in the Netherlands East Indies, 1816–1941," in *Colonial Counterinsurgency and Mass Violence: The Dutch Empire in Indonesia*, ed. Bart Luttikhuis and Dirk Moses (Abingdon, UK: Routledge, 2014), 25–44.

19. *Voorschrift voor de uitoefening van de Politiek-politionele Taak van het Leger (VPTL)* (Bandung 1928/1929), 27. Cf. 10–11, 26, 31, 33, 44, 88; Paul van 't Veer, *De Atjeh-oorlog* (Amsterdam: Arbeiderspers, 1969), 260. For more on the *VPTL* in English see Jaap A. de Moor, "Colonial Warfare: Theory and Practice; The Dutch Experience in Indonesia," *Journal of the Japan-Netherlands Institute* (1990): 98–114.

20. Douglas Porch, "Bugeaud, Galliéni, Lyautey: The Development of French Colonial Warfare," in *Makers of Modern Strategy: From Machiavelli to the Nuclear Age*, ed. Peter Paret (Princeton, NJ: Princeton University Press, 1986), 376–407, 390–392, 395, 404.

21. Thomas R. Mockaitis, "The Minimum Force Debate: Contemporary Sensibilities Meet Imperial Practice," *Small Wars & Insurgencies* 23, no. 4–5 (2012): 762–780; Kim A. Wagner, "Seeing Like a Soldier: The Amritsar Massacre and the Politics of Military History," in *Decolonization and Conflict: Colonial Comparisons and Legacies*, ed. Martin Thomas and Gareth Curless (London: Bloomsbury, 2017), 23–38.

22. Lyndall Ryan, "Martial Law in the British Empire," in Dwyer and Nettelbeck, *Violence, Colonialism and Empire in the Modern World*, 93–110, 93–94; Huw Bennett, "The Other Side of the COIN: Minimum and Exemplary Force in British Army Counterinsurgency in Kenya," *Small Wars & Insurgencies* 18, no. 4 (2007): 638–664, 645–646; David French, *The British Way in Counter-insurgency, 1945–1967* (Oxford: Oxford University Press 2011), 82, 134.

23. Groen, "Colonial Warfare," 39. This is *not* to say other forms of ethics did not influence military thinking and doctrine.

24. *VPTL*, 10. See also note 19.

25. Christophe Wasinski, "La volonté de réprimer. Généalogie transnationale de la contre-insurrection," *Cultures and Conflicts* 79–80 (2010): 161–180. Cf. Daniel Whittingham, "'Savage Warfare': C. E. Callwell, the Roots of Counterinsurgency, and the Nineteenth Century Context," *Small Wars & Insurgencies* 23, no. 4–5 (2012): 591–607, 604; Karma Nabulsi, *Traditions of War: Occupation, Resistance, and the Law* (Oxford: Oxford University Press, 1999), 16–18, 29–30. Please note that the translation "the will to put down" is Wasinski's own.

26. Carl von Clausewitz, *Vom Kriege. Hinterlassenes Werk des Generals Carl von Clausewitz*, ed. Werner Halhweg (1832–1834; Bonn: Dümller, 1952), 1:2, 89–90.

27. Martijn Kitzen, "Western Military Culture and Counterinsurgency: An Ambiguous Reality," *Scientia Militaria, South African Journal of Military Studies* 40, no. 1 (2012): 1–24, 3–6; Patrick Porter, *Military Orientalism: Eastern War through Western Eyes* (London: Hurst, 2009), 59–60.

28. Fritz Kalshoven, *Belligerent Reprisals* (Leiden: Martinus Nijhoff, 1971), 64–67; Shane Darcy, "The Evolution of the Law of Belligerent Reprisals," *Military Law Review* 175 (2003): 184–251, 187.

29. A. J. Birtle, *U.S. Army Counterinsurgency and Contingency Operations Doctrine, 1942–1976* (Washington, DC: Government Printing Office, 2006), 8–9, 12–13; Scheipers, "Counterinsurgency," 881–884, 890–892.

30. Daniel R. Headrick, *Power over Peoples: Technology, Environments, and Western Imperialism, 1400 to the Present* (Princeton, NJ: Princeton University Press, 2009), 257–302; Jan. C. Jansen and Jürgen Osterhammel, *Decolonization: A Short History* (original German ed. 2013; Princeton, NJ: Princeton University Press, 2017), 68–70, 81–89, 157.

31. P. M. H. Groen, *Marsroutes en dwaalsporen. Het Nederlands miliair-stratetegisch beleid in Indonesië 1945–1950* (The Hague: Sdu, 1991), 212–213.

32. Robbins, "Defeat," 112–114, 116–117; Philippe Pottier, "GCMA/GMI: A French Experience in Counterinsurgency during the French Indochina War," *Small Wars & Insurgencies* 16, no. 2 (2005): 125–146; Hubert Tourret, "L'évolution de la tactique du corps expéditionnaire français en Extrême-Orient," in *L'armée française dans la guerre d'Indochine (1946–1954): Adaptation ou inadaptation?*, ed. Maurice Vaïsse (Paris: Éditions Complexe, 2000), 173–188, passim.

33. V. J. Croizat, *A Translation from the French: Lessons from the Indo-China* War, vol. 2 (Santa Monica, CA: RAND Corp. Memorandum RM-5271-PR 1967), 12, makes this point explicitly. This is an English translation of official French military reflection from just after the end of the Indochina War.

34. For an overview see Bürgin, "From the Classics."

35. Frémeaux, "French Experience," 49, 57–59; Douglas Porch, *Counterinsurgency: Exposing the Myths of the New Way of War* (Cambridge: Cambridge University Press, 2013), 171, 172–175; Claire Mauss-Copeaux, "Violences militaires françaises en Algérie, 1954–1962," presentation at the 19th Salon International du Livre d'Alger (2014, updated July 2019: https://histoirecoloniale.net/violences-militaires-francaises-en.html).

36. Charles Townshend, "In Aid of Civil Power: Britain, Ireland and Palestine 1916–1948," in Marston and Malkasian, *Counterinsurgency in Modern War*, 21–38, 37; Kaushik Roy, *The British Army in India: From Colonial Warfare to Total War 1857–1947* (London: Bloomsbury, 2013), 137.

37. I. F. W. Beckett, *Modern Insurgencies and Counter-insurgencies* (London: Taylor & Francis, 2001), 91.

38. Gareth Curless, "The Sten Gun Is Mightier Than the Pen: The Failure of Colonial Police Reform after 1945," in *Decolonization and Conflict: Colonial Comparisons and Legacies*, ed. Martin Thomas and Gareth Curless (London: Bloomsbury, 2017), 79–98, 91.

39. Karl Hack, "The Malayan Emergency as Counter-insurgency Paradigm," *Journal of Strategic Studies* 32, no. 3 (2009): 383–414, 404, 409–412; Porch, *Counterinsurgency*, 246–267.

40. Croizat, *Translation*, 83, cf. 94.

41. Groen, *Marsroutes*, 214; Jaap A. de Moor, *Generaal Spoor. Triomf en tragiek van een legercommandant* (Amsterdam: Boom, 2011), 257–258; Croizat, *Translation*, passim.

42. Beckett, *Modern Insurgencies*, 25, 50–51; Pieter Lieb, "Few Carrots and a Lot of Sticks: German Anti-partisan Warfare in World War Two," in Carter and Malkasian, *Counterinsurgency in Modern Warfare*, 57–78.

43. Robert M. Cassidy, *Counterinsurgency and the Global War on Terror: Military Culture and Irregular Conflict*, paperback ed. (2006; Stanford, CA: Stanford University Press, 2008), 25–27.

44. Adrian R. Lewis, "The American Culture of War in the Age of Artificial Limited War," in *Warfare and Culture in History*, ed. Wayne E. Lee (New York: NYU Press, 2011), 187–218, 188.

45. Bruce Cronin, "Reckless Endangerment Warfare," 176.

46. John Ellis, *The Sharp End: The Fighting Man in World War Two*, rev. paperback ed. (1980; London: Pimlico, 1993), 67.

47. Robert H. Scales Jr., *Firepower in Limited War*, 2nd rev. ed. (1990; Novato, CA: Presidio, 1995), 51–52; National Archives UK (NA UK), War Office (WO) 291/113, "Lethal effect of artillery fire"; WO 291/166, "Accuracy and dispersion of fire from a 25-pdr troop"; WO 291/946, "Effects of bombardment—present state of knowledge" (1946); Croizat, *Translation*, 102, 279.

48. Museum Bronbeek Collections (BRO), Voorschriften (VS) 34, SROI Bandoeng, "stencil tactiek" no. 6, 40–41, 50; Croizat, *Translation*, 61–62, 78, 223–224.

49. J. de Moor, *Westerling's oorlog: Indonesië 1945–1950: De geschiedenis van de commando's en parachutisten in Nederlands-Indië 1945–1950* (Amsterdam: Boom, 1999), 25–30; Croizat, *Translation*, 84, 160.

50. Clayton, *Wars*, 83; Yannick Veilleux-Lepage and Jan Fedorowicz, "The Mau Mau Revolt in Kenya, 1952–1956," in Fremont-Barnes, *History of Counterinsurgency*, 1:177–204, 190.

51. Margo Klijn-Pot, ed., *KP'er in Zeist en oorlogsvrijwilliger in Nederlands-Indië. Herinneringen uit de jaren 1943–1950 van Kees Klijn* (Arnhem, Netherlands: privately published, 1997), 82, 93.

52. NA UK, WO 291/476, "Comparison of Rifle, Bren and Sten."

53. NA UK, WO 291/107, "Comparison of the 7½ lb and 10 lb 3" mortar bomb"; NA UK, WO 291/113, "Lethal effect of artillery fire."

54. BRO, VS 16, KL, OA 31, 20–22. It should also be noted that heavy machine-gun fire is especially lethal once one is hit. Ellis, *Sharp End*, 177.

55. Goscha, *Penguin History*, 244.

56. NA UK, WO 291/138, "Influence of ground cover on performance of HE projectile."

57. Ellis, *Sharp End*, 69.

58. Croizat, *Translation*, 289; Norbet Jung, "L'artillerie dans la lutte contre-insurrectionnelle en Algérie (1954–1962)," *Stratégique* 1–4 (2009): 409–424, 414–415.

59. Croizat, *Translation*, 193.

60. As quoted in Croizat, 275.

61. National Archives, The Hague, Strijdkrachten in Nederlands-Indië, 2.13.132, inv. no. 3375, III AVA KNIL, "Samenstelling korpsgeschiedenis," 28 March 1947 (hereafter NL-HaNA, followed by collection number and inventory number).

62. Bart Luttikhuis and C. H. C. Harinck, "Nothing to Report? Challenging Dutch Discourse on Colonial Counterinsurgency in Indonesia 1945–1949," in Dwyer and Nettelbeck, *Violence, Colonialism and Empire in the Modern World*, 265–286, 271–272, 278–280.

63. Annelot Hoek, "De verzwegen moordpartij in Palembang," *Vrij Nederland*, September 2017 issue, online publication 4 August 2017, https://www.vn.nl/onderzoek-palembang/.

64. NL-HaNA, SNI, 2.13.132/804, KNIL Inf. I, "De Guerilla en haar bestrijding," 26 March 1949, 4.

65. NL-HaNA, SNI, 2.13.132/3297, 2–12 RVA, quarterly report for Q1, Q2 and Q3, 1949.

66. NL-HaNA, SNI, 2.13.132/3353, KNIL inf. I, war diary January–March 1949.

67. Douglas Porch, "French Imperial Warfare," in Marston and Malkasian, *Counterinsurgency in Modern Warfare*, 79–100, 83; Birtle, *US Army*, 68; Croizat, *Translation*, 96, 99, 223.

68. NL-HaNA, SNI, 2.13.132/469, "Memorie van overgave TtTC Midden-Java," 16 March 1948, 3; NL-HaNA, SNI, 491, Buurman van Vreeden to Spoor, 29 June 1948, "Appreciatie van de toestand," 5, 10-.

69. Hack, "Malayan Emergency," 385.

70. Scales, *Firepower*, 26, 51; Porch, "French Imperial Warfare," 86; Jac Weller, *Fire and Movement: Bargain-Basement Warfare in the Far East* (New York: Crowell, 1967), 38–40; Croizat, *Translation*, 91–93, 96–97.

71. Croizat, *Translation*, 86–88; Christopher Griffin, "Major Combat Operations and Counterinsurgency Warfare: Plan Challe in Algeria, 1959–1960," *Security Studies* 19, no. 3 (2010): 555–589, 575–579, 588.

72. Henri Bergmans, ed., *Oost-Java. Gedenkboek 4e Infanterie Brigade* (Tilburg, Netherlands: Henri Bergmans, 1950), 471; S. A. Lapré, *Het Andjing Nica Bataljon (KNIL) in Nederlands-Indië (1945–1950)* (Ermerlo, Netherlands: privately published, 1987), 242–251, 250; Croizat, *Translation*, 64; Tourret, "L'évolution," 176.

73. Richard Stubbs, "From Search and Destroy to Hearts and Minds: The Evolution of British Strategy in Malaya 1948–1960," in Marston and Malkasian, *Counterinsurgency in Modern War*, 102–118, 103.

74. Croizat, *Translation*, 99.

75. NL-HaNA, SNI, 2.13.132/804, KNIL Inf. I, "De Guerilla en haar bestrijding," 26 March 1949, 4.

76. Clayton, *Wars*, 84–86.

77. Croizat, *Translation*, 94, 96–97.

78. For Indonesia: W. A. Schouten and H. B. Evers, "Het gebruik van de artillerie, ingedeeld bij de V-Brigade gedurende en na de politionele actie," *Militaire Spectator* 118, no. 4 (April 1949): 225–236; the detailed entries (though mostly lacking casualty numbers) of 2–12 RVA for Q1–Q3 1949 in NL-HaNA, SNI, 2.13.132/3297. For a tactically similar use of British airpower in Kenya: Stephen Chappell, "Air Power in the Mau Mau Conflict—the Government's Chief Weapon," *RUSI Journal* 156, no. 1 (2011): 64–70.

79. Kevin Boylan and Luc Olivier, *Valley of the Shadow: The Siege of Dien Bien Phu* (Oxford: Osprey, 2018), 63. Cf. Scales, *Firepower*, 39, 52; Croizat, *Translation*, 61–62, 78.

80. Croizat, *Translation*, 69, 71, 74, 95, 98, 102.

81. Clayton, *Wars*, 85.

82. Jung, "L'artillerie," 414.

83. Jung, 419. For the Challe plan: François-Marie Gougeon, "The Challe Plan: Vain Yet Indispensable Victory," *Small Wars & Insurgencies* 16, no. 3 (2006): 293–316. Also see Roel Frakking and Martin Thomas's chapter in this volume.

84. NL, BRO, VS 33, *Gevechtshandleiding Indonesië Anno 1949*, vol. 2, 1, 6, 21, 26, quote on 21.

85. Jan Hoffenaar, Joep van Hoof, and Jaap de Moor, *Vuur in beweging: 325 jaar veldartillerie, 1677–2002* (Amsterdam: Boom, 2002), 114–115; NL-HaNA, SNI, 2.13.132/1739, Periodical Reports HQ Military Aviation KNIL (ML-KNIL) August–December 1947;

NL-HaNA, SNI, 2.13.132/1740, Periodical Reports HQ ML-KNIL 1948; NA, SNI, 2.13.132/1741, Periodical Reports HQ ML-KNIL January–August 1949; Jung, "L'artillerie," 417.

86. Anton P. de Graaff, *Indonesië als eindstation. Met het vergeten leger in Indië* (Franeker, Netherlands: Van Wijnen, 2005), 30; Bergmans, *Oost-Java*, 75–84, quote on 82.

87. Croizat, *Translation*, 200.

88. Christopher Bayly and Tim Harper, *Forgotten Wars: Freedom and Revolution in Southeast Asia* (Cambridge, MA: Harvard University Press, 2007), 150–152.

89. Bayly and Harper, 179.

90. Bayly and Harper, 180.

91. NL-HaNA, Indisch Instructie Bataljon, 2.13.106/19, Van Ham, "Casueel commentaar op het rapport van luitenant Mahler," 14 June 1949, 1.

92. NL-HaNA, SNI, 2.13.132/804, KNIL Inf. I, "De Guerilla en haar bestrijding," 26 March 1949, 4.

8. COMPARING THE AFTERLIVES, POLITICAL USES, AND MEMORIES OF EXTREME VIOLENCE DURING THE WARS OF DECOLONIZATION IN FRANCE, THE NETHERLANDS, AND BRITAIN

1. All my thanks to the anonymous reviewer and to Esther Zwinkels, Stef Scagliola, and Huw Bennett for their answers to my questions regarding the Dutch and the British cases. I also wish to thank Christopher Mobley for his help with the first English version of this text.

Also a member of the PCA and a journalist, Henri Alleg was arrested in June 1957 and tortured. His book *La question*, dealing with his experiences in French captivity, was first published in 1958 and subsequently banned. His testimony is the last eyewitness account of Maurice Audin's ordeal. Jean-Paul Sartre, together with three other French literature Nobel Prize winners, supported Alleg. An article that Sartre wrote in support of Alleg ("A victory") became the preface to the book's English translation.

2. On the issue of assessing the exact figures for crimes such as forced disappearances see Raphaëlle Branche, *La guerre d'Algérie: Une histoire apaisée?* (Paris: Seuil, 2005), 204–217, http://raphaellebranche.fr/wp-content/uploads/2013/04/e%CC%81preuves.pdf.

3. Pierre Vidal-Naquet, *L'affaire Audin* (Paris: Minuit, 1958).

4. Magalie Besse and Sylvie Thénault, eds., *Réparer l'injustice: L'affaire Maurice Audin* (Paris: Institut Francophone pour la Justice et la Démocratie, 2019), 258.

5. Raphaëlle Branche, *La torture et l'armée pendant la guerre d'Algérie, 1954–1962* (Paris: Gallimard, 2001), 474.

6. Macron's statement was made after two other precautions had been taken. The president had consulted the French army and the diplomatic corps and did not go to see Audin until he was certain neither would react negatively to this declaration.

7. For the full declaration, dated 13 September 2018, see https://www.elysee.fr/emmanuel-macron/2018/09/13/declaration-du-president-de-la-republique-sur-la-mort-de-maurice-audin (accessed 1 March 2020; author's translation).

8. Eighteen months after the presidential declaration, the French National Archives published an online guide on "the missing of the Algerian war" in the French public archives, at https://francearchives.fr/fr/actualite/223693824.

9. The author was present in the room and can bear witness that the president has asked for forgiveness.

10. On the Dutch debates on the colonial past see Gert Oostindie, *Postcolonial Netherlands: Sixty-Five Years of Forgetting, Commemorating, Silencing* (Amsterdam: Amsterdam University Press, 2012).

11. Miguel Bandeira Jerónimo and António Costa Pinto, eds., *The Ends of European Colonial Empires: Cases and Comparisons* (London: Palgrave Macmillan, 2015).

12. On the issue of torture see Darius Rejali, *Torture and Democracy* (Princeton, NJ: Princeton University Press, 2007); Raphaëlle Branche, "The French Military in Its Last Colonial War: Algeria, 1954–1962, the Reign of Torture," in *Interrogation in War and Conflict: A Comparative and Interdisciplinary Analysis*, ed. Simone Tobia and Christopher Andrew (London: Routledge, 2014), 169–184; Huw Bennett, "The Other Side of the COIN: Minimum and Exemplary Force in British Army Counterinsurgency in Kenya," *Small Wars & Insurgencies* 18, no. 4 (2007): 638–664. More broadly, see Samy Cohen, ed., *Democracies at War against Terrorism* (Basingstoke, UK: Palgrave Macmillan, 2008), 280.

13. Harald Welzer and Claudia Lenz, "Opa in Europa. Erste Befunde einer vergleichenden Tradierungsforschung," in *Der Krieg der Erinnerung. Holocaust, Kollaboration und Widerstand im europäischen Gedächtnis*, ed. Harald Welzer (Frankfurt am Main: Fischer Taschenbuch Verlag, 2007), 7–40.

14. After the mid-2000s, in light of the wars in Afghanistan and Iraq, classic counterinsurgency doctrine, or COIN, was temporarily hailed as the silver bullet to fighting guerrillas before being criticized for not delivering on its promise. Here again, the past of the decolonization war was mobilized, but without major additions to the lexicon. This time, parts of Dutch military circles also advocated a "Dutch model" of counterinsurgency (partly inspired by colonial examples). On the Dutch case see Thijs Brocades Zaalberg, "The Use and Abuse of the 'Dutch Approach' to Counter-insurgency," *Journal of Strategic Studies* 36, no. 6 (2013): 867–897.

15. Daniel Branch, *Defeating Mau Mau, Creating Kenya: Counterinsurgency, Civil War and Decolonization* (Cambridge: Cambridge University Press, 2009).

16. On the specific issue of the memories of the repression of Algerian nationalists in Paris see Jim House and Neil Macmaster, *Paris 1961: Algerians, State Terror, and Memory* (Oxford: Oxford University Press, 2006).

17. On Algeria see Raphaëlle Branche, "To Forget and Remember: The Paradoxical Legacy of French Military Actions in Algeria," in *Oxford Handbook on Colonial Insurgencies and Counter-insurgencies*, ed. Gareth Curless and Martin Thomas (forthcoming in 2022). On Indonesia see Esther Zwinkel's PhD dissertation. On Kenya see David M. Anderson, "Making the Loyalist Bargain: Surrender, Amnesty and Impunity in Kenya's Decolonization, 1952–63," *International History Review* 39, no. 1 (2017): 48–70.

18. Stef Scagliola, "The Silences and Myths of a 'Dirty War': Coming to Terms with the Dutch-Indonesian Decolonisation War, 1945–1949," *European Review of History / Revue européenne d'histoire* 14, no. 2 (2007): 235–262.

19. For the Dutch case I had to rely on English publications. See Bart Luttikhuis and A. Dirk Moses, "Mass Violence and the End of the Dutch Colonial Empire in Indonesia," *Journal of Genocide Research* 14, no. 3–4 (2012): 257–276; Rémy Limpach, "Business as Usual: Dutch Mass Violence in the Indonesian War of Independence 1945–49," in *Colonial Counterinsurgency and Mass Violence: The Dutch Empire in Indonesia*, ed. Bart Luttikhuis and A. Dirk Moses (Abingdon, UK: Routledge, 2014), 64–90. See also Rémy Limpach, *De brandende kampongs van General Spoor* (Amsterdam: Boom, 2016).

20. On My Lai see Howard Jones, *My Lai: Vietnam, 1968, and the Descent into Darkness* (Oxford: Oxford University Press, 2017). For collective oblivion see Paul Bijl, *Emerging Memory: Photographs of Colonial Atrocity in Dutch Cultural Memory* (Amsterdam: Amsterdam University Press, 2009), 194–195.

21. Pierre Vidal-Naquet, *La torture dans la République: Essai d'histoire et de politique contemporaines, 1954–1962* (Paris: Minuit, 1972), 205.

22. Henry Rousso, *Le syndrome de Vichy, 1944–1987* (Paris: Seuil, 1987), 382.

23. Gert Oostindie, Ireen Hoogenboom, and Jonathan Verwey, "The Decolonization War in Indonesia, 1945–1949: War Crimes in Dutch Veterans' Egodocuments," *War in History* 25, no. 2 (2018): 254–276. See also the introduction to this volume.

24. Stef Scagliola, "Cleo's 'Unfinished Business': Coming to Terms with Dutch War Crimes in Indonesia's War of Independence," *Journal of Genocide Research* 14, no. 3–4 (2012): 419–439, 425.

25. Pieter Lagrou, "Victims of Genocide and National Memory: Belgium, France and the Netherlands, 1945–1965," *Past & Present* 154, no. 1 (1997): 181–222.

26. Erik Linstrum, "Facts about Atrocity: Reporting Colonial Violence in Postwar Britain," *History Workshop Journal* 84 (2017): 108–127.

27. Huw Bennett, "Escaping the Empire's Shadow: British Military Thinking about the Insurgency on the Eve of the Northern Ireland Troubles," in *Decolonization and Conflict: Colonial Comparisons and Legacies*, ed. Martin Thomas and Gareth Curless (London: Bloomsbury, 2017), 229–246.

28. Tom Buchanan, *Amnesty International and Human Rights Activism in Postwar Britain, 1945–1977* (Cambridge: Cambridge University Press, 2020); Brian Drohan, *Brutality in an Age of Human Rights: Activism and Counterinsurgency at the End of the British Empire* (Ithaca, NY: Cornell University Press, 2018), chap. 2 on the Cyprus ECHR cases; and A. W. B. Simpson, *Human Rights and the End of Empire: Britain and the Genesis of the European Convention* (Oxford: Oxford University Press, 2001), chaps. 18 and 19 on the Cyprus ECHR cases.

29. Stephen Hopgood, *Keepers of the Flame: Understanding Amnesty International* (Ithaca, NY: Cornell University Press, 2006).

30. Gerda Jansen Hendriks, "'Not a Colonial War': Dutch Film Propaganda in the Fight against Indonesia, 1945–49," in Luttikhuis and Moses, *Colonial Counterinsurgency*, 198–213.

31. Gielt Algra, Martin Elands, and Jan René Schoeman, "The Media and the Public Image of Dutch Veterans from World War II to Srebrenica," *Armed Forces & Society* 33, no. 3 (2007): 396–413.

32. These results are quoted in Algra, Elands, and Schoeman's article. They were derived from the opinion poll that was conducted by the Centre for Research and Expertise of the Veterans Institute in Doorn, Netherlands, in September 2005.

33. Sylvie Thénault, "L'état d'urgence (1955–2005). De l'Algérie coloniale à la France contemporaine: Destin d'une loi," *Le Mouvement Social* 218, no. 1 (2007): 63–78.

34. Louisette Ighilahriz (with Anne Nivat), *Algérienne* (Paris: Fayard, 2001).

35. Chris Lorenz, "Can a Criminal Event in the Past Disappear in a Garbage Bin in the Present? Dutch Colonial Memory and Human Rights: The Case of Rawagedeh," in *Afterlife of Events: Perspectives of Mnemohistory*, ed. Marek Tamm (Basingstoke, UK: Palgrave Macmillan, 2015).

36. David M. Anderson, "Mau Mau in the High Court and the 'Lost' British Empire Archives: Colonial Conspiracy or Bureaucratic Bungle?," *Journal of Imperial and Commonwealth History* 39, no. 5 (2011): 699–716.

37. David M. Anderson, *Histories of the Hanged: Britain's Dirty War in Kenya and the End of Empire* (London: Weidenfeld & Nicolson and W. W. Norton, 2005); Caroline Elkins, *Britain's Gulag: The Brutal End of Empire in Kenya* (London: Pimlico, 2005); Huw Bennett, *Fighting the Mau Mau: The British Army and Counter-insurgency in the Kenya Emergency* (Cambridge: Cambridge University Press, 2013).

38. Following the Kenyan case, thirty-three former members of the Cypriot guerrilla group Eoka also filed a suit against the UK government. In 2019, the government decided to settle the case out of court. See Helena Smith, "UK to Pay £1m to Greek Cypriots over

Claims of Human Rights Abuses," *Guardian*, January 23, 2019; and Jean Christou, "British Army Given 'Free Rein' to Torture Eoka Suspects," *Cyprus Mail*, November 18, 2018.

39. For more information on the program "Independence, Decolonization, Violence and War in Indonesia, 1945–1950" and its eight subprojects see www.ind45-50.org/en/about-programme. This volume is one of the outcomes of the program's subprojects.

40. For the king's statement see www.royalhouse.nl/documents/speeches/2020/03/10/statement-by-king-willem-alexander-at-the-beginning-of-the-state-visit-to-indonesia (accessed 10 May 2020). On the expected avoidance of apologies see Kysia Hekster, "Geen koninklijke excuses bij bezoek aan Indonesië," 1 March 2020, www.nos.nl/artikel/2325249-geen-koninklijke-excuses-bij-bezoek-aan-indonesie-maar-waarom-niet.html.

Index

Aceh, 88–89
Adel, Khedidja, 104–5, 117
Aden, 5, 11, 47
Afghanistan, 2, 124
Ailleret, General, 111
Akache, Chérifa, 109
Akfadou, 112
Akkache, Huguette, 106
Algeria
    Algerian Communist Party, 106, 162–63
    Armée de Libération Nationale (ALN), 61–62, 66–68, 103–4, 109, 113
    Armée Nationale du Peuple Algérien, 61
    Aurès Mountains, 52, 60, 104, 113, 118
    demographic patterns, 12, 108, 167
    Front de Libération Nationale (FLN), 13, 51–52, 59, 62, 68, 97–98, 103–4, 108, 111, 154
    Groupes Mobiles de Police Rurale (GMPR), 59–62, 69–70
    mainland France, ties to, 167
    Mouvement National Algérien, 13, 47, 61
    Operation Sauterelle, 60
    paramilitary organizations, 59–62
    Specialized Administrative Section (SAS), 62, 112
    tax collection challenges, 51
    Tifelfel women's prison, 104, 106, 113
    See also Algerian War of Independence
Algerian War of Independence
    accountability avoidance, 174–79
    Algiers battle, 164, 171
    Aurès region conflicts, 52, 60, 113, 118
    camp de regroupement usage, 103–5, 117
    community grievances, 59–62
    fatalities, 13–14, 61, 68, 144, 154, 160, 164
    French troop levels, 13, 157–58
    Front de Libération Nationale (FLN) involvement, 13, 51–52, 98, 103–4, 108, 111
    guerre révolutionnaire concept, 149
    guerrilla campaigns, 67, 98–99, 103, 105, 109, 149, 152, 158–59
    iconic atrocities, 10–11, 23, 144
    indirect heavy weapons usage, 154, 157–59
    information management, 66–67
    insurgent networks, 56, 66–67
    interior borderlands vulnerability, 52, 62–63, 69
    international recognition, 12–13, 171, 176
    Operation Sauterelle, 60
    paramilitary organizations, 59–62, 70
    rape patterns, 96–101, 103–18, 176
    torture usage, 1, 10–11, 23, 98, 103–7, 114, 144, 162–66, 171–72, 176
    See also Algeria; France
Allied Powers, 3–4, 18, 71–74, 77, 79, 81, 89, 94, 123, 145
Alloula, Malek, 115–16
Ambar, Galuh, 117
Amnesty International, 173
Anderson, David, 7, 177–78
Angola, 1
Anwar, Chairil, 74–75
Armed Forces of the Philippines (AFP), 126–27
Attlee, Clement, 39, 45
Audin, Josette, 162–66
Audin, Maurice, 162–66
Australia, 91, 159
Axis Powers, 123

Bali, 91
Balongsari (Rawagede), 175, 177
Bandung, 63, 75, 77–78, 85–86, 90
Banjoewangi, 102
Banten, 88
Bao Dai, 73–74, 76
Battle of Algiers, The (movie), 171
Bayly, Christopher, 124, 160
Beckett, Ian, 150
Beel, Louis, 42
Belgium, 3, 18, 172
Belloc, Hilaire, 124
Bellounis, Mohammed, 61–62
Ben Hamdani, 100, 112
Beni Chebana, 61
Benkhellat, Souhila, 114
Bennett, Huw, 177
Biddle, Stephen, 123
Bollardière, General, 171

225

226 INDEX

Bot, Ben, 174, 179
Bouaziz, Salima, 111
Boupacha, Djamila, 97–98, 103–4, 106, 111, 114
Branche, Raphaëlle, 107
Britain
    Aden campaigns, 5, 11, 47
    Colonial Office, 29, 33
    Colony Emergency Committee, 34
    Conservative Party, 36, 39–40
    Cyprus campaigns, 11, 44, 47–48, 173
    Dutch-Indonesian intervention, 3, 72, 75, 77–79, 85–91, 94, 131–32, 143–44
    Foreign Office, 29, 33, 177
    French-Indochina occupation, 72, 77–79, 85, 90, 94
    "Imperial Policing and Duties in Aid of the Civil Power" manual, 149
    Information Research Department (IRD), 28
    Joint Intelligence Committee (JIC), 33
    Labour Party, 25, 39, 97
    Movement for Colonial Freedom, 38–39
    Northern Ireland, conflict with, 47, 173
    Official Secrets Act, 32
    propaganda efforts, 28–30, 38–39, 41, 47
    Provincial Emergency Committee, 34
    Royal Air Force (RAF), 4, 6, 131, 133
    Royal Artillery, 128, 131
    Secret Intelligence Service, 33
    Security Office, 33
    Trades Union Congress, 39
    See also Malayan Emergency; Mau Mau uprising
Brockway, Fenner, 39
Bui Quang Chieu, 77
Burma, 91, 123, 132, 160
Bussemaker, Herman, 89

Calley, William, 170
Callwell, Charles, 124, 129
Cambodia, 65, 79
Cassidy, Robert, 150
Cédile, Jean, 79
Challe, Maurice, 62, 109, 158–59
Cherif, Larbi, 62
Chiang Kai-shek, 76, 83
Christison, Philip, 77–78, 83, 131, 160
Churchill, Winston, 45
Clausewitz, Carl von, 17, 146
Congo, 3
Constans, Colonel, 60
Constantine, 51, 60–61
Constantine Tribunal of the Armed Forces, 97, 100

Cornah, D.M., 44
Cribb, Robert, 89
Cronin, Bruce, 145, 150
Crossman, Richard, 45
Cyprus, 11, 44, 47–48, 173

Dalstein, Colonel, 66–67
Damascus, 81
D'Argenlieu, Thierry, 79, 82–84
De Beauvoir, Simone, 111
De Gaulle, Charles, 79, 169
De Jong, Piet, 170, 172
De Niet, G.J., 42
Debès, Pierre-Louis, 84
Democratic Army of Greece (GDA), 125
Depok, 78
Drees, William, 37, 43
Dreyfus, Alfred, 164
Drif, Zohra, 110–11
Drohan, Brian, 47

East Borneo, 38
East Timor, 67
Edelman, Maurice, 25
Elkins, Caroline, 177
Enloe, Cynthia, 105–7, 116
Erskine, George, 44–45
Esméralda, H. G., 106
European Convention on Human Rights (ECHR), 8, 47–48, 173
Excessennota report, 7–8, 139, 170, 174
Excesses of Rawagedeh, The (documentary), 174

Fanon, Frantz, 108, 116
Fasseur, Cees, 8
Favre, Bernard, 175
Felderhof, Henk, 6
Feraoun, Mouloud, 99
Fletcher, Eileen, 39–40
France
    Foreign Legion, 54, 148–49
    Franco-Prussian War, 122
    French Communist Party, 162
    Madagascar conflict, 49, 52–54, 69, 142–43, 152–53, 158, 160
    nuclear arsenal, 169
    rape criminality views, 113–14
    Vichy regime, 73, 172
    See also Algerian War of Independence; Indochina War

Frederick, William, 89
Front de Libération Nationale (FLN), 13, 51–52, 59, 62, 68, 97–98, 103–4, 108, 111, 154

Galama, Sikke, 106
Garne, Kheira, 104
Garne, Mohamed, 104, 114
Geneva Convention, 8, 173
Germany, 6, 18, 26, 47, 81, 110, 122–23, 145, 150, 172–73
Goedhart, Frans, 36, 38, 43
Gracey, Douglas, 78–79, 81, 83, 160
Greece, 47–48, 121, 125–26, 130, 139, 173
Greek National Army (GNA), 125–26
Griffith-Jones, Eric, 6
Griffiths, Major, 44–46
Guelma, 67, 81
Guergour, 61
Guomindang (GMD), 76

Haiphong, 83–85, 87
Haken, Jan, 25
Hale, Leslie, 39
Halimi, Gisèle, 103, 111
Hanoi, 65, 71, 83, 85
Harnoko, Darto, 117–18
Harper, Tim, 124, 160
Hatta, Mohammed, 3, 73–74, 83, 86, 93
Hawthorn, D.C., 132
Hendrix, W.J., 7, 120
Ho Chi Minh, 3, 74, 76, 79, 82–85, 93
Hola detention camp, 40, 43–44
Hollande, François, 165
Holocaust, 168
Hon Gay, 83
Hueting, Joop, 6, 170–71
Hukbalahap Rebellion, 121, 126–30
Human Rights Charter (United Nations), 8
Huot, Pierre, 65–66
Huynh Phu So, 77

Ighilahriz, Louisette, 106, 114, 176–77
Ikadjadjen, 61
Immerzeel, Bart, 89
India, 3, 12, 39, 77–78, 85–86, 90, 131–32, 135, 145
Indochina War
    Allied occupation, 72, 77–79, 85, 90, 94
    arson, 61, 152
    Chinese negotiations, 83
    Cité Hérault kidnappings, 81
    Cochinchina-Cambodia Division, 79
    Corps expéditionnaire français en Extrême-Orient (CEFEO), 79, 82–84, 95
    Dien Bien Phu battle, 124, 130–31
    fatalities, 13–14, 81–84, 90, 143–44, 150, 157, 160
    French troop levels, 13, 82, 156, 158
    guerrilla campaigns, 137, 140, 152, 158
    Haiphong battle, 83–85, 87
    indirect heavy weapons usage, 124, 130, 134–36, 154, 156–60
    interior borderlands vulnerability, 63
    international recognition, 12–13, 65, 170
    Japanese surrender power vacuum, 21, 71–74
    Military Directive No. 1, 83
    Operation Enfer, 84
    Phúc Yên curfew petition, 65–66
    Vietminh insurgents, 56, 65–66, 74, 82, 130, 148, 154, 157
    weapons shortages, 129
    See also France; Vietnam
Indonesia
    Allied occupation, 3–4
    demographic patterns, 12–13
    famine, 72–73
    forced prostitution, 110–11
    Heroes Day, 87–88, 132
    independence proclamation, 3, 36, 74, 93–94, 131
    Indonesian Air Force (AURI), 135
    Indonesian National Armed Forces (Tentara Nasional Indonesia) (TNI), 20, 59, 63–64, 130, 132, 138, 152
    Investigative Committee for Indonesian Independence, 73
    Japanese occupation, 3, 6, 21, 71–74, 88, 110, 131
    Mohammed Hatta leadership, 3, 73–74, 83, 86, 93
    National Committees (KNI), 74
    Negara Pasundan proclamation, 63–64
    Pao An Tui (PAT), 57–59, 64, 70
    People's Security Agency (BKR), 74
    peranakan elite, 94
    plantation guards (PG), 57–60, 69–70
    Republic of United States of Indonesia (RUSI) founding, 59
    Second World War damages, 71
    State of Eastern Indonesia (Negara Indonesia Timur), 91–92
    Sukarno leadership, 3, 36, 63, 73–74, 78, 83, 86, 93

INDEX

Indonesia (*continued*)
   UN Commission for Indonesia (UNCI), 138
   See also Indonesian War of Independence
Indonesian War of Independence
   accountability avoidance, 16–17, 24–32, 42, 46–48, 109, 170–71
   Allied occupation, 3, 72, 75, 77–79, 85–91, 94, 131–32, 143–44
   arson, 9, 64, 153
   baboe usage, 101–3, 106, 108, 112, 115, 117
   badan perdjuangan units, 74–75
   Depot Speciale Troepen (DST), 89, 91–92, 109
   DIRVO (Directie Verre Oosten: Directorate for the Far East), 31
   Dutch troop levels, 13, 26, 82, 130, 133–36, 139–40, 156–58
   Excessennota report, 7–8, 139, 170, 174
   fatalities, 13–14, 26, 37, 58, 73, 75–78, 86–93, 120–21, 131–32, 135–39, 143–44, 152–55, 158–61, 175
   federalism efforts, 90–93
   guerrilla campaigns, 3–4, 91, 93, 98–99, 105, 130, 132, 137, 140, 152, 155, 158
   iconic atrocities, 10–11, 23
   indirect heavy weapons (*technisch geweld*) usage, 121–22, 130–39, 152, 154–55, 158–60
   information management, 26–42, 46–47
   interior borderlands vulnerability, 63–64, 69
   international recognition, 12–13, 15, 41, 78, 110, 170
   Japanese surrender power vacuum, 21, 71–78
   Java military importance, 3, 6, 41, 63–64, 71–79, 85, 88–94, 137
   Netherlands Indies Civil Administration (NICA), 75
   Operation Kraai, 135
   Operation Product, 133–35
   paramilitary organizations, 57–59, 70
   pemuda militias, role of, 73–76, 78, 85–86, 88–90, 132
   "police actions", 3–4, 57, 93, 135–38, 160, 169
   prisoner of war (POW) camps, 14, 75–77, 86, 89, 91
   rape patterns, 96–98, 100–102, 104–19
   Royal Netherlands East Indies Army Air Force (ML-KNIL), 133–35, 138
   Royal Netherlands East Indies Army (KNIL), 58, 72, 75, 89, 91–92, 154–55
   scandal avoidance, 27, 35–38
   scandal management, 27, 40–43, 46
   South Sulawesi violence, 6, 10, 14, 37, 41, 91–93, 104, 120, 170, 177
   Staat van Oorlog en Beleg, 51
   Sudanese targeting, 63–65
   Sumatra military importance, 3, 6, 41, 63–64, 76–79, 88–90, 93–94, 137
   Surabaya battle, 6, 85–88, 90, 131–32, 153, 160
   United Nations intervention, 3–4, 25–26, 36, 41, 138
   See also Indonesia; Netherlands
International Committee of the Red Cross (ICRC), 38, 40, 154
International Conference for the Abolition of Torture, 173
Iraq, 2
Irish Republican Army (IRA), 173

Jakarta, 28, 75, 77–78, 85, 93
Japan, 3, 6, 21, 26, 55, 71–79, 82, 85–90, 92, 110, 123, 131–32
Jonkman, Jan Anne, 42

Kabylia, 61, 99, 107, 109, 113–14
Kalyvas, Stathis, 8, 51
Kedah, 56
Kenya
   demographic patterns, 12
   Hola detention camp, 40, 43–44
   Home Guard, 44, 46
   King's African Rifles (KAR), 44
   Police Reserve, 44
   See also Mau Mau uprising (Kenyan Emergency)
Kilcullen, David, 67
Klose, Fabian, 25
Koets, P.J., 31–32
Korean War, 121, 124

La guerre sans nom (documentary), 175
Lacoste-Dujardin, Camille, 113
Lafayette, 61
L'affaire Audin, 164–65
Lagrou, Pieter, 172
Laos, 65
Lawrence, Adria, 54
League of Nations, 169
Leclerc, Philippe, 79, 82–84
Lennox-Boyd, Alan, 40
Lenz, Claudia, 168
Les années algériennes (documentary), 175
Lieb, Pieter, 150
Limpach, Rémy, 2, 16, 107, 121, 139
Lion Cachet, Carel, 91
Logemann, J.A.A., 33
Loris-Rodionoff, Marius, 97, 100
Lovink, A.H.J., 41
Luttikhuis, Bart, 121
Lyautey, Hubert, 145, 148
Lyttelton, Oliver, 25

MacBride, Seán, 173
Macmillan Harold, 40
Macron, Emmanuel, 1–2, 162, 165–66, 178–79
Madagascar, 49, 52–54, 69, 142–43, 152–53, 158, 160
Magsaysay, Ramon, 127
Makassar, 91
Malang, 38
Malaya
   Chinese workforce, 55–56
   indirect heavy weapons usage, 139
   Japanese occupation, 55
   Malayan Communist Party (MCP), 26, 55
   Malayan National Liberation Army (MNLA), 55–56
   Malaysian Chinese Association (MCA), 55–56
   rubber industry, 29
   See also Malayan Emergency
Malayan Emergency
   accountability avoidance, 30–31
   Briggs Plan, 55
   British troop levels, 13, 156, 158
   communist insurgents, 3, 29, 55–56
   community grievances, 55–56
   fatalities, 13–14, 129, 144, 158
   guerrilla campaigns, 55–56, 129–30, 152
   iconic atrocities, 10–11
   indirect heavy weapons usage, 121, 127–28, 157, 159
   information management, 26–31, 33–35
   interior borderlands vulnerability, 52, 55–56
   international recognition, 12–13
   minimum force approach, 5–7, 145, 158
   Operation Nassau, 128
   Second World War ripple effects, 55
   villagization program, 10, 55–56, 69
   See also Britain; Malaya
Malewa, Deang, 92
Malino Conference, 63
Mallaby, A.W.S., 86–87, 131, 160
Mansbergh, Robert, 160
Mansergh, General, 132
Mao Tse-tung, 124
Massu, General, 171
Mau Mau uprising (Kenyan Emergency)
   accountability avoidance, 24–31, 46–48, 177–78
   British troop levels, 13, 158
   combat intensity, 15
   fatalities, 13–14, 45, 142–43, 158
   forced displacement, 10
   guerrilla campaigns, 152–53
   Hola detention camp violence, 40, 43–44
   iconic atrocities, 10–11, 23

   information management, 26–40, 46–47
   international recognition, 12–13
   mass internment, 9–10
   propaganda depictions, 38–39
   scandal avoidance, 27, 38–40
   scandal management, 27, 40, 43–46
   See also Britain; Kenya
McLean, Kenneth, 45–46
Medan, 57–58, 77, 89
Meester Cornelis, 37
Melouza, 61–62
Merouane, Omar, 10
Messali Hadj, 61
Mitchell, Neil, 30–31
Mollet, Guy, 66
Moluccan Islands, 75–76, 91, 109
Morlière, Louis, 84
Mountbatten, Louis, 78
Mouvement Démocratique de la Rénovation Malgache (MDRM), 53
Mozambique, 1, 7
Mus, Paul, 84

Nasution, Abdul Haris, 98, 124, 137
NATO, 169
Nazi Party, 6, 18, 26–27, 110, 145, 171–72
Neher, L., 43
Neitzel, Sönke, 18
Netherlands
   Colonial Office, 32
   Dutch News Agency ANP, 29
   Excessennota report, 7–8, 139, 170, 174
   geopolitical relevance, 12
   Jewish extermination rates, 172
   KUKB organization, 114–15
   Labor Party (PvdA), 29, 36, 42–43
   Ministry of Foreign Affairs, 31
   Ministry of Justice, 174
   Netherlands Institute for War Documentation, 174
   Netherlands Institute of Military History, 178
   Netherlands Naval Aviation Service (MLD), 133
   NIOD Institute for War, Holocaust and Genocide Studies, 178
   propaganda efforts, 28–30, 37, 41, 47
   Protestant Party ARP, 26, 29
   Regeringsvoorlichtingsdienst (RVD-Batavia: Government Information Service), 28
   Rijksvoorlichtingsdienst (RVD-The Hague: National Information Service), 28
   Royal Netherlands Institute of Southeast Asian and Caribbean Studies, 178
   Socialist Broadcasting Society (VARA), 29
   See also Indonesian War of Independence

Ngo Dinh Diem, 77
Ngo Dinh Huan, 77
Ngo Dinh Khoi, 77
Nobel Peace Prize, 173
Northern Ireland, 47, 173
Nu'mang, Sitti Hasanah, 104, 106, 113
Nyasaland, 43

Oeroeg (novel and movie), 174
Olivier, Dominique, 105–6
Operation Enfer, 84
Operation Kraai, 135
Operation Nassau, 128
Operation Product, 133–35
Operation Sauterelle, 60

Paget, Stephen, 129
Pahang, 56
Palar, Nico, 36, 138
Palembang, 154
Palestine, 39
Parlange, Gaston, 60
Pekalongan, 88
Peniwen, 38, 115–16
Perak, 55
Pesing, 36–37
Pham Quynh, 77
Philippines, 83, 126–30, 139
Picasso, Pablo, 98, 114
Pondaag, Jeffrey, 114–15
Pontecorvo, Gillo, 171
Portugal, 1, 5, 7, 12, 168
Potsdam Conference, 72
Protschky, Susie, 108, 115

Rawagede (Balongsari), 37, 174–75, 177
Report from Banaran: Experiences during the People's War, 137
Republic of Korea (ROK), 126
Roem, Mohammed, 76
Roman Catholic Political Party (KVP), 29
Roosevelt, Franklin, 79
Roosjen, A.B., 26
Rousso, Henry, 171
Royal Ulster Constabulary (RUC), 173
Russia, 6
Rwanda, 114

Safari (movie), 38
Saigon, 65, 78–82, 84
Salavar, António de Oliveira, 168
Sartre, Jean-Paul, 111
Schmitt, Maurice, 114, 176

Schuyt, Kees, 46
Semarang, 29, 75, 77–78, 85–86, 90, 135
September 11 terrorist attacks, 2
Sétif, 61, 81
Shipway, Martin, 5
Siam, 75, 91
Simatupang, T.B., 137
Simba (movie), 38
Singapore, 34, 89
Sjahrir, Sutan, 76
Soekowirjo, 99
Somalia, 124
Somer, J.M., 42
Somers-Heidhues, Mary, 89
Something of Value (movie), 38
Sorrow and the Pity, The (documentary), 171
Soustelle, Jacques, 52, 60
South Korea, 126, 139
South Sulawesi, 6, 10, 14, 37, 41, 91–93, 104, 120, 170, 177
Spoor, Simon, 2, 6, 32, 42–43, 57, 68, 91, 93, 133
Srebrenica, 174
Stam, W.H., 43
Stoler, Ann Laura, 108
Sudirman, General, 138
Suez Crisis, 38
Sukabumi, 99
Sukarno, 3, 36, 63, 73–74, 78, 83, 86, 93
Surabaya, 6, 75, 77, 85–86, 90, 131–32, 153, 160
Suriakartalegawa, 63
Syria, 81

Ta Thu Thau, 77
Taruc, Luis, 129
Tavernier, Bertrand, 175
Thomas, Martin, 5, 7
Ticsi, 61
Tillion, Germaine, 52
Tonkin, 82–84
Tønnesson, Stein, 71, 84
Trotskyism, 76–77
Truman, Harry, 79
Tunisia, 52

United Nations, 3–4, 8, 13, 25–26, 36, 41, 110, 126, 138, 173–74
Universal Declaration of Human Rights, 110

Valluy, Jean-Étienne, 84–85
Van der Goes van Naters, M., 43

Van Doorn, J.J.A., 7, 120
Van Maarseveen, Johan, 33, 41, 43
Van Mook, Hubertus, 63, 91–92
Van Randwijk, Henk, 36
Van Rij, C., 43
Vann, John Paul, 120, 123, 133
Vidal-Naquet, Pierre, 162, 164–65, 171
Vietnam
  Bao Dai government, 73–74, 76
  Cao Dai presence, 76
  communist insurgents, 3
  Democratic Republic of Vietnam (DRVN) founding, 74
  Dien Bien Phu fortress, 65, 124
  enemy-centric attrition strategy, 5–6
  famine, 72–73
  fatalities, 14
  Ho Chi Minh leadership, 3, 74, 76, 79, 82–85, 93
  Hoa Hao presence, 76–77
  independence proclamation, 3, 74, 76, 79, 93
  Indochinese Communist Party (ICP), 74, 76–77, 79, 85, 90, 94
  Mekong Delta, 158
  My Lai massacre, 170
  Nationalist Party of Vietnam (VNQDD), 76
  People's Army of Vietnam (PAVN), 65
  Second World War damages, 71
  Vietnamese Revolutionary League (Viet Cach), 76
  See also Indochina War

Wagner, Kim, 17
Walter, Dierk, 17
Wanita Lima Nama (novel), 110
Wasinski, Christophe, 146
Wati, Kawar, 110
Welter, Charles, 43
Welzer, Harald, 18, 168
Westerling, Raymond, 6, 10–11, 23, 37, 41, 89, 91–93, 120, 133, 140
Willem-Alexander, King, 2, 179
Wonosari, 137–39
Wood, Elizabeth, 107

Yalu River, 126
Yogyakarta, 37, 42, 117, 135, 138
Yugoslavia, 114, 174

Zegveld, Liesbeth, 115
Zighoud, Youcef, 61
Zola, Émile, 164

CPSIA information can be obtained
at www.ICGtesting.com
Printed in the USA
LVHW110002211222
735623LV00018B/616/J